A SELECTED PROSE

ROBERT DUNCAN

A SELECTED PROSE

Edited by Robert J. Bertholf

A NEW DIRECTIONS BOOK

ACKNOWLEDGMENTS
Portions of this book appear by arrangement with The University of California Press.

The following people helped in the preparation of the manuscript of this volume: Marta Werner, Nava Fader, Janet Sorenson, and Cynthia Kimball. The manuscript was watched over and helped along in many ways by Susan Michel.—RJB

Manufactured in the United States of America
New Directions Books are printed on acid-free paper.
First published clothbound by New Directions in 1995
Published simultaneously in Canada by Penguin Books Canada Limited

Library of Congress Cataloging in Publication Data

Duncan, Robert Edward, 1919–
    [Prose. Selections]
    A selected prose / Robert Duncan ; edited by Robert J. Bertholf.
        p.   cm.
    Includes bibliographical references and index.
    ISBN 0–8112–1278–5 (alk. paper)
    I. Bertholf, Robert J. II. Title.
PS3507.U629A6   1995
811′.54—dc20   94–12983
                                                                      CIP

New Directions Books are published for James Laughlin
by New Directions Publishing Corporation,
80 Eighth Avenue, New York 10011

Contents

Introduction

Writing prose was as much a part of Robert Duncan's life as writing poetry. The essays in this volume come from the early as well as the later periods of Duncan's life. The essays are not arranged in chronological order. Dates and the publishing history for each essay appear in a note. This is not a complete collection of Duncan's essays. He wrote an "Introduction" to Allen Upward's *The Divine Mystery,* for example, as well as completed and partially completed essays on James Joyce, Charles Olson, and William Shakespeare, and several statements of his poetics. The essays here present the persistent and guiding ideas of myth, poetics, and lineage that so actively inform his prose and the poetry.

Duncan lived and wrote in a complex web of personal and intellectual engagements. He was, as he said in many ways, a "derivative poet" who generated the forms of his poems and essays from a vast diversity of sources. But the central idea of both the poems and the essays is the freedom of the individual to create, to make decisions, and to act. Duncan fought against restrictions of the egoistical "I" as consistently as he fought against rigid, systematic thought. Both forces predicated a conclusion before the beginning of the first idea of a poem or essay. Restrictions of social mores and governmental regulations were as threatening to his process of creation as positing preconditions in the terms and forms of a poem or essay. He worked at redirecting the flow of an argument in writing to dislocate the logic of his own presentation. He wrote to declare the freedom of his mind and its attunement to a larger universe of language and meanings.

The collection begins with "Towards an Open Universe" (1966). This essay propounds the idea that cosmic energy and mythic presences are alive in the contemporary, daily enterprise. "[The Matter of the Bees]" (1972) comes in as a "coda" to the first five essays in finding in the lives of bees the actual life of the imagination. Other aspects of Duncan's poetics appear in the middle essays. "The Homosexual in Society" first appeared in 1944; the revised version (from 1959) in this volume was not published by Duncan in his lifetime. In both versions, Duncan holds fast to the principle of the necessity of human freedom. The same principle

vii

runs through the notes in "Pages from A Notebook," which provoked
Charles Olson to write his essay "Against Wisdom As Such." In "Ideas of
the Meaning of Form," Duncan again rejects convention and says that a
poem must project its form from within the energy of its content.

Duncan enjoyed defining and redefining his literary and artistic
heritage, his masters, and his contemporaries. The remaining essays
testify to this process. "Changing Perspectives in Reading Whitman" sets
out the spiritual traditions behind Duncan's thought deriving from
Dante on the one hand and from Whitman on the other. For him, both
poets projected personal freedom, a dynamic spiritual life, and a rich
intensity of democracy. Duncan first read Ezra Pound's *A Draft of XXX
Cantos* in 1937, and Pound's poetry substantiated Duncan's own writing;
so in "The Lasting Contribution of Ezra Pound," he pays tribute to the
power of Pound's poetry, "the sound and sense of the language." Like-
wise, Duncan admired Marianne Moore's articulation of the line, and her
abilities to manage a poetry crowded with particulars; he emphasizes
these points in "Notes on the Poetics of Marianne Moore." H.D. was a
monumental figure in Duncan's design of derivation. What started out in
1960 as a tribute for H.D.'s birthday exploded into "The H. D. Book," a
reinvestigation of the modernist movement with H.D.'s work at the cen-
ter of that movement, and "Rites of Participation" is an informative
chapter from that book. In "As Testimony: Reading Zukofsky These
Forty Years," Duncan says that reading Zukofsky's poetry was a "call to
order" for a new poetry. He calls Zukofsky an "enduring resource" for
his own poetry. Duncan met Charles Olson in Berkeley in 1947. In the
middle 1950s Duncan wrote an essay on Olson's work, "Notes on Poetics
Regarding *Maximus*" (1956), reprinted in *Fictive Certainties*. In "As an
Introduction," written in 1972, two years after Olson's death, Duncan
commands a profound understanding of Olson's sense of history and the
fullness of his poetic process.

Of the poets in Cid Corman's *Origin*, Charles Olson, Robert Creeley,
and Denise Levertov were the three he claimed again and again as his
contemporaries of the poetic line. That praise and the delineation of a
heritage in American poetry from Pound, Zukofsky, and William Carlos
Williams also appear in his review of Creeley's *For Love*. Duncan first met
Denise Levertov in 1955 and even before that had admired her poetry.
The "Introductory Notes for Denise Levertov" were written for a poetry
reading in San Francisco. Although Duncan never finished an essay on
Robin Blaser, he confirms Blaser's (as well as Spicer's) central role in the
formation of the "serial poem." In the "Preface" to Spicer's *One Night*

Stand, he traces out his relationship with Spicer by confirming the integrity of Spicer's vision of "primitive magic" in the guise of baseball, bridge, or detective stories.

In San Francisco, Duncan had many friends in the art world. He was closest to the work of Jess, his life companion. In this introduction to the exhibition catalog of the *Translation* series, "Iconographical Extensions" (1971), he vivifies Jess's power of transforming images from one place into a palace of color in painting. Harry Jacobus, a friend of both Jess and Duncan, receives praise for his integrity and command of colors so that the inner vision and the outer world correspond. Though the essay for an exhibition was written in 1961, Jacobus had been a close ally of Duncan and Jess since 1950. In "Of George Herms, His Hermes, and His Hermetic Art," Duncan applauds the artist for his precision and care in the "recycling of riches" of society into artistic forms, and in "Wallace Berman: The Fashioning Spirit" (1978) he points attention to Berman's strength of vision in complex collages.

But the tradition of poetry was never far from his attention. The essay on Beverly Dahlen's *The Egyptian Poems* recognizes in a young poet a servant of language who uncovers divine powers in her poems. She is as much a part of the line of poetry as Olson, Levertov, and Creeley were in his own generation. The final essay, "The Delirium of Meaning," is a ringing tribute to Jabès, his "delirium of finding meanings beyond meaning" in a rich spiritual tradition which is alive in contemporary French poetry. Intricate passages through these essays honor the reverberations of poetic vision in articulate language.

Robert J. Bertholf
The Poetry Collection
State University of New York, Buffalo
April 1994

Towards an Open Universe

I was born January 7, 1919, in the hour before dawn, in the depth of winter at the end of a war. When I think of the hour, from their obscurity the tree at the window, the patterned curtain, the table and chair, the bowl of golden glass upon the chest of drawers are just emerging into view. Sleeping and waking fuse, things seen in an inner light mingle with things searched out by eyes that are still dim. Day "breaks," we say, and the light floods out over the land. The shining planets and the great stars, the galaxies beyond us, grow invisible in light of our sun.

The imagination of this cosmos is as immediate to me as the imagination of my household or my self, for I have taken my being in what I know of the sun and of the magnitude of the cosmos, as I have taken my being in what I know of domestic things. In the coda of the poem "Apprehensions," the "First Poem" calls upon the birth of life itself in the primal waters and may call upon my birth hour:

> It is the earth turning
> that lifts our shores from the dark
> into the cold light of morning,
> eastward turning,
>
> and that returns us from the sun's burning
> into passages of twilight and doubt,
> dim reveries and gawdy effects.
> The sun is the everlasting center of what we know,
> a steady radiance.
>
> The changes of light in which we dwell,   *life = series of colors*
> colors among colors that come and go,

First published in *Contemporary American Poetry: Voice of America Forum Lectures*, ed. Howard Nemerov (Washington, D.C.: The Voice of America, 1964); the same book was republished as *Poets on Poetry*, ed. Howard Nemerov (New York: Basic Books, 1966). The essay was included in *Fictive Certainties: Essays by Robert Duncan* (New York: New Directions, 1985).

are in the earth's turning.

Angels of light! raptures of early morning!
your figures gather what they look like
out of what cells once knew of dawn,
first stages of love that in the water thrived.

So we think of sperm
as spark-fluid, many milliond,
in light of the occult egg striking
doctrine.
            Twined angels of dark,
hornd master-reminders of from-where!
your snake- or animal-red eyes
store the fire's glare.

O flames! O reservoirs!

In the very beginnings of life, in the source of our cadences, with the
first pulse of the blood in the egg then, the changes of night and day must
have been there. So that in the configuration of the living, hidden in the
exchanging orders of the chromosome sequences from which we have
our nature, the first nature, child of deep waters and of night and day,
sleeping and waking, remains.

We are all the many expressions of living matter, grandchildren of
Gaia, Earth and Uranus, the Heavens. Late born, for the moon and
ocean came before. The sea was our first mother and the sun our father,
so our sciences picture the chemistry of the living as beginning in the
alembic of the primal sea quickened by rays of the sun and even, beyond,
by radiations of the cosmos at large. Tide-flow under the sun and moon
of the sea, systole and diastole of the heart, these rhythms lie deep in our
experience and when we let them take over our speech there is a monoto-
nous rapture of persistent regular stresses and waves of lines breaking
rhyme after rhyme. There have been poets for whom this rise and fall,
the mothering swell and ebb, was all. Amoebic intelligences, dwelling in
the memorial of tidal voice, they arouse in our awake minds a spell, so
that we let our awareness go in the urgent wave of the verse. The rhym-
ing lines and the repeating meters persuade us. To evoke night and day
or the ancient hypnosis of the sea is to evoke our powerful longing to fall
back into periodic structure, into the inertia of uncomplicated matter.
Each of us, hungry with life, rises from the cast of seed, having just this

unique identity or experience created in the dance of chromosomes, and having in that identity a time; each lives and falls back at last into the chemistry of death. *rhythm is limited, rhythm is life*

Our consciousness, and the poem as a supreme effort of consciousness, comes in a dancing organization between personal and cosmic identity. What gnosis of the ancients transcends in mystery the notion Schrödinger brings us of an aperiodic structure in *What Is Life?*: ". . . the more and more complicated organic molecule in which every atom, and every group of atoms, plays an individual role, not entirely equivalent to that of others."[1] "Living matter evades the decay to equilibrium," Schrödinger titles a section of his essay of 1944. "When is a piece of matter said to be alive?" he asks, and answers: "When it goes on 'doing something,' moving, exchanging material with its environment." *action = life*

What interests me here is that this picture of an intricately articulated structure, a form that maintains a disequilibrium or lifetime—whatever it means to the biophysicist—to the poet means that life is by its nature orderly and that the poem might follow the primary processes of thought and feeling, the immediate impulse of psychic life. As I start here, first with night and day, then with a genesis of life, and would go forward to the genesis and nature of consciousness, my mind balks at the complication. It is not that we are far afield from the poem. Each poet seeks to commune with creation, with the divine world; that is to say, he seeks the most *real* form in language. But this most real is something we apprehend; the poem, the creation of the poem, is itself our primary experience of it. *life = poem, we = poem*

We work toward the Truth of things. Keats's ecstatic "Beauty is truth, truth beauty" rises from the sureness of poetic intuition or of recognition, our instant knowing of fitness as we work in the poem, where the descriptive or analytic mind would falter. Here the true is beautiful as an arrow flies from its bow with exact aim. Dirac in "The Physicist's Picture of Nature" tells us: "It is more important to have beauty in one's equations than to have them fit experiment."[2] What is at issue here is that the truth does not lie outside the art. For the experimenter it is more important to have beauty in one's experiments than to have them fit mathematics.

The most real, the truth, the beauty of the poem is a configuration, but also a happening in language, that leads back into or on towards the beauty of the universe itself. I am but part of the whole of what I am,

[1] (1944; Cambridge: Cambridge Univ. Press, 1969), p. 60.
[2] *Scientific American* (May 1963): 47.

background?

true should not look for art itself, but rather than with the truth is why it by adhering to already established & exterior norms

cites physicists, equations →

and wherever I seek to understand I fail what I know. In the poem "Atlantis" I had this sense of the fabulous as an intuition of the real:

> The long shadow thrown from this single ob-
> struction to its own light!
> Thought flies out from the old scars of the sea
> as if to land. Flocks that are longings
> come in to shake over the deep water.
>
> It's prodigies held in time's amber
> old destructions
> and the theme of revival the heart asks for.
>
> The past and future are
> full of disasters, splendors
> shaken to earth, seas rising to overshadow
> shores and roaring in.

Beauty strikes us and may be fearful, as there is great beauty in each step as Oedipus seeks the heart of tragedy, his moment of truth, as he tears out his eyes, and sees at last. But this is a heroic and dramatic gesture and may obscure what I would get at. For in our common human suffering, in loss and longing, an intuition of poetic truth may arise. In the poem "A Storm of White" I spoke from my grief, let grief have its voice, in the loss of a cat, a beloved person of my household. He had died of pneumonia within a few weeks of our moving to a house on the coast north of San Francisco.

A STORM OF WHITE

> neither
> sky nor earth, without horizon, it's
> a-
> nother tossing, continually in-
> breaking
>
> boundary of white
> foaming in gull-white weather
> luminous in dull white,   and trees

ghosts of blackness or verdure
that here are
      dark whites in storm.

white white white   like
      a boundary in death advancing
that is our life,   that's love,
      line upon line
breaking in radiance, so soft- so dim-
      ly glaring, dominating

"What it would mean to us if
      he died," a friend writes of one she loves
and that she feels she'll
      outlive those about her.

      The line of outliving
    in this storm   bounding
obscurity from obscurity,   the foaming
      —as if half the universe
(neither sky nor earth, without
      horizon)   were forever

breaking into being another half,
      obscurity   flaring into a surf
upon an answering obscurity.
      O dear gray cat that died in this cold,
      you were born on my chest
      six years ago.

The sea of ghosts dances. It does not
      send your little shadow to us.
I do not understand this
empty place in our happiness.

Another friend writes in a poem
(received today, March 25th 58):

      "Death also
can still propose the old labors."

It is not that poetry imitates but that poetry enacts in its order the order of first things, as just here in this consciousness, they may exist, and the poet desires to penetrate the seeming of style and subject matter to that most real where there is no form that is not content, no content that is not form. "A change of cadence," so the early Imagists realized, "means a new idea." But idea means something seen, a new image: here it is the Way, in which action, vision, and thought have their identity.

In the turn and return, the strophe and antistrophe, the prose and the versus of the choral mode, are remembered the alternations of night and day and the systole and diastole of the heart, and in the exchange of opposites, the indwelling of one in the other, dance and poetry emerge as ways of knowing. Heraclitus wrote the opposites or alternates large and imagined them as phases of a dynamic unity: "God is day, night, winter, summer, war, peace, satiety, hunger, and undergoes alteration in the way that fire, when it is mixed with spices is named according to the scent of each of them."

The Christian Hippolytus accuses Heraclitus of teaching "that the created world becomes maker and creator of itself." The Greek word for "created" being *poieitos* and for "creator" *poieiteis*, the created world is a poem and the creator a poet.

We begin to imagine a cosmos in which the poet and the poem are one in a moving process, not only here the given Creation and the Exodus or Fall, but also here the immanence of the Creator in Creation. The most real is given and we have fallen away, but the most real is in the falling revealing itself in what is happening. Between the god *in* the story and the god *of* the story, the form, the realization of what is happening, stirs the poet. To answer that call, to become the poet, means to be aware of creation, creature, and creator coinherent in the one event. There is not only the immanence of God, His indwelling, but there is also the imminence of God, His impending occurrence. In the expectancy of the poem, grief and fear seem necessary to the revelation of Beauty.

Central to and defining the poetics I am trying to suggest here is the conviction that the order man may contrive or impose upon the things about him or upon his own language is trivial beside the divine order or natural order he may discover in them. To see, to hear, to feel or taste— this sensory intelligence that seems so immediate to us as to be simple and given—comes about in a formal organization so complicated that it remains obscure to our investigation in all but its crudest aspects. To be alive itself is a form involving organization in time and space, continuity and body, that exceeds clearly our conscious design. "It is by avoiding the rapid decay into the inert state of 'equilibrium,' that an organism appears so enigmatic," Schrödinger writes, "so much so, that from the earliest times of human thought some special nonphysical or supernatural force was claimed to be operative in the organism."[3]

There is not a phase of our experience that is meaningless, not a phrase of our communication that is meaningless. We do not make things meaningful, but in our making we work towards an awareness of meaning; poetry reveals itself to us as we obey the orders that appear in our work. In writing I do not organize words but follow my consciousness of—but it is also a desire that goes towards—orders in the play of forms and meanings toward poetic form. This play is like the play of actors upon a stage. Becoming conscious, becoming aware of the order of what is happening is the full responsibility of the poet. The poem that always seems to us such a highly organized event is in its very individuality ("idiocy" the classical Greek would have said), in its uniqueness, crude indeed compared with the subtlety of organization which in the range of contemporary linguistic analysis the study of syntax, morphology, etymology, psychology reveals in the language at large from which the poem is derived. The materials of the poem—the vowels and consonants—are already structured in their resonance, we have only to listen and to cooperate with the music we hear. The storehouse of human experience in words is resonant too, and we have but to listen to the reverberations of our first thought in the reservoir of communal meanings to strike such depths as touch upon the center of man's nature. *what is this?*

Man's nature? Man's speech? Carlyle in his essay "The Hero as Poet" saw the inherent music of our common speech:

> All speech, even the commonest speech, has something of song in it: not a parish in the world but has its parish-accent;—the rhythm or *tune* to which the people there *sing* what they have to say! Accent is a kind of chaunting; all men have accent of their own,—though they only *notice* that of others. Observe too how all passionate language does of itself become musical. All deep things are Song. It seems somehow the very central essence of us, Song; as if all the rest were but wrappages and hulls! The primal element of us; of us, and of all things. The Greeks fabled Sphere-Harmonies: it was the feeling they had of the inner structure of Nature; that the soul of all her voices and utterances was perfect music. Poetry, therefore, we will call *musical Thought*. The Poet is he who *thinks* in that manner. . . . See deep enough, and you

[3] Schrödinger, *op. cit.*, p. 70.

see musically; the heart of Nature *being* everywhere music, if you can only reach it.[4]

This music of men's speech that has its verity in the music of the inner structure of Nature is clearly related to that beauty of mathematics that Schrödinger and Dirac feel relates to the beauty of the inner structure of the physical universe.

The dancer comes into the dance when he loses his consciousness of his own initiative, what *he* is doing, feeling, or thinking, and enters the consciousness of the dance's initiative, taking feeling and thought there. The self-consciousness is not lost in a void but in the transcendent consciousness of the dance. "Night and Day address each other in their swift course, crossing the great brazen threshold," Hesiod sings in his *Theogony;* "the one will go inside, the other comes out." As consciousness is intensified, all the exciting weave of sensory impression, the illustration of time and space, are "lost" as the personality is "lost"; in focus we see only the dancer. We are aware only in the split second in which the dance is present. This presentation, our immediate consciousness, the threshold that is called both *here-and-now* and *eternity,* is an exposure in which, perilously, identity is shared in resonance between the person and the cosmos.

In 1950, with his essay "Projective Verse,"[5] Charles Olson called for a new consideration of form in the poem where the poet as he worked had to be "instant by instant, aware."

> And if you also set up as a poet, USE USE USE the process at all points, in any given poem always, always one perception must must must MOVE, INSTANTER, ON ANOTHER!

In the poem this instant was the attention of "the HEAD, by way of the EAR, to the SYLLABLE." The mind was not to be diverted by what it wanted to say but to attend to what was happening immediately in the poem.

> With this warning, to those who would try: to step back here to this place of the elements and minims of language is to engage speech where it is least careless and least logical.

---

[4] *On Heroes and Hero-Worship and the Heroic in History* (1840).
[5] *Human Universe and Other Essays*, ed. Donald Allen (New York: Grove Press, 1967), pp. 51-61.

At the same time the poem demanded a quickening of "the HEART, by way of the BREATH, to the LINE." Here Olson too was thinking of the dance:

> Is it not the PLAY of a mind we are after, is it not that that shows whether a mind is there at all? . . . And the threshing floor for the dance? Is it anything but the LINE?

This play of heart and mind we see as the play of life itself in the extension of our language as life plays in the extension of our lifetime upon the threshold of consciousness between what man is and his Cosmos—the very fire of Heraclitus upon the hearth where the imagination of what man is and what the cosmos is burns. Our gods are many as our times are many, they are the cast and events of one play. There is only this one time; there is only this one god.

If the sea is first mother of the living, the sun is first father, and fire is his element. Here too death and life, the heat of our blood and the light of our mind, in one reality. That I have seen in poems as the fire upon the hearth, the genius of the household, as if the secret of our warmth and companionship were hidden in a wrathful flame.

FOOD FOR FIRE, FOOD FOR THOUGHT

good wood
that all fiery youth burst forth from winter,
    go to sleep in the poem.
Who will remember thy green flame,
    thy dream's amber?

Language obeyd flares tongues in obscure matter.
    We trace faces in clouds: they drift apart,
    palaces of air—the sun dying down
        sets them on fire;

    descry shadows on the flood from its dazzling mood,
    or at its shores read runes upon the sand
        from sea-spume.

This is what I wanted for the last poem,
a loosening of conventions and return to open form.

Leonardo saw figures that were stains upon a wall.
Let the apparitions contain in the ground
　　　play as they will.
You have carried a branch of tomorrow into the room.
Its fragrance has awakend me—no,

　　it was the sound of a fire on the hearth
　　leapd up where you bankt it, sparks of delight
　　　　Now I return the thought!
　　to the red glow, that might-be-magical blood,
　　palaces of heat in the fire's mouth
"If you look you will see the salamander,"
　　　to the very elements that attend us,
　　　fairies of the fire, the radiant crawling . . .

That was a long time ago.
No, they were never really there,

　　tho once I saw—Did I stare
　　into the heart of desire burning
　　and see a radiant man? like those
　　fancy cities from fire into fire falling?

We are close enough to childhood, so easily purged
of what we thought we were to be,

flamey threads of firstness go out from your touch.

Flickers of unlikely heat
at the edge of our belief bud forth.

There is an emotion, a realization, but it is also a world and a self,
that impends in the first stirrings of a poem. In a poem like "A Storm of
White" or "Food for Fire, Food for Thought," the voice may seem to rise
directly from or to the incoming breakers that had become a moving
whiteness into which I stared or the flickering light and shadow cast upon
a wall by a fire on the hearth I had forgotten, waking in the night, still
close enough to the sleeping mind that I dreamed in what was happen-
ing. In "A Poem Beginning with a Line by Pindar," the germ of the poem
quickened as I was reading one evening the *Pythian Odes* translated by
H.T. Wade-Grey and C.M. Bowra. I have an affinity with Pindar, but

here it was my inability to understand that began the work or it was the work beginning that proposed the words I was reading in such a way that they no longer belonged to Pindar's *Pythian I*: "The light foot hears you, and the brightness begins." In Pindar it is the harp of Apollo that the light foot of the dancer hears, but something had intruded, a higher reality for me, and it was the harp that heard the dancer. "Who is it that goes there?" the song cried out.

I had mistaken the light foot for Hermes the Thief, who might be called The Light Foot, light-fingered, light-tongued. The Homeric Hymns tell us that he devised the harp of Apollo and was first in the magic, the deceit, of song. But as Thoth, he is Truth, patron of poets. The infant Hermes, child of Zeus and the lady Maia—Alexandrian gnostics of the second century saw Zeus as the One God and the lady as Maya, name and personification of the Buddha's mother and also of the Great Illusion—-this genius of childhood in his story resolves: "I too will enter upon the rite that Apollo has. If my father will not give it me, I will seek— and I am able—to be a prince of robbers." First crossing the threshold of the Sun, he steals a tortoise. "Living, you shall be a spell against mischievous witchcraft," he says: "but if you die, then you shall make sweetest song." Then staring at the shell, he conceives song's instrument: "As a swift thought darts through the heart of a man when thronging cares haunt him, or as bright glances flash from the eye, so glorious Hermes planned both thought and deed at once."[6]

The poet is such a child in us. And the poem, the instrument of music that he makes from men's speech, has such a hunger to live, to be true, as mathematics has. Numbers and words were both things of a spell. To dream true, to figure true, to come true. Here poetry is the life of the language and must be incarnate in a body of words, condensed to have strength, phrases that are sinews, lines that may be tense or relaxed as the mind moves. Charles Olson in his essays toward a physiology of consciousness has made us aware that not only heart and brain and the sensory skin but all the internal organs, the totality of the body is involved in the act of a poem, so that the organization of words, an invisible body, bears the imprint of the physical man, the finest imprint that we feel in our own bodies as a tonic consonance and dissonance, a being-in-tune, a search for the as yet missing scale. Remembering Schrödinger's sense that the principle of life lies in its evasion of equilibrium, I think too

---

[6] *The Homeric Hymns*, trans. Hugh Evelyn-Whik (Cambridge: Harvard Univ. Press, 1908). Published as part of the Loeb Classical Library.

of Goethe's Faust, whose principle lies in his discontent, not only in his search but also in his search beyond whatever answer he can know. Our engagement with knowing, with craft and lore, our demand for truth is not to reach a conclusion but to keep our exposure to what we do not know, to confront our wish and our need beyond habit and capability, beyond what we can take for granted, at the borderline, the light fingertip or thought-tip where impulse and novelty spring.

This exposed, open form ("Projective Verse," Olson named it in poetry) began to appear in the 1940s. With the *Pisan Cantos* of Ezra Pound and *Paterson* of William Carlos Williams, with the *Symphony in Three Movements* of Stravinsky, I began to be aware of the possibility that the locus of form might be in the immediate minim of the work, and that one might concentrate upon the sound and meaning present where one was, and derive melody and story from impulse not from plan. I was not alone, for other poets—Louis Zukofsky, Charles Olson, Denise Levertov, Robert Creeley—following seriously the work of Pound and Williams, became aware, as I was, that what they had mastered opened out upon a new art where they were first ones working. In music John Cage, Pierre Boulez, or Karlheinz Stockhausen seem in the same way to realize that Stravinsky, Schönberg, and Webern stand like doors, mastering what music was, opening out upon what music must be.

It is a changing aesthetic, but it is also a changing sense of life. Perhaps we recognize as never before in man's history that not only our own personal consciousness but also the inner structure of the universe itself has only this immediate event in which to be realized. Atomic physics has brought us to the threshold of such a—I know not whether to call it certainty or doubt.

The other sense that underlies the new form is one that men have come to again and again in their most intense or deepest vision, that the Kingdom is here, that we have only now in which to live—that the universe has only now in which to live. "The present contains all that there is," Whitehead says in *The Aims of Education:*

> It is holy ground; for it is the past, and it is the future. . . . The communion of saints is a great and inspiring assemblage, but it has only one possible hall of meeting, and that is the present; and the mere lapse of time through which any particular group of saints must travel to reach that meeting-place, makes very little difference.[7]

[7] *The Aims of Education and Other Essays* (New York: The Macmillan Co., 1929), p. 3.

Pages from A Notebook

1.

On Revisions. In one way or another to live in <u>the swarm of human</u> <u>speech</u>. This is not to seek perfection but to draw honey or poetry out of all things. After Freud, we are aware that unwittingly we achieve our form. It is, whatever our mastery, the inevitable use we make of the speech that betrays to ourselves and to <u>our hunters (our readers)</u> the spoor of what we are becoming.

I study what I write as I study out any mystery. A poem, mine or another's, is an occult document, a body awaiting vivisection, analysis, X-ray.

<u>My revisions are my new works, each a poem a revision of what has</u> <u>gone before. In-sight. Re-vision.</u>

I have learnd to mistrust my judgment upon what I have done. Too often what I thot inadequate proved later richer than I knew; what I thot slavishly derivative proved to be "mine."

On Quality and Poems. A longing grows to return to the open composition in which the accidents and imperfections of speech might awake intimations of human being.

He searches for quality like a jeweler—and he is dependent one suspects on whether his emotion (which he polishes) is a diamond or no. That is, he would attempt to cut any stone diamond-wise, to force his emotion to the test. He would discover much if he also would cut paper-crowns or scatter the pebbles and litter of a mind wherever he goes.

On the Secret Doctrine. There are neglected, even scornd, books in which one begins to find the Gnosis of the modern world. These stories (Macdonald calld his early novel *Phantastes*), fantasies, disclose for the explorer the thread of wisdom. The world of childhood created by Hans

First published as *The Artist's View*, 5 (July 1953), and then reprinted in part in *The New American Poetry*, ed. Donald M. Allen (New York: Grove Press, 1960).

Christian Andersen, George Macdonald, or L. Frank Baum. The power of these works lies not solely in their images of the subconscious, in their being our inherited dreams. But there is another source of mystery, of true "magic"—for these hold a kernel, a secret of the soul. These fantasies are re-inventions of soul.

Where there is a soul, all the world and body become the soul's adventure or trial. The body is real and all real things perish. But realities give birth to unrealities. As Plato discoverd, or St. Augustine discoverd in the City of God, unrealities, fantasies, mere ideas, can never be destroyd. Soul is the body's dream of its continuity in eternity—a wraith of mind. Poetry is the very life of the soul: the body's discovery that it can dream. And perish into its own imagination.

Why should one's art then be an achievement? Why not, more an ✗ adventure? On one hand one produces only what one knows. Well, what else can one accomplish. The thrill is just that one did not know one knew it. But now I like to wander about in my work, writing so rapidly that I might overlook manipulations and design; the poetic experience advancing as far as one can (as far as one dares) toward an adventure. All design here is a recovery if it belongs to ones art; a discovery if it belongs to ones adventuring courage. Courage? Courage to travel on roads of no glory; to dwell in the storm which Shakespeare saw in the idiot's mind; a poor boob; to be even inarticulately simple. *i. e. me ∺*

On Publishing. Could it be that when poetry no longer has any cultural value; when poetry no longer furnishes the gentleman's library with its elegance or the English professor with his livelihood; that a poetry will remain, cherished only by unimportant people who love or adventure.

Poems are now, when they are "ours," fountains: as in Oz, of life or of forgetfulness of self-life. What we expected poetry to be when we were children. A world of our own marvels. Doors of language. Adoration. We dreamd not originally of publishing. What a paltry concern. No child of imagination would center there. But we dreamd of song and the reality of romance.

It is the marvelous of *The Pisan Cantos* that reassures me. Even after a lifetime of the struggle for publication and importance, because of his love for poetry, for song and for romance, Pound dwells in the innermost enchantment of mind. He has been initiated into a world transformd and inhabited by spirits.

On Suffering. I once dreaded happiness, for I thot that to be happy was to be contented. Coleridge writes in his *Table Talk* on the great evil of too entire domestication.

The domestic world might have been our achievement. The poet, the adventurer, dreads achievements, eschews rest. But for the imagination all "achievements" are unreally worlds; apparent entireties of domestication are in themselves undomesticated Africas. Our love is both the storm and the hearth of our emotional being.

I once dreaded happiness, for I thot that ones being, ones art, sprang full grown from suffering. But I found that one suffers happiness in that sense. There is no magic of poetry that will remain magic because one has sought wisdom. The wisdom of the heart is, one finds, an other magic. It was the disappearance of dread itself that made suffering unessential—as, indeed, happiness had become unessential.

And then (I am not domestic by nature) the home is the sheerest product of my imagination, a triumph of soul—at every point magically imaginary. I mean, of course, that happiness itself is a forest in which we are bewilderd, run wild, or dwell, like Robin Hood, outlawd and at home. *※*

On Science. Croce thinks with Vico that poetry is a kind of thot primitive to science, and that the imagination creates in poetry an inarticulate ground from which particulars and exactitudes are distinguishd. But poetry is not primitive to anything but poetry. Only ideas of poetry develop from the ideas of poetry. For the poet, science seems like poetry itself a primitive conceiving of things. *flipping gen. relationship w/ science on its head*

Medicine can cure the body. But soul, poetry, is capable of living in, longing for, choosing illness. Only the most fanatic researcher upon cancer could share with the poet the concept that cancer is a flower, an adventure, an intrigue with life.

The magnificence of Freud is that he never seeks to cure an individual of being himself. He seeks only that the individual may come to know himself, to be aware. It is an underlying faith in Freud that every "patient" is Man Himself, and that every "disease" is his revelation. *loves Freud*

On Christianity. It is true that our salvation lies in Christ. That is, in the god who is crucified (lost) and then resurrected (saved). The outrage of the Christians upon humanity is that they sought to impose salvation as the sole adventure of life. Christian fury loosed upon those who do not desire to be saved thru Christ is the very hell, exactly the hell, which they condemn all non-Christians to. At times I would rather be burnd or physically tortured for my disinterest in or disavowal of salvation than to be subjected to Xtian argument. "It is not my intention to enter the city of man's salvation."

Yet one must honor Christ as one honors salvation. This non-Christian's view is just that he would not, in honoring Christ, dishonor or displace any of the other gods, dreams, goddesses, eternities of human vision. If one views all religions as human inventions, projections and pageants of the imagination, then Christ may be included, adored; one may even, seeking salvation there, come into heaven without casting a world into hell.

But if Christ, heaven, or hell are real, in the sense that Christian belief demands, then we are all damnd. And I should knowingly choose an eternity of hell fire. For I find many gods more loveable than Jehovah, and I find Lao-tzu and Buddha more wise; and Confucius more reasonable than Christ.

On Children Art and Love. Created by the imagination, the parent's love might well have gone along with the child, but the parent, we notice, more often refuses love there; holds out in loving. Parental love goes only as the child goes along with the parent.

This is the crippling of the imagination or rather its starvation. The world of wonders is limited at last to the parent's will (for will prospers where imagination is thwarted); intellectual appetites become no more than ambitions; curious minds become consciences; love, hatred, affection, and cruelty cease to be responses and become convictions. And the adventure of life becomes a self-improvement course.

It is the key to our own inner being that the child offers us in his self-absorption. He would eagerly share himself with us, were we not so determined that he be heir to our achievement.

Human learning is not a fulfillment but a process, not a development but an activity. Andersen, Macdonald, Baum tell us that wisdom belongs to the child as well as to us. But we have turnd from, and indeed "willingly" forsaken, wisdom for what we might acquire.

Every moment of life is an attempt to come to life. Poetry is a "participation," a oneness. Can the ambitious artist who seeks success, perfection, mastery, ever get nearer to the universe, can he ever know "more" or feel "more" than a child may?

To be a child is not an affair of how old one is. "Child" like "angel" is a concept, a realm of possible being. Many children have never been allowd to stray into childhood. Sometimes I dream of at last becoming a child.

A child can be an artist, he can be a poet. But can a child be a banker? It is in such an affair as running a bank or managing a store or directing a war that adulthood counts, an experienced mind. It is in the world of these pursuits that "experience" counts. One, two, three, times and divided by. The secret of genius lies in this: that here experience is not made to count. Where experience knows nothing of counting, it creates only itself out of itself.

On Lions. The Christians thot of the lion as Christ the King: because the lion was a terrible power and at the same time a beast of great beauty.

For me, the Lion is the Child, the unfetterd intellect that knows in his nobility none of the convictions and dogmas which human mind inflicts itself with—what is the human desire to humiliate even its own being?

[margin, handwritten: Christians chose symbol of that misrepresents]

For me, the Lion is sexual appetite that knows no contradiction within itself. The dream of myself as Emperor of the World. Laura Riding suggests that in Story one is Emperor of the World, creator of all things; that wisdom comes in abdicating. The freedom of the individual lies in his institution of anarchy where before he was sole ruler.

Muse Amused. To bemuse, I think of a sphinx, smiling to myself. Only the inscrutable amuses.

2.

Notes Midway on My Faust.

Faust is right when he sez everything is Truth. But each of us finds everything beyond his conception. And even of the everything with which we compose our minds we have constructed designs of which we knew nothing, edifices of much that we had named lies we have fitted, ourselves, into monuments of eternal truth.

The malice of churches, the malice of witches: how can they exceed each other? The wisdom of the parent, the idiocy of fan-dancers, the idiocy of poets: how can they exceed each other?

The only thing a student can learn from a teacher is what he can teach his teacher. What can a teacher learn from a student?

My *Faust* is not a very divine Comedy. At times in writing it I am dismayd by the cheap turns that seem to suffice: but if one must have revelation, one must accept that what is reveald may not be disgraceful in any glamorous sense.

Writing is compounded of wisdom and intuition. Faust seeks to wrench himself free from the world of wisdom and to achieve pure intuition. My lot is not Faust's lot, but the play's lot: this conflict unresolved. But then the trouble of the soul is not in this carcass a tug of war or a choice of two worlds. Everywhere dissenting, contradictory voices speak up, I find. I don't seek a synthesis, but a mêlée. It is only as I have somewhat accepted my inconsequential necessities that I have been able to undertake a play. But a play is a play here—a prolongd charged aimless, constantly aimd, play ground. Only play for me did not mean slides, games, teeter-totters and tots; but moods, cities, and desires. In the jungle of words and the life in doubts afterwords, I have discoverd certain bright courses after my own heart: not to be saved; and then to portray carnal pleasures that the world denies, and we deny ourselves. Well, part of the drama of holding back and of immersing oneself is the sheer sexual set-to of marriage and our dreams. There is no contradiction between the two, but we set them to in order to avoid the perplexity, the "peril of our souls" in freedom. The problem is that we dread all inconsequential experience; our taboo is at root against unintelligible passions.

I have "selected" my works, weeded out the poetry which is not all of a tone, and composed a works that has a remote consistency. But resurrect everything: and one will discover my true book—no pleasure for aesthetes. A composite indecisive literature, attempting the rhapsodic, the austere, the mysterious, the sophisticated, the spontaneous, "higglety-pigglety" as Emory Lowenthal sez.

The host of my heroes, gods, and models betrays an unsettled spirit. (Enter two Devils and the Clown runs up and down crying.) Two Devils? What a simple distraction.

Where I am ambitious only to emulate, imitate, reconstrue, approximate, duplicate: Ezra Pound, Gertrude Stein, Joyce, Virginia Woolf, Dorothy Richardson, Wallace Stevens, D. H. Lawrence, Edith Sitwell, Cocteau, Mallarmé, Marlowe, St. John of the Cross, Yeats, Jonathan Swift, Jack Spicer, Céline, Charles Henri Ford, Rilke, Lorca, Kafka, Arp, Max Ernst, Saint-John Perse, Prévert, Laura Riding, Apollinaire, Brecht, Shakespeare, Ibsen, Strindberg, Joyce Cary, Mary Butts, Freud, Dali, Spenser, Stravinsky, William Carlos Williams, and John Gay.

[handwritten margin note: everything, even the rejects, are his work]

Higglety-pigglety: Euripedes and Gilbert. The Strawhat Reviewers, Goethe (of the *Autobiography*—I have never read *Faust*) & H.D. The despair of all sincere folk, the dismay of all greatness. "All"? What I lack in pretension I make up in wit.

3.

In Complete Agreement on Writing

The Hive. Charlemagne, emperor of the world, sleeping in his chamber surrounded by his golden bees, the *fleur de lys*. Words, the royal apis. The name, immortality, a noun, prerogative of kings. And the comb of un-knowing design. The hive of human being: it is this in part we work in composing. Poets, we hear languages like the murmuring of bees. Swarm in the head. Where the honey is stored. An instinct for words where, like bees dancing, in language there is a communication below the threshold of language.

There is a natural mystery in poetry. We do not understand all that we render up to understanding.

Working. I notice basic states, senses for language: all of them possibilities for work. Surety, "the line learnd in the hand"; inspiration, "when they seemingly arrange themselves"; confusion, "I do not seek a synthesis but a mêlée"; violence, "Driven by the language itself, alive with such forces, / he violates, desiring to move / the deepest sound."; intoxication, "losing so many values / just for that sound"; sight, "She hesitates upon the verge of sound. She waits upon a sounding impossibility, upon the edge of poetry." Despair, grief, anger, fear—invaluable preparations for being seized by the language to work purposes we had not contemplated.

I make poetry as other men make war or make love or make states or revolutions: to exercise my facilities at large.

*

But here they all come now fussing and worrying, scolding, correct-ing, striving, sizing up, hovering over, demanding of. Jimmy Broughton calld them the tch tch frumps. "What does it mean? Should it be? Is it great? Or small? Or anything at all? Is it worth? Is it right? Is it wrong? Is it really a song? At all. Is it original? Is it sane? Is it obscure? Is it really yours? Is it universal? Is it sense? Or nonsense?" Here they all come: should, ought to, have to, must, one two, wish it were, like and, little cousin, don't like.

Out they go, all of them! Bit noses, aesthetes, entrepreneurs, authorities, fat burghers haggling over the sales counters and auctions of literature.

It Finally Dawnd. It was a painful lesson. To give up greatness when one was not capable of it; to surrender fame when fame was out of the question. Yet what a relief at last to dwell in ignominious defeat. Once it dawnd on me that I might, without talent, become what the most sadistic busybodies calld me—an ersatz piece of goods; a provincial poetaster; a bounder, a dilettante: I found myself freed from all responsibilities.

Here I am, at last, I said. Why who cares now, not I, that I imitate or pretend, or sit a great frog in the mighty puddle of my own front room. Here I need not be mature. I can be, as Virginia Admiral used to accuse, wet behind the ears, adolescent indeed. I shall live out my life in this small world, with my imaginary genius, doing as I please, as fancy will; all pretension and with my wits at an end at last.

*

Do I believe in God? heaven? hell? salvation? damnation? What a trickery this is, to ask a poet. In centaurs? in lovers? in suffering? in metamorphosis? How obscene are these creations of the treacherous imagination. Xtians have been murdering Jews, Moslems and heathen Chinese for centuries to establish the kingdom of their imagination on earth. As Joyce sez, their poor little magic nation. To make a living poetry. A living universal poem, an inspiration realized, is a scourge for all.

I am a poet, self-declared, manqué.

I have never been and never will be baptized, converted, psychoanalyzed, initiated, graduated, endowd, sacramented or insured. I sin in my own sight. I pray to myself. All else were discourtesy. Self-excommunicated from the sacraments of high poetry.

How invaluable these terms of theology are in making divorce with the Western World. But they are valueless for all else. If God's eye is on the sparrow, what is the sparrow's eye on? Or do we care a damn about sparrows after all?

Sounds and the Sea. A Poet cares about sparrows. To hear them chatter. Chirpings of song and sounds in the ear.
  The beat of the heart: inside.
  The pounding of the sea: outside.
  Pulses of poetry reflecting.

4.

Descriptions Of Imaginary Poetries.

1. Where giant wordlings interrupt the stuttering machine-gun-wit; the pale insensible bland body phrases loom, as islands in the line-of-fire. Not targets, but meaningless casualties. Luminous blobs in a splattered night scene. Too accidental for inspiration, too clumsy for lyric.

2. Gaps.
      Regular straining.
Great rips in the febrile goods..
  Gapes
  A leftover intending.

3. My god, we thot after four minutes, how much more of this can there be? O a pure pure tedium. With and without ideas. A pure lovely tedium.

4. The poet can hardly lift these words.
  Not because they are heavy, but because he is so weak.

5. Unfolding phrases, like chairs closing into themselves. Furnitures walking, shifting sides over legs, backs. A gate closed in order to open. Irregular measures of meaning. The words, all cream and curds, all slick and sheen.
  Drop and drop of acid. A bitter cool smooth move ball bearing. A heavy wooden convertible structure.

6. A field of targets and archers.
  Bright. Black red and white concentric circles the bulls eyes. Looking not watching. Sing sting sing slings of fortune. Birds fly far afield in far off sky. A shout arises. Almost. Halloo. Elegiac victories.
  And all this refers to one's extreme of youth. How extreme youth is.

7.   Wide awake and confusions.
     Then drowsy illness. Ill, at ease.
     Then. Deep imageless sequence of words as blackout.
     Two words startled like deep sleeping
     deer started up from
     deep started up from
     deep thicket of words. Aroused.
     Confusion, like the breaking and smashing and trampling of
     a thicket of words.
     A weary after statement of wide awake confused
     aroused.

8.   Two or three occasional
     endearing clear
     statement of a tea pot, a
     sculptural head, a cat asleep.

Ideas of the Meaning of Form

Phases of meaning in the soul may be like phases of the moon, and, though rationalists may contend against the imagination, all men may be one, for they have their source out of the same earth, mothered in one ocean and fathered in the light and heat of one sun that is not tranquil but rages between its energy that is a disorder seeking higher intensities and its fate or dream of perfection that is an order where all light, heat, being, movement, meaning and form, are consumed toward the cold. The which men have imagined in the laws of thermodynamics.

But if our life is mixed, as the suspicion comes from the Gnostics and from Blake, and rays of many stars that are suns of all kinds, Aie! if we are so many fathered, or if, as theosophists have feared, we were many mothered in the various chemistries of the planets, still let the war be done and the adultery rage on, for <u>my soul is sick with fear and conten-</u> <u>tion whenever I remember the claim of mind against mind and some ass</u> <u>praises me because a line rimes who would despise me if he knew the</u> <u>meanings, and I am aroused myself toward thoughts of vengeance and</u> <u>triumph.</u> Thus, I say, "Let the light rays mix," and, against the Gnostics, who would free the sparks of spirit from what is the matter, and against the positivists and semanticists who would free the matter from its inspirational chaos, I am glad that there is night and day, Heaven and Hell, love and wrath, sanity and ecstasie, together in a little place. Having taken thought upon death, I would be infected by what is.

despises critics?

> she said, Sir, it is a most beautiful fragrance,
> as of all flowering things together;

Thus, H.D., fifteen years ago, in *The Flowering of the Rod*: "But Kasper knew the seal of the jar was unbroken." And William Carlos Williams in the close of "Asphodel":

First published in a mimeographed version for Warren Tallman's classes at the University of British Columbia, 1961; it was revised and published in *Kulchur* 4 (1961). The essay appeared in *Fictive Certainties: Essays by Robert Duncan* (New York: New Directions, 1985).

Asphodel
  has no odor
    save the imagination
but it too
  celebrates the light.
    It is late
but an odor
  as from our wedding
    has revived for me
and begun again to penetrate
  into all crevices
    of my world.

The end of masterpieces . . . the beginning of testimony. Having their mastery obedient to the play of forms that makes a path between what is in the language and what is in their lives. In this light that has something to do with all flowering things together, a free association of living things then—for my longing moves beyond governments to a cooperation; that may have seeds of being in free verse or free thought, or in that other free association where Freud led me to remember their lives, admitting into the light of the acknowledged and then of meaning what had been sins and guilts, heresies, shames and wounds;

  that may have to do with following the sentence along a line of feeling until the law becomes a melody, and the imagination, going where it will—to the stars! may return to penetrate, a most beautiful fragrance, into all the crevices of our world:

  in this light I attempt to describe what I most abhor, what most seems to exclude or mistake the exuberance of my soul.

CONVENTION, CONFORMITIES, AND REGULATED METERS

Form, to the mind obsessed by convention, is significant in so far as it shows control. What has nor rime nor reason is a bogie that must be dismissed from the horizons of the mind. It is a matter of rules and conformities, taste, rationalization, and sense. Beyond, as beyond in the newly crowded Paris or London of the Age of Reason, lies the stink of shit and pestilence. Wherever the feeling of control is lost, the feeling of form is lost. The reality of the world and men's habits must be constricted to a realm—a court or a salon or a rationale—excluding whatever is

inclusion of fear

feared. It is a magic that still survives in Christian Science and the New Criticism, a magic that removes the reasonable thing from its swarming background of unreason—unmentionable areas where all the facts that reason cannot regulate are excluded and appear as error, savage tribes, superstitions, and anarchical mobs, passions, madnesses, enthusiasms, and bad manners. Metaphor must be fumigated or avoided (thought of as displaying the author's fancy or wit) to rid the mind of the poetic, where metaphor had led dangerously toward Parcelsus' universe of psychic correspondences, toward a life where men and things were beginning to mix and cross boundaries of knowledge. Poets, who once had dreams and epiphanies, now admit only to devices and ornaments. Love, that had been a passion, had best be a sentiment or a sensible affection. Rational piety and respect for God stood strong against divine inspiration and demonic possession. The struggle was to have ideas and not to let ideas have one. Taste, reason, rationality rule, and rule must be absolute and enlightened, because beyond lies the chiaroscuro in which forces cooperate and sympathies and aversions mingle. The glamor of this magic haunts all reasonable men today, surrounding them with, and then protecting them from, the shadows cast by the enlightenment, the darkness of possibilities that control cannot manage, the world of thought and feeling in which we may participate but not dominate, where we are used by things even as we use them.

This frame of mind still holds a dominant place today. In literary circles (literary societies were an expression of this prophylactic genius against experience) there are so many mentors of wit and taste, of what ought to be, "hoping with glory to trip up the Laureate's feet," whose meters must perform according to rules of iamb and spondee, these phantasms of the convention triumphing over the possible disorder or music that threatens in the contamination of actual stresses in the language.

later, this seems not so random

So, one Miss Drew (selected by me at random from a library recommended-currents shelf to represent up-to-date academic opinion about form in poetry) defining the art of the poet: "A metrical scheme is itself simply a mechanical framework, a convention, within which and against which, the poet orders his individual poetic movement," reacts throughout against any thought that there might be, as Carlyle was not afraid to think, a music in the heart of things that the poet sought. What Carlyle saw was that the key to that music lay in the melody (which we must take it Miss Drew has never heard) of the language itself, where "all speech, even the commonest speech, has something of song in it: not a

[handwritten margin notes: poetry = Song w/a capital S]

parish in the world but has its parish-accent;—the rhythm or *tune* to which the people there *sing* what they have to say." But Carlyle in those lectures in 1840 was concerned with the return of the heroic spirit. Miss Drew is a latter-day believer in men cut down to the proper size, a mistress of that critical demon that Pound in his *Cantos* calls Pusillanimity.

Contrast the voice and spirit of Carlyle, where imagination appears as an intuition of the real: "All deep things are Song. It seems somehow the very central essence of us, Song; as if all the rest were but wrappages and hulls! The primal element of us; of us, and of all things. The Greek fabled Sphere-Harmonies: it was the feeling they had of the inner structure of Nature; that the soul of all her voices and utterances was perfect music. Poetry, therefore, we call *musical* thought. The Poet is he who *thinks* in that manner. At bottom, it turns still on power of intellect; it is a man's sincerity and depth of vision that makes him a Poet. See deep enough, and you see musically; the heart of Nature *being* everywhere music, if you can only reach it." Against which the voice and spirit of Miss Drew: "The convention sets up a pattern of recurrent sound effects which is pleasant to the ear. It is an element in a larger movement, his rhythm. Rhythm means flow, and flow is determined by meaning more than meter, by feeling more than feet. It represents the freedom the poet can use within his own self-imposed necessity. It is the personal voice speaking through the formal convention."

[handwritten margin notes: form as "self-imposed necessity"; this is great; ha!]

What we see in the contrast is, in scope of imagination, style, intellect, unfair perhaps. Carlyle is so obviously a mind troubled by genius; Miss Drew is so obviously a mind troubled only by, as she calls it, "a self-imposed necessity." But the genius of convention, that was brilliant in the 17th and 18th centuries, in our own is liable to come out small or trivial. Carlyle's thought opens a vista toward what our own inspired science of linguistics has made part of our responsibility, if we are concerned with the nature of things. Carlyle's thought going toward the inner structure of Nature had intuitions of the inner structure of language. The science of Sapir and Whorf has its origins in the thought of "The Hero as Poet." Just as, exemplified in Miss Drew, one of the stands of the conventional, of all reasonable men, is against the heroic.

"Pound's cult of *Imagism*," Miss Drew goes on, "demanded no rhythmical stress at all, only a clear visual image in lines alleged to be in the pattern of the musical phrase. When read aloud, these patterns couldn't possibly be distinguished from prose. The result was a flood of poems such as William Carlos Williams' 'The Red Wheelbarrow,' which proves perhaps only that words can't take the place of paint."

[handwritten margin notes: For my paper]

It is of the essence of the rationalist persuasion that we be protected, by the magic of what reasonable men agree is right, against unreasonable or upsetting information. Here, in order to follow Miss Drew's intelligence, we must be ignorant of (aggressively oppose the facts) or innocent of (passively evade the facts) history (what Imagism actually was), poetics (what Pound actually did say about tone and duration, stress and phrase), gestalt (what a pattern actually is in time, and how poetry and music have common characteristics by reason of that extension), linguistics (what the actual patterns of vowel and consonant, stress and pitch, are in the language); and, finally, we must be determined to read "The Red Wheelbarrow" to fit Miss Drew's determination that "these patterns couldn't possibly be distinguished from prose."

The base evil of Miss Drew's mind is that it must depend upon our taking its authority. Her evocation throughout of "mechanical framework," "orders his movement," "determined," "imposed," "alleged" and then "ought" and "ought not," "couldn't possibly," "can't" is the verbal effluvia of a mind holding its own ("self-imposed necessity") against experience. For were we to question her authority in light of the poem, we would find that there is some difference in movement between the poem she seems to have read that went as follows: "So much depends upon a red wheel barrow glazed with rain water beside the white chickens" and the actual poem. But it is part of her conviction that the appearance on the page of a line is a matter of convention, must indicate either following or disobeying what men have agreed on. Any other meaning, that the line might be a notation of how it is to be read, is intolerable.

So she must overlook or deny the lines as meaningful notation, where syllabic measures of variable number alternate with lines of two syllables to form a dance immediate to the eye as a rhythmic pattern:

> four syllables (two one-syllable words + one two-syllable word)
> one two-syllable word
> three syllables (three one-syllable words)
> one two-syllable word
> three syllables (three one-syllable words)
> one two-syllable word
> four syllables (one two-syllable word + two one-syllable words)
> one two-syllable word.

She must overlook, fail to hear, or deny the existence of riming vowels in "glazed" and "rain," "beside" and "white" that give a balanced emphasis to the measure in the close; much less an ear for the complex or subtle relations that syncopate the opening lines between "so much" and "barrow," "depends" and "red wheel," "a" and "upon."

At every level her mind was excited to resist against Williams's "so much depends." Her goal in criticism was not to explore the meaning and form of the poem but to stand against it; to remain independent of red wheelbarrow, vowels and consonants, count of syllables and interchange of stresses, juncture, phrase.

"Whether this kind of thing pleases," she decides firmly, "must be a matter of personal taste, but it should not be called *verse, since that word means that the rhythm turns and repeats itself; just as prose means that it runs straight on.*"

But criticism like this is a monster of poor sort. Though I am unread in contemporary verse of the conventional persuasion outside of the work of Marianne Moore, T.S. Eliot, and Robert Lowell, I realize that beyond these there is marshaled an imposing company of arbiters and camp followers, lady commandos of quatrains right! and myrmidons of the metaphysical stanza, holding the line against any occurrence of, much less the doctrines of, poetic genius or romantic imagination, handing out prizes (booby and otherwise) to balance the accounts and bolster standards. Schoolmarms and professors of literature affronted by the bardic presumptions of Dame Edith Sitwell.

Were our songs of the universe and our visions of that great Love who once appeared to Dante holding his smoking heart in his hand, were our feelings and thoughts that had flowed out of whatever originality they might have had into their origins in phrases of a melody, were our dreams and our architectures to come home at last, members of no more than a classroom education?

Convention, anyway, in these circles of literary critics and schoolmasters is a proper mode, and seldom rises to any height above the general conventionality, having its roots (like the unconventionality of "beats") in what other men think. But in the vitality of poets, of Marianne Moore or of Robert Lowell, some personal necessity rather than social opportunity gives substance and meaning to their conventional verse. The rigorously counted syllables, the certainty of end rimes, the conformation of stanzas arise along lines, not of a self-imposed necessity but of a psychic need.

Stanza must conform to stanza in the work of Marianne Moore wherever the charge of emotion is carried, because awareness at all depends upon a character structure that proves itself in awareness. "Tell me the truth,/especially when it is/unpleasant," she says in "Light Is Speech," and there is the sense of facing the facts, of "Test me, I will resist." Power over things, which is the keynote of the aesthetic of the Man of Reason, is at least related to the power to survive things that inspires Marianne Moore's art. It is not subtlety of movement and inter-relation but the challenge of obstacles and particulars that informs her dance. "No more fanatical adjuster," she remarks in lines that keep their own "constant of the plumbline, of the tilted hat/than Escudero." Her metaphor is never a device but a meaningful disclosure. She is not conventional then by social class or by prejudice, but by nature. But to be conventional by nature leaves her personal and vulnerable, erecting around herself an armored modesty, that can show also an irritable sense of possible violation. In her strength and in her weakness she shows her likeness to this constellation I have been drawing of the genius of defensive Reason.

Robert Lowell, too, is not merely conventional as a matter of what men approve but holds his line and establishes his rime at the edge of disaster. His precisions arise not from a love of the melos, the particles that contribute to the melody, but from a mistrust throughout of free movements. When in *Life Studies* his line grows irregular, it conforms to the movement straining for balance that a drunk knows. Betrayal is immanent:

> In the ebb-
> light of morning, we stuck
> the duck
> -'s web-
> foot, like a candle, in a quart of gin we'd killed.

The notation of these lines is as accurate as in William Carlos Williams, and the art as admirable. But the concept of the verse is not free, but fearful. Where in the later poetry of Williams the end juncture makes possible a hovering uncertainty in which more may be gathered into the fulfillment of the form, in the *Life Studies* of Lowell the juncture appears as a void in measure that is some counterpart of the void in content. How /we feel/can this/foot/get across to/that/line. There.

[margin annotation: good explanation of "free verse" vs. "fear verse"]

In *O to Be a Dragon* Marianne Moore sees in "Combat Cultural" terms which relate directly to the rise in the seventeenth and eighteenth centuries of the Reasonable Convention confronted by intolerable threat:

> I recall a documentary
> of Cossacks: a visual fugue, a mist
> of swords that seemed to sever
> heads from bodies—feet stepping through
> harp-strings in a scherzo. . . .

As, perhaps another conventional soul, Charles Bell, writing in *Diogenes 19*, speaks of "the transformations of Renaissance and Baroque" that filled architecture of churches "with voluptuous riot," bringing religion into a vertigo, "the dramatic contrasts of assertive ego of later religious music, of Gabrielli and Bach." And we recall that the rationalist aesthetic was an heroic effort to find balance against this admission of vertigo, against the swirl of a vastly increased vision of what man might be.

"However," Marianne Moore pauses, and begins her next stanza:

> the quadrille of Old Russia for me:
> with aimlessly drooping handkerchief
> snapped like the crack of a whip;

The tension, the reality of the verse, depends upon its being sufficiently haunted by the thought of its energy as a violence and the thought of its form as repose for the poet to take her stance. But the "aimlessly drooping handkerchief / snapped like the crack of a whip" is an image of the unnecessary conventionality of Marianne Moore's later work where recognition and admiration have disarmed her of the struggle that gave reality to her vigorous lines. Challenged, she may be aroused to display her backbone, to bristle her armatures. But window shopping among the ads of *The New Yorker*, it is not to the aepyornis or rock challenged by time that the figure refers but to the qivies with winning ways.

In her career Marianne Moore began, in certain poems like "An Octopus" or "In the Days of Prismatic Color," with some promise of a free verse, where movement of language had the vigor of a feeling and thought that was not self-conscious. Here the number of lines in the stanza can vary with the immediate sense of movement, and the actual kept feeling of the tempo gives measure rather than the systematic repeated count of syllables or the emphasis of rimes at the end of lines. It is the uneasy definition of what is "sophistication" and what are "the initial great truths" that is one proposition of the poem; it is "the days of Adam and Eve," of "complexity . . . committed to darkness," of smoke, modified color, even murkiness, on the one hand; and "when Adam was alone," where color keeps its place in "the blue-red-yellow band/of in-candescence" on the other. These poems imagine terms of a nature where things may mingle still, though the soul is troubled and the mind already resolved to outlast unsureness.

But in the work in which she found what was typical or original, the metaphor is that of animal or hero who survives by resistance of his spine (backbone) and his spiny armature (protective character structure). Conventionality breeds personality. She conforms to her own society. Individuality, yes, but dependent throughout upon rules and orders even as it insists upon its individuality. Her splendid achievement is to excite our admiration of her performance, her risky equilibriums, and her resistance to deeper thought and feeling where personality is lost. Her skill and her craft are unexcelled. But they depend upon increased self-consciousness, and they divert then the attention of the poet and our attention in reading from the question they beg of the avoidance of emotions too common to be personalized.

In the resolution of "In the Days of Prismatic Color" we note the conditions were already potential where truth is identified with what resists but not with the experience that is resisted: "The wave may go over it if it likes," she says, where "it" is Truth and the wave is experience. "Know that it will be there when it says,/'I shall be there when the wave has gone by'." She evokes in her most famous poetry, with its images of rigorists and armored animals, a heroism of the isolated remnant, a constantly reiterated picture of her own personality as determined in a "little-winged, magnificently speedy running-bird" poetry, increasingly specialized. These poems were practices meant to insure habitual virtues. Vision and flight of the imagination were sacrificed to survival in terms of personal signature.

In pieces like "Hometown Piece for Messrs. Alston and Reese," "Enough," and "In the Public Garden," she sacrifices character to the possibilities of what America loves in public personality. What had been a display of bony determination and admirable protective structure becomes now a projection of loveable peculiarity, a profession of charming helplessness. In her career she has performed a range that once in history had its hopeful beginnings in Dryden, then its heroic dimensions in the rage of Pope and Swift, and at last, its social occasions in our own day when "a British poet," as Auden writes in the Introduction to his 1956 *Book of Modern American Verse,* "can take writings more for granted and so write with a lack of strain and over-seriousness." We remember, for it applies here, too, the "aimlessly drooping handkerchief" of "Combat

The Enlightenment is the historical source of the oppression of thought.?

Cultural" in this professional lack of over-seriousness, which is the secret superior possibility for Auden.

The vital phase of Rational Genius came as it met straight on the threat of an overwhelming expansion in consciousness that followed the breakthrough in the Renaissance on all levels. The inspiration of Reason was to close off consciousness in an area that was civilized, European, superior in race, practical and Christian (or at least rational in religion). The neo-Platonism and Hermeticism that had begun with Gemisthus Plethon, Ficino, and Pico della Mirandola and appeared in the Rosicrucianism of the early 17th century carried men's religious thought across barriers of right belief, church, and civilization, into realms of imaginative synthesis. The agreement of reasonable men was to quarantine the fever of thought. Rationalism erected a taboo of social shame that still lasts against the story of the soul, against the dream and inner life of men the world over, that might be read were the prejudices of what's right and what's civilized lost. Only in the fairy-tales and lore of the common people or in the ritual and lore of cults whose members incurred the cost in their thought of their being outcast and shamed did the great imagination survive. Churchgoer or atheist, the rational man was immune to revelation.

Ideas of race, of nation and progress, held and still in many circles hold against the recognition that mankind is involved in one life. Respectable critics and versifiers have been as shocked by the "Buddhism" of Allen Ginsberg or Kerouac as they are by the "sex." When the wall broke, and where it broke, orthodoxy or atheism was swept aside, and men began again to read inner meaning and experience in the arts of all places and times, the message of the soul in African masks, in Aeschylus or in Lady Murasaki, even as they read it in the lore of Catholic saints and Protestant mystics, letting the light from Asia come into their souls to wed and mingle with the light from Rome. It was against this flood of information that threatened once men began to explore the world that the genius of Reason was evoked. Against the imagination then.

The plagues and panics that swept men in their physical existence after 1492 had their counterparts in the plaguing contacts with fellow civilizations in America, Africa, and Asia, and the panic that swept Christendom as time before Christendom and space beyond Christendom began to be real and men found their psychic resistances invaded. Up swirled minds and emotions, sciences and art, in a convulsive imagination. There were fearful architectures, gestures, efforts to hold what was not understood and might not be tolerable—in one swirling rhythm. So, in Milton's thundering syntax, the heaped-up effort at architecture, majesty, and vastness, takes over the drama from even Satan, and leaves Adam and Eve impoverished in their identity and as overwhelmed as they are disobedient. How Eve is dwindled in conception from the vital conception of Lady Macbeth or Cleopatra.

There is then a lovely release in the Restoration. The beauty of what the Age of Enlightenment meant we can hear still in the "Ode on the Death of Henry Purcell," where Dryden and John Blow build their musical monument to the genius of art over chaos. Angels sing where demons had lurked in chaos. Had it held, had the lights and shadows played as they do in Watteau's pastoral charades, had all of humanity come in under the charm of the rational imagination, masked and playing in a masque, Eskimos and Congo warriors in costumes of the Commedia dell'arte, might it have been like that? a lovely surety gathering its strength in chaos and uncertainty, to banish care? But the art was based on care. Convention, as long as it was heroic, something greater and finer than what we mean today by conventional verse and conventional manners, held its own and needed care, could take nothing for granted. Those shepherds and milkmaids were what could stand against any thought of those who actually herded the sheep or milked. In a painting by Longhi, Venetian revelers give dimension that is real to a rhinoceros, an animal nature momentarily held in its place.

The crisis of the Enlightenment was the crisis that Keats saw recapitulated in Coleridge's collapse from the inspiration of "The Ancient Mariner" and "Cristabel" to the psychic despair, the rationalist obsession, of later years. "The Ancient Mariner" had evoked the revelation of the soul in terms of world exploration; "Cristabel" had evoked the revelation of the soul in the terms of psychic threat that came from sexual lore condemned by Christendom.

"Negative Capability," Keats wrote in a letter, December 21st, 1817: "that is, when a man is capable of being in uncertainties, mysteries, doubts, without any irritable reaching after fact and reason—Coleridge, for instance, would let go-by a fine isolated verisimilitude caught from the Penetralium of mystery, from being incapable of remaining content with half-knowledge."

Science, too, in Newton, sought fact and reason, some order that did not verge upon uncertainty. Whitehead in *Adventures in Ideas* notes that "Literature preserves the wisdom of the human race; but in this way it enfeebles the emphasis of first-hand intuition." It is against some first-hand intuition that men strove to render wisdom sensible and the immediate experience passing, haunted by some premonition of the uncertainty principle in physical measurements that our own science must face, of the uncertainty of self-knowledge in terms of our psychology and physiology, of the uncertainty of our role in life raised by information of evolution. A psyche that is not all to be lightened! a universe that is not all to be ours!

Fact and reason are creations of man's genius to secure a point of view protected against a vision of life where information and intelligence invade us, where what we know shapes us and we become creatures, not rulers, of what is. Where, more, we are part of the creative process, not its goal. It was against such intolerable realizations that these men took thought. The rationalist gardener's art is his control over nature, and beauty is conceived as the imposed order visible in the pruned hedgerow and the ultimate tree compelled into geometric globe or pyramid that gives certainty of effect.

The poet's art was one of control over the common speech, forcing natural metaphor from all hint of meaningful experience or intuition of the universe and maintaining it as a form of speech, and disciplining syntax and line away from the energies of the language itself into balanced phrases, regular meters and heroic couplets. —As too, in military arts, manoeuvres and disciplines occupy the conscious mind. Men are drilled in order that there be an authority, removing them from immediate concern in the acts of killing and destruction involved. A Frederick the Great may be on the edge of knowing that his wars are devastations, not drills. But to such modern triumphs of the conventional mind as Roosevelt or Eisenhower decisions are matters of reason and plan. Disease, death, terror, and the ruin of cities are not experienced but dealt with, where rational theory wages its war. The question of the use of disease as a weapon has already been decided by reasonable men who developed the diseases to use and who appointed the military power to use them. Wrathful inspiration (divine or demonic) will not move our rulers to war, nor will some romantic drive to power or suicidal imagination: it is convention, what reasonable men agree upon, that will decide all. War, too, becomes rational.

The game of tennis and the minuet both subject the Yahoo of the animal man to the manners and rules of a court and give authority to that trained horse (and house-broken, too, I hope) of the rational faculty that is a Houyhnhnm. But this Yahoo and this Houyhnhnm is one man divided against himself, fantasy of the Enlightenment in his formal wig performing his ritual dance towards the riddance of Yahoos who know nothing of tennis or minuet. I think of those wigs that marked men of fashion and wit from the uneducated and impoverished mob, the conventional wig and the unconventional cap alike perched on the universally lousy scalp.

But my point here is that the minuet, the game of tennis, the heroic couplet, the concept of form as the imposing of rules and establishing of regularities, the theories of civilization, race, and progress, the performances in sciences and arts to rationalize the universe, to secure balance and class—all these are a tribal magic against a real threat of upset and things not keeping their place.

The tonal scale of Mozart, where, even among the given notes on the piano, scales are established, so that certain notes are heard as discordant in relation to other notes, threatening to harmony, is a scale imagined to hold its own against threat. A change in mode, in what was permitted, once threatened demonic disorder. Now, unconventional usages threatened loss of reason or insurrection. It is an architecture built up of symmetries, for the mind feels even visual departures from the norm will bring vertigo and collapse. There must be regular sequences and a repetition of stanzas, because thought must not wander, possibility must contain the reassurance of an end to possibilities.

Even in that beginning that I pictured as a kind of health realized by this creation of "Reason" after the whirling orders of the early seventeenth century, there is an uneasy strain. Dryden in his Preface to *All for Love* needs the reassurance of "a subject which has been treated by the greatest wits of our nation" and "their example has given me the confidence to try myself." Then there must be—why?—"the middle course," "motive," "the excellency of moral," "all reasonable men have long since concluded"—these are the terms of the conventional art at its youthful beginning. The tenor throughout is prophylactic. "Since our passions are, or ought to be, within our power," Dryden proposes. In all fields, in poetry as in government or religion, the goal is system or reason, motive or morality, some set of rules and standards that will bring the troubling plenitude of experience "within our power." As long as the battle is for real, where so much depends upon control of self or of environment, there is pathos and even terror in the reasonable man, for there is so much in man's nature and experiences that would never be within his authority.

Frost is right in his sense that the meters and rimes of regulation verse have a counterpart in the rules, marked areas of the court (establishing bounds and out-of-bounds), and net of the tennis game. ("I would *but couldn't one see free verse as even more challenging?*

as soon write free verse as play tennis with the net down.") But, for those who see life as something other than a tennis game, without bounds, and who seek in their sciences and arts to come into that life, into an imagination of that life, the thought comes that the counterpart of free verse may be free thought and free movement. The explorer displays the meaning of physical excellence in a way different from that displayed by the tennis player.

Linnaeus, who, as Ernst Cassirer describes him in *The Philosophy of the Enlightenment,* "selected arbitrarily certain qualities and features according to which he tries to group the plant world," removing his specimens from the field in which they had their living significance, has a counterpart in anthologists of our day who strive to rise above schools and movements, to remove poetry from any reference to its environment and living associations, and to present what suits their taste—orders that display their acumen and avoid any reference to what is. The stamp or flower collection, the tasteful anthology, the values, weights, standards— all these are justly subject, if we are concerned not with what "all reasonable men have long since concluded" is good, but with what is actually happening, to the criticism science had to make in time of Linnaeus. As given by Cassirer: "He thinks he can give us a picture of the sequence, organization, and structure of this world on the basis of this procedure of mere arrangement, of analytical classification. Such a picture is possible only by a reversal of his procedure. We must apply the principle of connection rather than that of analytical differentiation; instead of assigning living creatures to sharply distinguished species, we must study them in relation to their kinship, their transition from one type to another, their evolution and transformations. For these are the things which constitute life as we find it in nature."

So, a Cecil Hemley wishes that a Donald Allen's anthology had shown better taste, and would group the "best" of Allen's anthology with poets who never in their lives or thoughts were connected with Olson or Creeley or myself or Denise Levertov. Cecil Hemley reflects that he does not have a "taste" for the work of Robert Creeley. Since he has no other conceivable route to knowledge of that work, taste must suffice. But I can have no recourse to taste. The work of Denise Levertov or Robert Creeley or Larry Eigner belongs not to my appreciations but to my immediate concerns in living. That I might "like" or "dislike" a poem of Zukofsky's or Charles Olson's means nothing where I turn to their work as evidence of the real. Movement and association here are not arbitrary, but arise as an inner need. I can no more rest with my impressions of

Maximus than I can indulge my impressions at any vital point: I must
study thru, deepen my experience, search out the challenge and salva-
tion of the work.

What form is to the conventional mind is just what can be imposed,
the rest is thought of as lacking in form. Taste can be imposed, but love
and knowledge are conditions that life imposes upon us if we would come
into her melodies. It is taste that holds out against feeling, originality that
tries to hold out against origins. For taste is all original, all individual
arbitration. Dryden's "reasonable men" who "have long since concluded"
are a bogie of his own invention (though they may be devoutly believed
in at Oxford or Harvard today) and lead at last to the howling dismay
and scorn of Pope, Swift, and Gibbon, who must hold out everywhere
against rampant Stupidity, Madness, and Superstition in the universe of
man's psychic life. In the "Ode on the Death of Henry Purcell" the
illusion is fresh, and the conflicts of conscience and intellect have not yet
appeared, or, perhaps, are subsumed in the honest fact that the work is a
tomb or memorial to its own genius.

How strangely Shakespeare's voice in Prospero's contrasts with Dry-
den's in that period when charm (a device, yes, but a reality of the psyche,
no) is replaced by wit:

> Now my Charmes are all ore-throwne,
> And what strength I have's mine owne.

contrasted with Dryden's "their example has given me the confidence to
try myself." Shakespeare who imagined something of that Negative Ca-
pability that Keats defines must rest not upon example but upon prayer,
having his art by a grace that was not the grace Dryden knew of men's
manners, but a mystery.

> Now I want
> Spirits to enforce; Art to inchant,
> And my ending is despaire

The Enlightenment was to correct even the spelling in its effort to post-
pone the knowledge.

The Homosexual in Society

INTRODUCTION

Seymour Krim has urged me to reprint this early essay as "a pioneering piece," assuring me "that it stands and will stand on its own feet." At the time it was printed (*Politics*, August 1944) it had at least the pioneering gesture, as far as I know, of being the first discussion of homosexuality which included the frank avowal that the author was himself involved; but my view was that minority associations and identifications were an evil wherever they supersede allegiance to and share in the creation of a human community good—the recognition of fellow-manhood.

Blind lifeliness—what Darwin illuminates as evolution—has its creative design, and in that process a man's sexuality is a natural factor in a biological economy larger and deeper than his own human will. What we create as human beings is a picture of the meaning and relation of life; we create perspectives of space and time or a universe; and we create ideas of "man" and of "person," of gods and attendant powers—a drama wherein what and who we are are manifest. And this creation governs our knowledge of good and evil.

For some, there are only the tribe and its covenant that are good, and all of mankind outside and their ways are evil; for many in America today good is progressive, their professional status determines their idea of "man" and to be genuinely respectable their highest concept of a good "person"—all other men are primitive, immature, or uneducated. Neither of these perspectives was acceptable to me. I had been encouraged by my parents, by certain teachers in high school, by friends, through Socialist and Anarchist associations, and through the evidence of all those artists, philosophers and mystics who have sought to give the truth of their feeling and thought to mankind, to believe that there was an entity in the imagination "mankind," and that there was a community of thoughtful men and women concerned with the good of that totality to

Originally appeared in *Politics*, I, 7 (August 1944). The revisions were made in 1959. The expanded version was first published in *Jimmy & Lucy's House of "K,"* 3 (January 1985).

whom I was responsible. The magazine *Politics* represented for me during the Second World War an arena where intellectuals of that community were concerned, and I came to question myself in the light of the good they served.

It was not an easy essay to write. As a form an essay is a field in which we try ideas. In this piece I try to bring forward ideas of "homosexual," "society," "human" and, disguised but evident, my own guilt; and their lack of definition is involved with my own troubled information. Our sense of terms is built up from a constant renewed definition through shared information, and one of the urgencies of my essay was just that there was so little help here where other writers had concealed their own experience and avoided discussion.

Then too, the writing of the essay was a personal agony. Where we bear public testimony we face not only the community of thoughtful men and women who are concerned with the good, but facing the open forum we face mean and stupid men too. The involved disturbed syntax that collects conditional clauses and often fails to arrive at a full statement suggests that I felt in writing the essay that I must gather forces and weight to override some adversary; I have to push certain words from adverse meanings which as a social creature I share with the public to new meanings which might allow for an enlarged good. In the polemics of the essay it is not always possible to find the ground of accusation unless we recognize that I was trying to rid myself of one persona in order to give birth to another, and at the same time to communicate the process and relate it to what I called "society," a public responsibility. I was likely to find as little intellectual approval for the declaration of an idealistic morality as I was to find for the avowal of my homosexuality. The work often has value as evidence in itself of the conflict concerned and of the difficulty of statement then just where it is questionable as argument. I had a likeness to the public and shared its conflicts of attitude—an apprehension which shapes the course of the essay.

I feel today as I felt then that there is a service to the good in bringing even painful and garbled truth of the nature of our thought and feeling to the light of print, for what I only feel as an urgency and many men may condemn me for as an aberration, some man reading may render as an understanding and bring into the wholeness of human experience. Reading this essay some fifteen years later, I need courage to expose the unhappiness of my writing at that time, for I am not today without conflicting feelings and have the tendency still to play the adversary where I had meant only to explore ideas. In preparing the text then

I have eliminated certain references that were topical at the time but would be obscure now and have cut where economy was possible without losing the character of the original; but I have not sought to rewrite or to remedy the effect.

[Robert Duncan's footnotes for the 1944 publication of this essay have been indicated by asterisks and set in a typeface different from the rest of the text. Duncan also added footnotes when he made revisions to the text in 1959. These notes have been indicated by numbers.]

THE TEXT

I propose to discuss a group whose only salvation is in the struggle of all humanity for freedom and individual integrity; who have suffered in modern society persecution, excommunication; and whose intellectuals, whose most articulate members, have been willing to desert that primary struggle, to beg, to gain at the price if need be of any sort of prostitution, privilege for themselves, however ephemeral; who have been willing rather than to struggle toward self-recognition, to sell their product, to convert their deepest feelings into marketable oddities and sentimentalities.

Although in private conversation, at every table, at every editorial board, one *knows* that a great body of modern art is cheated out by what amounts to a homosexual cult; although hostile critics have at times opened fire in attack as rabid as the attack of Southern senators upon "niggers"; critics who might possibly view the homosexual with a more humane eye seem agreed that it is better that nothing be said.[1] Pressed

---

[1] 1959. At a round table on Modern Art held in San Francisco in 1949 a discussion emerged between Frank Lloyd Wright and Marcel Duchamp where both showed the courage of forthright statement, bringing the issue publicly forward, which I lamented the lack of in 1944. *Wright* (who had been challenged on his reference to modern art as "degenerate"): "Would you say homosexuality was degenerate?" *Duchamp*: "No, it is not degenerate." *Wright*: "You would say that this movement which we call modern art and painting has been greatly or is greatly in debt to homosexualism?" *Duchamp*: "I admit it, but not in your terms . . . I believe that the homosexual public has shown more interest or curiosity for modern art than the heterosexual—so it happened, but it does not involve modern art itself."
What makes comment complicated here is that, while I would like to answer as Duchamp does because I believe with him that art itself is an expression of vitality, in part I recognize the justice of Wright's distaste, for there is a homosexual clique which patronizes certain kinds of modern art and even creates because, like Wright, they believe both homosexuality and the art they patronize and create to be decadent and even fashionably degenerate.

to the point, they may either, as in the case of such an undeniable homosexual as Hart Crane, contend that he was great despite his "perversion"*—much as my mother used to say how much better a poet Poe would have been had he not taken dope; or where it is possible they have attempted to deny the role of the homosexual in modern art, defending the good repute of modern art against any evil repute of homosexuality.

But one cannot, in face of the approach taken to their own problem by homosexuals, place any weight of criticism upon the liberal body of critics for avoiding the issue. For there are Negroes who have joined openly in the struggle for human freedom, made articulate that their struggle against racial prejudice is part of the struggle for all; there are Jews who have sought no special privilege or recognition for themselves as Jews but have fought for *human* rights, but there is in the modern American scene no homosexual who has been willing to take in his own persecution a battlefront toward human freedom. Almost coincident with the first declarations for homosexual rights was the growth of a cult of homosexual superiority to heterosexual values; the cultivation of a secret language, the *camp,* a tone and a vocabulary that are loaded with contempt for the uninitiated.

Outside the ghetto the word "goy" disappears, wavers, and dwindles in the Jew's vocabulary as he becomes a member of the larger community. But in what one would believe the most radical, the most enlightened "queer" circles, the word "jam" remains, designating all who are not wise to homosexual ways, filled with an unwavering hostility and fear, gathering an incredible force of exclusion and blindness. It is hard (for all the sympathy which I can bring to bear) to say that this cult plays any other than an evil role in society.[2]

---

*Critics of Crane, for instance, consider that his homosexuality is the cause of his inability to adjust to society. Another school feels that inability to adjust to society causes homosexuality. What seems fairly obvious is that Crane's effort to communicate his inner feelings, his duty as a poet, brought him into conflict with social opinion. He might well have adjusted his homosexual desires within society as many have done by "living a lie" and avoiding any unambiguous reference in his work.

[2] 1959. The alienation has not decreased but increased when the "Beat" cult projects its picture of themselves as saintly—junkies evoking an apocalyptic crisis in which behind the mask of liberal tolerance is revealed the face of the hated "square." Their intuition is true, that tolerance is no substitute for concern; but their belief that intolerance is more true, dramatizes their own share in the disorder. "Goy," "jam," and "square" are all terms of a minority adherence where the imagination has denied

But names cannot be named.[3] There are critics whose cynical, back-biting joke upon their audience is no other than this secret special reference; there are poets whose nostalgic picture of special worth in suffering, sensitivity, and magical quality is no other than this intermediate

---

fellow-feeling with the rest of mankind. Where the community of human experience is not kept alive, the burden of meaning falls back upon individual abilities. But the imagination depends upon an increment of associations.

Where being "queer" or a "junkie" means being a pariah (as it does in beat mythology), behavior may arise not from desire but from fear or even hatred of desire; dope-addiction may not be a search for an artificial paradise, an illusion of magical life, but an attack upon life, a poisoning of response; and sexual acts between men may not mean responses of love but violations of inner nature. Ginsberg (who believes the self is subject to society), Lamantia (who believes the self has authority from God), and McClure (who believes the self is an independent entity) have in common their paroxysms of self-loathing in which the measure of human failure and sickness is thought so true that the measure of human achievement and life is thought false.

But this attitude had already appeared in the work of urban sophisticates like Edmund Wilson and Mary McCarthy where there was an observable meanness of feeling. Robert Lowell's "Tamed by Miltown, we lie on Mother's bed" expresses in the *realism* of neurotic inhibition what Allen Ginsberg's "Creation glistening backwards to the same grave, size of universe" expresses in the *surrealism* of psychotic exuberance. "Mother your master-bedroom / looked away from the ocean" and "O Mother . . . with your nose of bad lay with your nose of the smell of the pickles of Newark" dramatizes with the difference of class the common belief in oedipal grievance.

[3] 1959. That even serious socio-sexual studies are curbed is shown by the following letter written by an eminent poet when I wrote in 1945 asking if I could attempt an essay on his work in the light of my concept that his language had been diverted to conceal the nature of his sexual life and that because he could never write directly he had failed to come to grips with immediacies of feeling:

> ". . . I am very sorry but I must ask you not to publish the essay you propose. I'm sure you will realize that the better the essay you write, the more it will be reviewed and talked about, and the more likelihood there would be of it being brought publicly to my attention in a way where to ignore it would be taken as an admission of guilt.
>
> "As you may know, I earn a good part of my livelihood by teaching, and in that profession one is particularly vulnerable. Further, both as a writer and as a human being, the occasion may always arise, particularly in these times, when it becomes one's duty to take a stand on the unpopular side of some issue. Should that ever occur, your essay would be a very convenient red-herring for one's opponents. (Think of what happened to Bertrand Russell in New York).
>
> "I hope you will believe me when I say that for myself personally I wish I could let you publish it, and that anyway I hope the other essays will be as good as you would like them to be."

My own conviction is that no public issue is more pressing than the one that would make a man guilty and endanger his livelihood for the open knowledge of his sexual nature; for the good of humanity lies in a common quest through shared experience toward the possibility of sexual love. Where we attend as best we can the volitions and fulfillments of the beloved in sexual acts we depend upon all those who in arts have portrayed openly the nature of love; and as we return ourselves through our writing "sixth sense"; there are new cult leaders whose special divinity, whose supernatural and visionary claim is no other than this mystery of sex.[4] The law has declared homosexuality secret, inhuman, unnatural (and why not then supernatural?). The law itself sees in it a crime—not in the sense that murder, thievery, seduction of children, or rape are seen as

---

to that commune of spirit we come close to the sharing in desire that underlies the dream of universal brotherhood. Undeclared desires and private sexuality feed the possibility of sexual lust which has many betrayals, empty cravings, violations, and wants to void the original desire.

That this eminent poet was not wrong in speaking of his professional vulnerability were his sexual nature openly avowed can be verified by the following passage from a letter of an eminent editor after reading "The Homosexual In Society" concerning my poem "Toward An African Elegy" which he had previously admired and accepted for publication:

> ". . . I feel very sure we do not wish to print the poem, and I regret very much to decline it after an original acceptance. I must say for the record that the only right I feel in this action is that belatedly, and with your permission, I read the poem as an advertisement or a notice of overt homosexuality, and we are not in the market for literature of this type.
>
> "I cannot agree with you that we should publish it nevertheless in the name of freedom of speech; because I cannot agree with your position that homosexuality is not abnormal. It is biologically abnormal in the most obvious sense. I am not sure whether or not state and federal law regard it so, but I think they do; I should not take the initiative in the matter, but if there are laws to this effect I concur in them entirely. There are certainly laws prohibiting incest and polygamy, with which I concur, though they are only abnormal conventionally and are not so damaging to a society biologically."

Both these men are leaders in just that community of thoughtful men and women I imagined; both have had and deserved highest honors as literary figures; and, while I believe one to be mistaken in his belief that sexual forthrightness is not a primary issue for the social good; and the other to be as misled by the unhappy conventions of his thought as by the atmosphere of guilty confession that he gathered from my essay; both, like I, are concerned not with the minority in question but rightly with what they consider the public good, an intimation of the human good. Much understanding yet is needed before men of good intentions can stand together.

[4] 1959. I find myself in this passage accusing certain "critics," "poets," and "new cult leaders" of what I might be suspected of in my poetry myself. "Suffering, sensitivity, and magical quality" are constants of mood; divinities and cults, supernatural and visionary claims, and sexual mystery are all elements in subject matter that give rise to poetic inspiration for me. In recent years I have had an increased affinity with imaginative reaches of religious thought, searching gnostic and cabalistic speculation for a more diverse order.

The Demon of Moral Virtue exacts his dues wherever he is evoked. Where we seek the Good he urges us to substitute what will be men's good opinion of us. I may have felt then that I might redeem my sexuality as righteous in the sight of certain critics, if I disavowed my heterodoxy in religious imagination as wicked or deluded.

human crimes—but as a crime against the way of nature.* It has been lit up and given an awful and lurid attraction such as witchcraft was given in the 17th century. Like early witches, the homosexuals, far from seeking to undermine the popular superstition, have accepted and even anticipated the charge of demonism. Sensing the fear in society that is generated in ignorance of their nature, they have sought not understanding but to live in terms of that ignorance, to become witch doctors in the modern chaos.

To go about this they have had to cover with mystery, to obscure the work of all those who have viewed homosexuality as but one of the many ways which human love may take and who have had primarily in mind as they wrote (as Melville, Proust, or Crane had) mankind and its liberation. For these great early artists their humanity was the source, the sole source, of their work. Thus in *Remembrance of Things Past*, Charlus is not seen as the special disintegration of a homosexual but as a human being in disintegration, and the forces that lead to that disintegration, the forces of pride, self-humiliation in love, jealousy, are not special forces but common to all men and women. Thus in Melville, though in *Billy Budd* it is clear that the conflict is homosexual, the forces that make for that conflict, the guilt in passion, the hostility rising from subconscious sources, and the sudden recognition of these forces as it comes to Vere in that story—these are forces which are universal, which rise in other contexts, which in Melville's work have risen in other contexts.

It is, however, the body of Crane that has been most ravaged by these modern ghouls and, once ravaged, stuck up cult-wise in the mystic light of their special cemetery literature. The live body of Crane is there, inviolate in the work; but in the window display of modern poetry, in so many special critics' and devotees' interest, is a painted mummy, deep sea green. One may tiptoe by, as the visitors to Lenin's tomb tiptoe by, and, once outside, find themselves in a world in his name that has celebrated the defeat of all that he was devoted to. One need only point out in all the homosexual imagery of Crane, in the longing and vision of love, the absence of the private sensibility that colors so much of modern writing. Where the Zionists of homosexuality have laid claim to a Palestine of their own—asserting in their miseries their nationality; Crane's suffering, his rebellion and his love are sources of poetry for him, not because

_____

*"Just as certain judges assume and are more inclined to pardon murder in inverts and treason in Jews for reasons derived from original sin and racial predestination." *Sodom and Gomorrah*, Proust.

they are what makes him different from his fellow-men, but because he saw in them his link with mankind; he saw in them his share in universal human experience.[5]

What can one do in the face of this, both those critics and artists, not homosexual, who are, however, primarily concerned with dispelling all inhumanities, all forces of convention and law that impose a tyranny over man's nature, and those critics and artists who, as homosexuals, must face in their own lives both the hostility of society in that they are "queer" and the hostility of the homosexual élite in that they are merely human?

For the first group the starting point is clear, that they must recognize homosexuals as equals, and, as equals, allow them neither more nor less than can be allowed any human being. There are no special rights. For the second group the starting point is more difficult, the problem more treacherous.

In the face of the hostility of society which I risk in making even the acknowledgment explicit in this statement, in the face of the "crime" of my own feelings, in the past I publicized those feelings as private and made no stand for their recognition but tried to sell them as disguised, for instance, as conflicts arising from mystical sources.[6] I colored and

---

[5] 1959. The principal point is that the creative genius of a writer lies in his communication of personal experience as a communal experience. He brings us to realize our own inner being in a new light through the sense of human being he creates, or he creates in us as we read a new sense of our being. And in Melville, Crane, and Proust I saw their genius awaken a common share in homosexual desire and love, in its suffering and hope, that worked to transform the communal image of man.

Professors of literature do not always have minds of the same inspiration as the minds of writers whose work they interpret and evaluate for consumption; and an age of criticism has grown up to keep great spirits cut down to size so as to be of use in the self-esteem of sophisticated pusillanimous men in a continual self-improvement course. Thus Freud's courageous analysis of his motives and psychic dis-ease has furnished material for popular analysts like Fromm to be struck by how normal their psyches are compared to Freud's, how much more capable of mature love they are.

Homosexuality affords a ready point at which a respectable reader disassociates himself from the work of genius and seeks to avoid any sense of realizing his own inner being there. Some years after my essay, Leslie Fiedler, whom I take to be heterosexual, was able to gain some notoriety by writing about homosexual undercurrents in American literature, playing, not without a sense of his advantage, upon the cultural ambivalence between the appreciation of literature as a commodity of education and the depreciation of genius as it involves a new sense of being, and upon the sexual ambivalence in which the urbane American male can entertain the idea of homosexuality providing he is not responsible, providing he preserves his contempt for or his disavowal of sexual love between males.

[6] 1959. But there is no "explicit" statement here! What emerges is a "confession" (analyzed further below) instead of what was needed and what I was unable to say out.

perverted simple and direct emotions and realizations into a mysterious realm, a mysterious relation to society. Faced by the inhumanities of society I did not seek a solution in humanity but turned to a second outcast society as inhumane as the first. I joined those who, while they allowed for my sexual nature, allowed for so little of the moral, the sensible, and creative direction which all of living should reflect. They offered a family, outrageous as it was, a community in which one was not condemned for one's homosexuality, but it was necessary there for one to desert one's humanity, for which one would be suspect, "out of key." In drawing rooms and in little magazines I celebrated the cult with a sense of sanctuary such as a medieval Jew must have found in the ghetto; my voice taking on the modulations which tell of the capitulation to snobbery and the removal from the "common sort"; my poetry exhibiting the objects made divine and tyrannical as the Catholic church has made bones of saints, and bread and wine tyrannical.[7]

While I had found a certain acceptance in special circles of homosexuals and opportunities for what Kinsey calls "contacts," this was a travesty of what the heart longed for. I could not say "I am homosexual," because exactly this statement of minority identity was the lie. Our deepest sexuality is free and awakens toward both men and women where they are somehow akin to us. Perhaps the dawning realization that we are all exiles from paradise, and that somehow goods have their reality in that impossible dream where all men have come into their full nature, gave rise to and a thread of truth to the feeling of guilt that prompts this voice.

[7] 1959. I am reminded in the foregoing passage of those confessions of duplicity, malice, and high treason made before the courts of Inquisition or the Moscow trials. "Society" appears as the merciless "hostile" judge; what I meant to avow—the profound good and even joyful life that might be realized in sexual love between men—becoming a confession that I had "disguised," "colored," "perverted," "celebrated the cult" and even in my work exhibited objects of alienation from the common law. Some remnant of Protestant adherence suggests there was Holy Roman wickedness, "divine and tyrannical as the Catholic Church has made."

Might there be a type of social reaction to which "confession" of "witches," "Trotskyites," and my confession as a "homosexual," conform? In the prototype there is first the volunteered list of crimes one has committed that anticipates the condemnation of church or party or society. Then there is the fact that what one confesses as a social "crime" has been held somewhere as a hope and an ideal, contrary to convention. The heretic is guilty in his love or his righteousness because he has both the conventional common mind and the imagination of a new common mind; he holds in his own heart the adversary that he sees in the actual prosecutor. Often there was torture to bring on the confession, but it enacted the inner torture of divided mind. "Names cannot be named" I exclaim in this essay, and perhaps akin to that felt necessity is the third phase in which "witches" and "Trotskyites" eventually named their accomplices in heresy, throwing up their last allegiance to their complicity in hope.

The Jungian revival of alchemy with its doctrine of the *nigredo* and the related

After an evening at one of those salons where the whole atmosphere was one of suggestion and celebration, I returned recently experiencing again the aftershock, the desolate feeling of wrongness, remembering in my own voice and gestures the rehearsal of unfeeling. Alone, not only I, but, I felt, the others who had appeared as I did so mocking, so superior in feeling, had known, knew still, those troubled emotions, the deep and integral longings that we as human beings feel, holding us from archaic actions by the powerful sense of humanity that is their source, longings that lead us to love, to envision a creative life. "Towards something far," as Hart Crane wrote, "now farther away than ever."

Among those who should understand those emotions which society condemned, one found that the group language did not allow for any feeling at all other than this self-ridicule, this "gaiety" (it is significant that the homosexual's word for his own kind is "gay"), a wave surging forward, breaking into laughter and then receding, leaving a wake of disillusionment, a disbelief that extends to oneself, to life itself. What then, disowning this career, can one turn to?

What I think can be asserted as a starting point is that only one devotion can be held by a human being seeking a creative life and expression, and that is a devotion to human freedom, toward the liberation of human love, human conflicts, human aspirations. To do this one must disown *all* the special groups (nations, churches, sexes, races) that would claim allegiance. To hold this devotion every written word, every spoken word, every action, every purpose must be examined and considered. The old fears, the old specialties will be there, mocking and tempting; the old protective associations will be there, offering for a surrender of

---

surrealist cult of black humor or bile has complicated the contemporary sense of a belief that in some phase the psyche must descend against its nature into its adversary. It is an exciting idea just as a great destruction of the world by war is an exciting idea. Part of the force which "Beat" poets have is the authority which we give after Freud and Jung to the potency of crime.

"Being a junkie in America today," Ginsberg writes, "is like being a Jew in Nazi Germany." This leads to humorous comment, like the parody of Marx, that "Marijuana is the opium of the people," or that "Opium is the religion of the people." But the revelation of Ginsberg's formula is that in taking to junk he is trying to become like a Jew in Germany. He cannot realize in his Jewishness a sufficient extreme of persecution (even he cannot quite believe in racial guilt—the American idea of the melting pot as virtue is too strong). The "fuzz" cannot live up to the projection of wrath that might externalize inhibition as rank and unjust punishment and satisfy his guilt without calling his need to account. So he takes up "the angry fix." "Holy Burroughs" and heroin addiction will surely test the frustrating tolerance of a liberal state and reveal beneath the "Moloch whose breast is a cannibal dynamo."

one's humanity congratulation upon one's special nature and value. It must be always recognized that the others, those who have surrendered their humanity, are not less than oneself. It must be always remembered that one's own honesty, one's battle against the inhumanity of his own group (be it against patriotism, against bigotry, against—in this special case—the homosexual cult) is a battle that cannot be won in the immediate scene. The forces of inhumanity are overwhelming, but only one's continued opposition can make any other order possible, will give an added strength for all those who desire freedom and equality to break at last those fetters that seem now so unbreakable.

REFLECTIONS 1959

In the fifteen years since the writing of "The Homosexual in Society," my circumstances have much changed. Life and my work have brought me new friends, where the community of values is more openly defined, and even, in recent years, a companion who shares my concern for a creative life. Distressed where I have been distressed and happy where I have been happy, their sympathy has rendered absurd whatever apprehension I had concerning the high moral resolve and radical reformation of character needed before I would secure recognition and understanding. It is a kinship of concern and a sharing of experience that draws us together.

The phantasmic idea of a "society" that was somehow hostile, the sinister affiliation offered by groups with whom I had no common ground other than the specialized sexuality, the anxiety concerning the good opinion of the community—all this sense of danger remains, for I am not a person of reserved nature; and conventional morality, having its roots in Judaic tribal law and not in philosophy, holds homosexual relations to be a crime. Love, art, and thought are all social goods for me; and often I must come, where I would begin a friendship, to odd moments of trial and doubts when I must deliver account of my sexual nature that there be no mistake in our trust.

But the inspiration of the essay was toward something else, a public trust, larger and more demanding than the respect of friends. To be respected as a member of the political community for what one knew in one's heart to be respectable! To insist, not upon tolerance for a divergent sexual practice, but upon concern for the virtues of a homosexual relationship! I was, I think, at the threshold of a critical concept: sexual love wherever it was taught and practiced was a single adventure, that troubadours sang in romance, that poets have kept as a traditional adherence, and that novelists have given scope. Love is dishonored where sexual love between those of the same sex is despised; and where love is dishonored there is no public trust.

It is my sense that the fulfillment of man's nature lies in the creation of that trust; and where the distrusting imagination sets up an image of "self" against the desire for unity and mutual sympathy, the state called "Hell" is created. There we find the visceral agonies, sexual aversions and possessions, excitations and depressions, the omnipresent "I" that bears true witness to its condition in "Howl" or "Kaddish," in McClure's *Hymns to St. Geryon* or the depressive "realism" of Lowell's *Life Studies*. "We are come to the place," Virgil tells Dante as they enter Hell, "where I told thee thou shouldst see the wretched people, who have lost the good of the intellect." In Hell, the homosexuals go, as Dante rightly saw them, as they still go often in the streets of our cities, looking "as in the evening men are wont to look at one another under a new moon," running beneath the hail of a sharp torment, having wounds, recent and old, where the flames of experience have burned their bodies.

It is just here, when he sees his beloved teacher, Brunetto Latini, among the sodomites, that Dante has an inspired intuition that goes beyond the law of his church and reaches toward a higher ethic: "Were my desire all fulfilled," he says to Brunetto, "you had not yet been banished from human nature: for in my memory is fixed . . . the dear and kind, paternal image of you, when in the world, hour by hour, you taught me how man makes himself eternal. . . ."

"Were my desire all fulfilled . . ." springs from the natural heart in the confidence of its feelings that has often been more generous than conventions and institutions. I picture that fulfillment of desire as a human state of mutual volition and aid, a shared life.

Not only in sexual love, but in work and in play, we suffer from the dominant competitive ethos which gives rise to the struggle of interests to gain recognition or control, and discourages the recognition of the needs and interests which we all know we have in common. Working for money (and then, why not stealing or cheating for money?) is the "realistic" norm, and working for the common good is the "idealistic" exception. "I have always earned my living at manual labor," an old friend writes. And his voice breaks through, like a shaft of sunlight through an industrial smog, the oppressive voices of junkies and pushers, petty thieves and remittance men of social security with their need and misery set adrift of itself. Oppressive, because these are sensitive young men and women I am thinking of, some of them the artists and poets of a new generation.

The sense of this essay rests then upon the concept that sexual love between those of the same sex is one with sexual love between men and women; and that this love is one of the conditions of the fulfillment of the heart's desire and the restoration of man's free nature. Creative work for the common good is one of the conditions of that nature. And our hope lies still in the creative imagination wherever it unifies what had been thought divided, wherever it transforms the personal experience into a communal good, "that Brunetto Latini had not been banished from human nature."

[The Matter of the Bees]

There is a legend in my mind that seems to me to be from a lecture in a course of study with Ernst Kantorowicz—from the period that the writing of *Caesar's Gate* belongs to then—or it may have originated in my mind's wandering during such a lecture—a legend of Charlemagne's looting the tombs of the Avar kings upon the Danube and of his finding there the mystery of a sign that is carried forward into the regalia of the French kings—the enigmatic *fleurs-de-lis*. In the legend we find, back of the *fleurs-de-lis*, the emblematic irises that we take to be flowers, are a flock of bees. Myths are the dream data of history, and the events of legend are more persistent than any but the most commanding of actual events. In this dream of the extension of Charlemagne's kingdom into its dream of empire, the kingdom of the Avars stands at the limits of geographical reality as it fades into the irreal, even as the ancient Celtic world stands at the limits of historical reality. In such a realm, he found the tombs of the Avar kings to be sacred hives, and the bodies of those kings, like the carcass of that lion that Samson slew and found again aswarm with bees and filled with honey, were covered with a hoard of bees of gold.

The tomb houses the dead and is, as a house is, an extension in the terms of an architecture of the death style or life style of a person, a soul-space, even as the actual carnal body is thought of often as being a soul's house or prison or tomb, either making manifest in its plan the intent of an inhabiting presence or masking in its disguise the true self or encumbering in its concretion and weight the longing for ecstatic flight the soul knows. Were the hives that men built for bees made after the model of men's dwellings in the beehive hut and tomb style of the ancient world? Or were the habitats of men derived from the model of hives they had been, even as they had been inspired to be beekeepers, inspired to make for the bees? Was there in the ancient world an imitation of the bees in men's world?

In the teachings of certain occultist schools in our own time, bees are

First published in *Caesar's Gate: Poems 1949-50* (Berkeley: Sand Dollar, 1972).

the signature in the work of the evolution of species of the artists of that work—or the Artist, for they were of one mind—who were *Bees* of an other order that had come in from outer space to the environs of Earth in its formation to start in its chemistry the code in which they would perpetuate themselves. But not only in the lore of such fantasts, in dream too and in poetry, in the researches of biological sciences—in the curious speculations of Denis Saurat's *La religion des géants et la civilisation des insectes* and in von Frisch's careful studies recounted in his *The Dance Language and Orientation of Bees,* I have pursued this lore of the bee-world from my own earliest memories in which the garden is alive with their hum and the sunlight swarms with them—an environment of revery, sound, and light, that must have provided a stage of Poetry in me—to the dark pages in which my mind in Poetry seems to be a hive or a swarm with ideas. I have a bee in my bonnet, as the common expression goes, but such a bee, for me, is only a scout and soon will return to arouse a host of foragers to return to the field.

From my childhood I had from my mother's oldest sister another teaching, in which the soul was itself a swarm of entities, as she called them, that were—it was ever her reference—most like bees. In the literalizing mind of the child I was and of that storyteller she was, in which the *as if* proposition of the simile led only too directly to be taken as the revelation of an actual reality, they were in fact bees. And the animal body was their hive, built up cell by cell in that intricate and wonderful chemical architecture, the design secreted by a correspondingly intricate society of invisible beings. The body—my body then, what I was—was a colony, ordered, even as societal bees are, in a matriarchal and totalitarian state or *Mutterrecht.* Bachofen's picture of such a primordial society of man is the picture of man living in imitation of the insect world, or, as my aunt would have seen it, man living in imitation of his own soul which was such a society.

The *anima* as image of the soul in the teachings of contemporary depth psychology is an archetypal Woman-Idea. But in the teaching of my aunt the *anima* is not thought of as an image but as an animating social force, a cloud or gathering of beings—each man a walking city, a conglomerate of individual cell-lives. The composition of this commune must have been predominantly female, if it was a bee-world. At the center, there would be the queen and the royal chamber in which the larval princesses slept, and from that realm the swarm of workers, undeveloped females, whose sexuality had been translated into a buzzing activity, nurses, scouts, foragers, builders, warriors, went out to make the life of the hive, building the combs, story upon story, researching the sources of pollen, returning to store the honey in the combs, forcing the queens in their cells with the royal jell. It is an Old Wives' Tale, for sure, out of some Amazonian history, in which the males or drones have no other role but their mating to perform, to idle in dream time until the one moment of truth, the queen's call—the sexual Muse's call—the frenzy and the ecstatic flight, the aroused vision and the intoxicating scent of the sting that drive him on to his rape of the virginal queen, his rapture and coming upon his death in her. The female, triumphant in being conquered, absorbs into her own body the store of his semen, fertile for her lifetime. The female alone in this order belongs to the immortal commune of the species. Hers the communion; hers the work. She builds and repairs the combs, commands the swarm, and feeds the pupae in their cells. She researches the field, she finds the food and returns. Only the female bears the sting—at once a lure and a deadly weapon—that is, for us, the very sign of the bee.

But I cannot find this account in any of my sources of the drone's death in mating, his being torn apart and his leaving his genitals in her. It was an Old Husbandman's Tale then that the beekeeper Watkins told me in 1942—"The males come in at her in full flight like dive-bombers in their excitement," he said: "And when they hit, you can hear it in the distance like a gunshot. He explodes in midair, and she, having her fill of him . . ." The image has remained of the Bee Queen, like the praying mantis, as a Demon-Bride, a Scorpion of the Air, devouring her ecstatic Groom even as she takes his seed; and the myth of the drone, an Attis fantasy of a Love-Death and sexual mutilation in one rite.

Back of my aunt's science fantasy, as back of the occultist doctrines, we find remnants of a tradition from forgotten religion and magic in which man worshiped bees. A.B. Cook, in his *Zeus,* tells us that the *histiátores* or "entertainers" of Artemis at Ephesus were called by the citizens *essênes,* a title that properly denotes "king bees." Were these sacred drones or entertainers the bards of the hive? And the priestesses of Demeter were "bees," as were the women initiated into her mysteries, foragers in the field and storers of the honey in the comb.

Psyches are butterflies, but souls are also bees. Our scholar shows us Hermes consulting with a soul bee [*Zeus,* I, p. 469, fig. 325] and calls our attention to another figure in Jane Harrison's *Prolegomena to the Study of Greek Religion* where we find (p. 443) the drawing of an embossed gold plaque bearing the figure of a woman with seraphic wings and a bee body from the waist down, a genius that is female, not male, an angelic power that may belong to the mysteries of the soul's creativity, as genius does, and to that imagination in which Worlds are created. The hive, the honey, and the love-death sting, that haunt Poetry, may belong then to the inner mysteries of Poetry itself as a Creative Art.

"Only from the side of death (when death is not accepted as an extinction, but imagined as an altogether surpassing intensity)"—so Rilke writes to a young girl, as a drone, dreaming of his love-death, might write—"only from the side of death, I believe, is it possible to do justice to love." And in that extraordinary letter that Rilke writes to his Polish translator, Witold von Hulewicz, on the meaning of the *Duino Elegies,* the poet speaks directly of the bees. In his account, as in my aunt's fantasy science, all sense of the *as if* passes over into the mode of revelation. What appears as simile in the common sense is in truth the apprehension of a higher reality. The process of Rilke's poetics is to create a sense in us of the pre-eminence of that other world; but it is also to convert this world into the food of the other. "Yes, for our task is to stamp this provisional, perishing earth into ourselves so deeply," he writes, "so painfully and passionately, that its being may rise again, 'invisibly,' in us. We are the bees of the Invisible. *Nous butinons éperdument le miel du visible, pour l'accumuler dans la grande ruche d'or de l'Invisible."* The work of the *Elegies* has to do then with this alchemy in which the elements of our world are transmuted into the honey-gold of an other. The hive of this order may be the skull, and it combs the tissues of the brain, for thought is one of the Invisibles into which the things of our world pass and are stored like honey. Appearing in thought, the "Angel" of the *Elegies* appears in the Invisible.

"He" is of the same order as the *Bees* that come in from outer space, the impersonation of the cosmos as it haunts the mind and seeds itself there. Like the Bee-genii of the hoard of the Avar kings, he belongs to the enigmas of the outer boundaries of a consciousness, the powerful lord of a peripheral center. "He" appearing to us at Ephesus a "King Bee," in the higher order of the Hive is the Queen. Thus, in the poet's dream of his love-death, aroused to flight, he goes, inspired, into the ascent to a Lord, his Death, that is, in his higher gnosis, a deadly Female Power.

"The Angel of the *Elegies* is the creature in whom the transformation of the visible into the invisible already appears complete. . . . The Angel of the *Elegies* is the being who vouches for the recognition of a higher degree of reality in the invisible—Therefore 'terrible' to us, because we, its lovers and transformers, still depend on the visible. All the worlds of the universe are plunging into the invisible as into their next-deepest reality."

But the "wine" is called *"milk,"* and the vessel containing it, a *"honey-jar."* The honey in speech is sweet in the vowels stored in the consonant articulations of the syllabic comb, mellifluous and intoxicating in the melodic sequence of those cells. The nurses of Apollo, the god of this delirium in language, in that rite are bees. The honey is bitter with the herb in its transsubstantiation, and the bee-prophetesses in that magic arouse and disturb Hermes to pass the gift of prophecy to Apollo. They are, these nurses, as the god Hermes tells of them, sisters of one mind—their heads heavy with pollen, their wings beating the air at the edge of the visible. "They are in a word 'Melissae,'" Jane Harrison comments: "honey-priestesses, inspired by a honey intoxicant"—nurses not only of Apollo then, but of Dionysos too, for they are the nurses of a musical high, a delirium of song—"they are bees, their heads white with pollen; they hum and buzz, swarming confusedly."

And so we see them again, swarming in the body of the lion in the mystery of Samson, as if within a dead language or a dead culture. We see them swarming in the formation of the body of our world, storing there the honey of an invisible presence at work in the alchemical generations of the evolution of species. We see them as if the Head were a Hive, alive with thought, and at the center, directive of all—we are drunk on the terrible honey of a sweet suggestion—the Eros that moved us in the beginning of the Visible and that we have posed as a King Bee were to be discovered to be in truth, in the Invisible, *their* Queen. In the swarm of our thought, a fateful thought stirs—"bee-like, death-like, a wonder!" Jane Harrison quotes from the chorus of Euripides's drama *Hippolytus*, as they sing of the power of the goddess. "How terrible is the advent of Aphrodite!" She brings the soul into that flaming bed in the thunder where in death the Dionysian seed is delivered up to her.

For the terror of her presence is felt thruout the field,

> And swift as a bee's flight
> Is the path of fate she commands.

The chief priestesses of the Great Mother were still "bees" in the first century of our era, Cook tells us and quotes from a commentary on Pindar: *"Melissam vero a patre primam sacerdotem Matri Magnae constitutam, unde adhuc eiusdem Matris antistites Melissae nuncupantur."* In the body of language, of a dead world, meanings stir, words we almost know—*Magna, Mater, pater, primas, sacerdos, Melissae*—it is as if we came upon bees generated out of a corpse. Latin and Greek are not *Classical* languages for me, but *dead* languages, and I consult my dictionaries reluctantly. *Antistites* are female overseers or chief priestesses of the temple that is now in ruins. But I do not want to translate. It is the bee-hum out of the dead language that I bring into the poem. It is the sounding of a magic of the dead speaking, the spectral voice of Augustine in his words, where I recognize, even as he addresses the theme of the fortunate fall—*O felix culpa*—he addresses the bee: *O vere beata et mirabilis apis!*

There remains the generation of lives out of the carcass of a dead bull or ox. The legend was Egyptian in origin the Greeks thought—was it the legend of the generation of Greek meanings out of buried Egypt? Was it the story of the *apis* in Apis, of the generation of a pun?

Ovid in his account of the origin of animal sacrifice in his *Fasti* [I.363–380] tells us the story of Aristaeus, who wept because he saw his bees killed, root and branch, and the unfinished hives abandoned, and who is, at last, instructed by Proteus, the Old Man of the Sea, to bury the carcass of a cow in the earth—"the buried carcass will give the thing you seek of me." Swarms of bees hive out of the putrid beeve: one life butchered gives birth to a thousand—*"mille animas una necata dedit."*

In the rites, Cook tells us, the buried bull was the center of a vital force, radiating outward especially through the head and the horns. King Bees come from the spinal marrow, or better still from the brain. The flesh becomes bees. In the body of that bull slain by Mithra, out of whose carcass all the things of our world are to come, certain *bees* appear, working there.

Is it then this bee I have so often taken central to my fantasy that has come into this darkness? But, even as I think to see but dimly that wriggling form crawling into the walnut shell or tiny skull—or is it a hole in the dark screen?—I doubt that I am seeing a bee. No! It is a wasp.

A white, Anglo-Saxon Protestant, I had laid claim to the bee, the royal insignia, the hieroglyph of the Pharaoh, staked out a claim to a mine in the ancient world. Now I see clearly, it is a wasp burrowing into its mine in the darkness. INSECT the print reads even as I hear the word *"INSECT,"* as if dictated. [The instructor had ordered us to produce a word to stand for the dream image we are using in the operation. "I do not know what it gives, / a vibration that we can not name," H.D. writes in her *Tribute to the Angels*: "my patron said, 'name it';"

I said, I can not name it,
there is no name;

he said,
"invent it."

Had he asked us to name it?] But even as I read the word INSECT from
the screen where it has appeared, it sounds like *"INCEST."* Did the voice
dictating the word say *"INCEST"*?

I am building a construction starting with the dream scene that this
image of a bee belongs to. The hole with the wriggling bee, working its
way in there, has passed on, for now I see the landscape of the sunny
hillside sloping down toward the sea in Santa Barbara just beyond the
Tallant's great house where we often went in childhood summers, and,
left to myself, for happy hours, lying in the haze of lavender bushes
and sage, the hum of bees around me, I watched them in their comings
and goings, climbing into the flower clusters, into flowery throats, and,
beyond, the gleam of the bay. This is it. It appears in a vignette, as in an
old film—framing the triangle of sea at the left of the vista, the horizon as
the upper side, and the hillslope as the hypotenuse—a broken shard of
mirror. I hear now the order to produce a word for it. Hadn't there been
this producing of a word before? And before that a first dream scene? I
can not recall.

CRAFTY is the word. I want to write "Child" or "Childhood" in-
stead. I try to force the thought—"CHILDHOOD." But the word
"CRAFTY" remains. I try to read it to read "Craft," the poet's craft. It
won't turn out that way. My anxiety is there again, it had to do before
with a word's not turning out right. "It means the artist's cunning in his
craft," I argue to my imaginary reader. And as I fret the meaning here, I
almost miss the directive that has already been issued—when did I hear
him tell us to find the opposite?—but now, perhaps in recall, I do hear
this directive quite clearly. "Find its opposite. Put it there."

The opposite is . . . ? It won't come to me. I look again into the
blue luminous blank area that is there in the dark screen of this interior
cinema, until I see emerge a blue-green vase. No, it is a jar. When is a
door not a door? It is, I recognize, even as the lines come to me in the
dream, a jar that "made the slovenly wilderness / Surround that hill,"
from Wallace Stevens's poem. As it turns out, it becomes a vase, a work of
wondrous craftsmanship—Is the work of art the opposite of the craft
that has gone into its working? A Tiffany vase of ultramarine blue. How

does it relate to the Sea? Does it stand as a blue emptiness as the opposite
to that blue fullness of the sea's reflection?

The instructor is telling us to move the two figures, one to the left—
the scene of the sea and the hill, the vignette of the sunny world of nature
alive with bees in their foraging—and the other—the wonderful work of
art, the blue vase—to the right. The one on the left hand, the other on
the right hand: I feel them on my hands even as I see them before me.
"Move them apart upon an axis as far as you can."

They move to opposite sides of the horizon line, as far apart as my
hands reach. They are now, I see, two shining "discs." I am not sure of
that word "disc"—should it have been *"balances"*? The word "disc" came
from a line in an old poem of mine—"Beauty is a bright and terrible
disk." They are dishes, I decide—the grail was a disc or dish, I read
somewhere—the two dishes of the pair of scales in Libra. The dark
screen into which I have been looking is now the night sky. And the
figure I am looking at is that composite constellation I gazed into night
after night at Stinson Beach, in which Scorpio reaches up at the hori-
zon line out of the Pacific, her raised claws becoming the two scales.
And below, just above the horizon, the deadly curve of the Scorpion's
tail to the left with its sting ever present to my mind, underlying the
balance.

But the instructor had from the first directed us to find a synthesis of
opposites in a "higher consciousness." He instructs us now to form an
equilateral triangle, locating the apex of two sides moving from the pair
of opposites. I move up from the two dishes of the constellation Libra
and at the apex find a hook from which the Scales is suspended. Yes, it is
a hook. A fish hook! That little skull I had seen in the beginning returns
to me. It is the skull of a fish. At the Apex, the Fish is hooked. *"Flippity has
gone to glory!"* I hear the voice reading from Baum's *The Sea Fairies* that
passage that always delighted me:

> ". . . I've seen fishes gather around a hook and look at it carefully for a long
> time. They well know it is a hook, and that if they bite the bait upon it they
> will be pulled out of the water. But they are curious to know what will
> happen to them afterward, and think it means happiness, instead of death.
> So finally, one takes the hook and disappears, and the others never know
> what becomes of him."
>
> "Why don't you tell 'em the truth?" asked Trot.
>
> "Oh, we do. The mermaids have warned them many times, but it does
> no good at all. The fish are stupid creatures."

"But I wish I was Flippity," said one of the mackerel, staring at Trot with his big, round eyes. "He went to glory before I could eat the hook myself."

But this Place of the Hook is where Christ must be! I try to see Him there, to place Him there at the Apex. The hook must be really a nail. But if his head were there, it is the place of the crown of thorns. I do see His head now, and the crown briefly. No, what I see now is a nail, driven into His forehead. There was no nail driven into His head there. It is the counterpart of the Sting of the tail in Scorpio below. The Sting above. The nail was not there nor was there a nail in the story there where now I drive the nail into the center of His brow. [Later as I recounted the dream to the group, it seemed that I saw the nails as they were, driven into his hands, which, left and right, are in the place of the opposites, the dishes of the Scales.] There is a PAIN (the word appears) at the Apex. I feel a stabbing pain at the tear duct of my left eye. And the warm resonance of pain at the back of my skull.

I return now determined to see the hook in the place of the nail, and once I see the hook and hold it in mind, it is a shepherd's crook. And shepherd's crook becomes a Bishop's Crozier.

My head curving upon its neck to look down over its body below comes into the Place of the Crozier. There it is the curved head of a violin. And from my temples and where my ears were, there are tuning pegs. I am a violin. Strings from the tension of my head descend toward the region below where the music is drawn from me by the bow.

Going deep into that figure, losing myself in that figure, I am becoming the curved figurehead of my torso upon the bow of a ship. Adrift upon waters I have known before in dreams, I am sailing out from this dream to islands beyond my figuring in shadow and mists. Is it once more northward toward Britain after the loss of Atlantis as I used to make up that dream in childhood to go on my way from the routes dictated by my parents' theosophical interests outward into uncharted seas? I am going out there.

But the instructor is, even now, telling us to return to our own consciousness of our being here in this room, in this body, to wait in ourselves, attend to the body, undoing the fantasy until, released, we open our eyes. I had been drifting out into a fusion of elements I desired and elements I feared, into the distances of fairy seas, shadowy, perilous, beckoning, as if I might come home beyond myself. Now I have been brought back from the music to the instrument. I have to dissolve the hold of the pegs, dissolve that figure of my head—it was a spell. Now my skull returns. In the Place of the Skull, there had been a sting and a hook. And at last, letting these go, I manage to open my eyes. Retracing in my mind the sequence of instructed images.

Changing Perspectives in Reading Whitman

When I was invited to participate in this celebration of Whitman's sesqui-centennial, I had thought that I would write a formal lecture, a compan-ion piece for a lecture I had done in 1965 in homage to Dante upon his seventh centennial. Whitman, like Dante, was a poet central to my thought, a perennial source from which my own art as a poet drew. And there were formal parallels that might have been made: Whitman, like Dante, projected a poem central to his civilization and his vision of the ground of ultimate reality—*Leaves of Grass*, like *The Divine Comedy*, being not an epic narrative but the spiritual testament of a self-realization. Whitman, as Dante did in his *De Vulgari Eloquentia*, wrote, in the Preface of the 1855 edition of *Leaves of Grass*—to which I would add the essay "Slang in America," written in 1885—a poetics grounded in a science of the language of the common people. Whitman's statement that "view'd freely, the English language is the accretion and growth of every dialect, race, and range of time, and is both the free and compacted composition of all" is directly comparable to Dante's sense of the illustrious vernacu-lar, the language in which the spirit of Man was embodied most wholly; and Whitman's "It is curiously in embryons and childhood, and among the illiterate, we always find the groundwork and start, of this great science, and its noblest products" agrees closely, indeed, with Dante's sense that "our first true speech" is "that to which children are accus-tomed by those who are about them when they first begin to distinguish words . . . that which we acquire without any rule, by imitating our nurses."

Whitman in *Democratic Vistas*, like Dante in *De Monarchia*, had writ-ten a definitive—even *the* definitive—politics of his time ("his time" being the time created in his poetic vision). Whitman, like Dante, had this vision of Time, of Self and World, in his poetic conversion, through the me-dium of a falling-in-love, where the inspiration of that falling-in-love

First appeared in *The Artistic Legacy of Walt Whitman: A Tribute to Gay Wilson Allen*, ed. Edwin Haviland Miller (New York: New York University Press, 1970). The essay was included in *Fictive Certainties: Essays by Robert Duncan* (New York: New Directions, 1985).

being never exorcised in a sexual satisfaction, longing had been the seed of a creative desire transforming the inner and outer reality. Freud has made us aware, even wary, of such a process of sublimation, and simple Freudians, those who do not go along with Freud's mythic imagination toward his deeper vision of the work of Eros and Thanatos in Creation, think of sublimation as a removal from the primary genital fact, which is real, a flight from what is sexual and actual into higher thought and abstraction. The generation of poets who were contemporary with psychoanalysis also had a bias against abstraction; Pound, Williams, and we as their progeny have sought to test language, as if many of its functions were unreal or unsound or unsavory, against a control taken, in mimesis of the empiricism presumed in the scientific method, from the observable "objective" world. But I would see the process at work in Dante's and Whitman's falling-in-love in light of another reading out of Freud, in which Eros and Thanatos are primary, at work in the body of the poem even as they are at work in the body of the man, awakening in language apprehensions of what we call sexuality and spirituality. Parts of language, like parts of the physical body, will be inspired; syllables and words, like cells and organs, will be excited, awakened to the larger identity they belong to.

Longing had been the seed, for Whitman as for Dante, of a creative desire, a new life, transforming the inner and outer reality of a poetic vision. As words belong to language and cells to animal bodies, poets come to belong to a poetry. But, here, just where Dante had begun with the foundation-stone of his *Vita Nuova*, creating in the world of ultimate poetic realities his Beatrice and establishing in the world of actual histories the poetic riddle of that reality, Whitman does not venture. Dante had cast over and through the real the enchantment of a commanding romance; he had established a *locus solus* in the daughter of Folco Portinari, wife of Simone de' Bardi, for the persona of Universal Being. Whitman, again and again, resolves to release man from romantic entanglement. The particularity and uniqueness, the painfulness, of Whitman's Beloved is released into the presence of the Beloved in throngs of men, a vision of democracy in which the Beloved is equally apprehended in all the variety and generative potentiality of mankind.

Inviting as such a fitting of parallels might be, the very fitting misfits. It is not only that generations of poets over seven hundred years have raised the imagination of the poet Dante again and again, and that our imagination of him has all the resource of that increment of associations, nor that Dante himself drew upon three generations of poets, a tradition in which the Spirit of Romance had grown from the schools of Provence to thirteenth-century Florence, nor that in turn he had a guide in the spirit of Virgil, and with Cavalcanti and Lapo Gianni, he belonged to a school, a "scene" or "movement" of the thirteenth century with advanced ideas about love and the nature of poetry. Whitman too is very much the member of such a movement in poetry in the nineteenth century; he comes to fulfill and he sees himself as fulfilling, as Dante came to fulfill the meaning of the troubadors, the vision of the poet that begins, for Whitman, in Carlyle's *On Heroes, Hero-Worship and the Heroic in History* and passes on through Emerson's writings. We have only to read Whitman's essays on the Bible, on Shakespeare, on the work of his own contemporaries, to realize how firm his grasp is of literary realities; he has here the largeness of mind and at the same time the keenness of perception that Dante has.

But Whitman nowhere presents the architectural ordering of universe and spirit that Dante presents. One had only, with Dante, to present the fittings of parts in a designated passage to arrive at its relevance; the design of reality in Dante was established in orders given and giving order to one's thought if it be but appropriate to the object. Whitman presents no such a settled business. He is the grand proposer of questions not to be settled, the poet of unsettling propositions. And as I worked on this previous to the lecture my notes became very dense, and in that density the sense of the task of unwinding the threads grew—out of hand. The *Leaves of Grass* in its nine editions grows, not toward a definitive architecture, but as a man grows, composed and recomposed, in each phase immediate and complete, but unsatisfied. It was my impulse then when I came to the lecture itself, as now again in preparing the lecture for its written version to be published, to let impulse and association enter into the composition, the talk *one* edition, the written homage another—and beyond that surely other editions of one essay—interleafing thoughts of the moment with the reading of passages of notes, designing the whole, in the case of the lecture, to take place within an hour's time.

The variety, the denseness, the suggestiveness of Whitman's thought lead me everywhere into an unwinding of themes in which the complexity from which I drew took over. His thought moves not toward conclusion and summary but toward involvement and the apprehension of the variety and copiousness of forces at work—Dante's rose and Whitman's "unseen buds."

Dante begins in such a dark thicket—"How hard a thing it is to tell what a wild, and rough, and stubborn wood this was." He means here just the actual density of his own life and of his own times. Virgil and Beatrice come to lead him out of the density of the contemporary disorder into the grand architectonic orders of the eternal as the imaginations of the Roman Empire and then of Christendom—the Empire become a Church—knew it. Avicenna, St. Thomas Aquinas, and Joachim of Fiori had furnished blueprints of the orders of the real mind and history, "goods of the intellect," which underlie Dante's poetics. But Dante had come to know, had thoroughly known, in his own lifetime, the end of all hope in the actual of just those orders which most gave his work order: pope and emperor, vicars of the orders in which the temporal and eternal are united in one reality, had profoundly betrayed that unity; and, for Dante, the temporal, the actual, was left a dark thicket, a disunity between the ideal and the real. Only in the Other World, the Hell and Heaven of the Imagination, can the architecture of that Reality in which the Ideal is embodied be raised. Dante was writing the monumental memorial of a perished hope, the mausoleum of Christendom, even as Shakespeare was to write the mausoleum of Renaissance man, of the magician or Prince.

Whitman did not believe he came at the end of a civilization but at the beginning, even, before the beginning, at the apprehension of what was yet to come. He does not represent his time but announces its coming. "America," for Whitman, is yet to come. And this theme of what America is, of what democracy is, of what the sexual reality is, of what the Self is, arises from an urgency in the conception of the Universe itself, not a blueprint but an evolution of spirit in terms of variety and a thicket of potentialities. His own work in poetry he sees so, moved by generative urgencies toward the fulfillment of a multitude of latent possibilities. And so we are actually in the throes, the throes in which the ideal and the reality are at work—now that's something to lecture from, to talk from, not recollections in tranquility, nor summations of study, but to be in the throes of a poetry in which the poet seeks to keep alive as a generative possibility a force and intent hidden in the very beginning of things, long before the beginning of the poem, the *Leaves of Grass* having its form not, as the *Commedia* had, as the paradigm of an existing eternal form, but as the ever flowing, ever Self-creative ground of a process in which forces of awareness, Self-awareness, of declaration, and of longing work and rework in the evolution of what they are, the evolution of a creative intention that moves not toward the satisfaction of some prescribed form but towards the fulfillment of a multitude of possibilities out of its seed. Whitman begins to see as we do, the flow of some prescribed form but toward the fulfillment of a multitude of as a field of being, not toward progress and improvement but toward variety and awareness of variety. The good of the earth and the sun? "There are millions of suns left."

> There was never any more inception than there is now,
> Nor any more youth or age than there is now;
> And will never be any more perfection than there is now,
> Nor any more heaven or hell than there is now.

The very wild and rough and stubborn wood which Virgil rescues Dante from—the matter of the poet's person and his world—Whitman determines to be the poet of. Taking his Self and his Law, Poetics and Politics, not in the architecture of an Other World, but in an identification with the creative forces working within masses and populations, the poet was to work toward the Wedding of the Ideal and the Actual, even as Blake had proposed a poetic marriage of Heaven and Hell in the Actual. Whitman saw within the actuality of These States the idea of an America latent and at work. Not a poetry commemorative of an established order or a poetry striving to perfect an order out of chaos, but a poetry creative "in the region of imaginative, spinal and essential attributes, something equivalent to creation . . . imperatively demanded."

In this the work of the new literature was Democracy itself at work. It was not the democracy that had appeared in the days of Adams and Jefferson; it was not a democracy that had appeared in Whitman's youth or after the Civil War. Intimations were everywhere; but there were intimations too of "the appalling dangers of universal suffrage in the United States." It was not a democracy which had appeared by the end of his life. The potentiality was there, but it involved, not only generation, but "the need, a long period to come, of a fusion of the States into the only reliable identity, the moral and artistic one"—it involved a radiational force in which a mutation of spirit would take place: "the fervid and tremendous IDEA, melting everything else with resistless heat, and solving all lesser and definite distinctions in vast, indefinite, spiritual, emotional power."

Democracy Whitman saw at work in the whole of evolution. In his old age he was to recognize a companion in Darwin, but he found himself

closest to Hegel. In his homage to Carlyle, Whitman calls upon the
Hegelian vision as an anchor for steadying the Carlylean ship:

> According to Hegel the whole earth, (an old nucleus-thought, as in the
> Vedas, and no doubt before, but never hitherto brought so absolutely to the
> front, fully surcharged with modern scientism and facts, and made the sole
> entrance to each and all,) with its infinite variety, the past, the surroundings
> of to-day, or what may happen in the future, the contrarieties of material
> with spiritual, and of natural with artificial, are all, to the eye of the *ensem-*
> *blist,* but necessary sides and unfoldings, different steps or links, in the
> endless process of Creative thought, which, amid numberless apparent fail-
> ures and contradictions, is held together by central and never-broken
> unity—not contradictions or failures at all, but radiations of one consistent
> and eternal purpose. . . .

Democracy was the politics of the ensemble, as Hegel's was the phi-
losophy of the ensemble, and Whitman saw his *Leaves of Grass* as belong-
ing to the poetics of the ensemblist. The word "ensemblist" he italicizes.
Dreaming of the ensemble of created and creating forms, Whitman was
the poet of primary intuitions, ancestor of Whitehead's *Process and Re-*
ality and of our own vision of creation where now we see all of life as
unfoldings, the revelations of a field of potentialities and latencies to-
ward species and individuals hidden in the DNA, a field of generations
larger than our humanity. Back of our own contemporary arts of the
collagist, the assembler of forms, is the ancestral, protean concept, wider
and deeper, of the poet as devotée of the ensemble. Back of the field as it
appears in Olson's proposition of composition by field is the concept of
the cosmos as a field of fields. Our field in which we see the form of the
poem happening belongs ultimately to, is an immediate apprehension of
or sense of locality in "the infinite variety, the past, the surroundings of
to-day, or what may happen in the future," the grand ensemble Whitman
evokes.

Whitman was a nineteenth-century poet, and he comes on with
many other attitudes and ideas that seem conventions of his day. We find
him talking about progress and ideals, even in the most moving passages,
in a tone of assumed moral enthusiasm that, out of tune with our own
sense of proprieties, reminds us that he belongs to the Victorian age. He
delights in the fact that he is a man of diversities—but, very important in
this discussion where I am often swept along by Whitman's spirit and
thought, he was a man of contradictions and he calls up inner contradic-

tions in the reader. His ideals, as you will appreciate, the very ideals of the potentialities of Democracy, of "America," of "scientism," as he calls it, and of *"men* here worthy the name . . . athletes" and "a strong and sweet Female Race, a race of perfect Mothers"—they are the staunchly held core of Whitman's popular appeal—have revealed potentialities of their own in the century since *Leaves of Grass* and *Democratic Vistas.* The truth of forces "a long time to come," of creative change distributed over vast populations and periods of time and written in microscopic terms out of a great variation of individual types, is one truth of the ideal: the forcing of an ideal in any immediate event will be untrue. In the late nineteen-thirties, as I came into some kind of social consciousness, ideas of Whitman's had come also to be the ideas of established and increasingly coercive governments. Totalism—*ensemblism*—is haunted when we return to it today in the dark monstrosities of socialistic and democratic totalitarianism.

Is it the deadly boast of the Chauvinist, the patriotic zeal of a spiritual imperialism, that fires Whitman's "The Americans of all nations at any time upon the earth have probably the fullest poetical nature. The United States themselves are essentially the greatest poem"? Presidents, congresses, armed forces, industrialists, governors, police forces, have rendered the meaning of "America" and "the United States" so fearful— causing fear and filled with fear—in our time that no nationalistic inspiration comes innocent of the greed and ruthless extension of power to exploit the peoples and natural resources of the world that has spread terror, misery, and devastation wherever it has gone.

Yet, reading these passages of the 1855 Preface, stronger than the contradiction, the mysterious message comes through, translating the transforming meanings. It comes as one of the great prophecies of the nature of our American experience. Yes, all that we would most disown remains, and unless we do come to change the meaning of "nation," of "state," of "America," of "at any time upon the earth," so that these are terms of "the fullest poetical nature," we must disown. What, in the light of "the fullest poetical nature" does Whitman mean by "America"?

> The American poets are to enclose old and new for America is the race of races . . . the expression of the American poet is to be transcendent and new. It is to be indirect and not direct or descriptive or epic. Its quality goes through these to much more. Let the age and wars of other nations be chanted, and their eras and characters be illustrated and that finish the

verse. Not so the great psalm of the republic. Here the theme is creative and has vista.

It was the nation of nations, the race composed of all races. It was the first time that out of no time and no where, yet out of every time then and every where, a nation had appeared. The United States of Adams and Jefferson saw itself as a mixture of European peoples, yes, but predominantly an extension of English dreams on a new continent. But in Whitman's time—it is the crux of the Civil War—the slave was freed, admitted into the community of the free, potentially the spiritual son of those who had proclaimed a Land of the Free and brother of those who continued that faith; Africa was admitted along with Europe into the unity, the "one nation." In the course of the nineteenth-century immigration, it became apparent that all the peoples of the world were represented in this one people. The nation of many nations, "the race of races"—no other country in the world has so many of the peoples of the world among its citizens.

Writing the poem "The Soldiers," I came to read Whitman's lines "The United States themselves are essentially the greatest poem" and "The Americans of all nations at any time upon the earth" in a new inspiration. Whitman's genius here is oracular. Prophetic. The oracular mode enters poetry and history where profound contradictions come into play. In the widening of what we call the credibility gap, incredible transformations may come into the statement of the truth. Oracles are to be read many ways or both ways. And here, where "the greatest poem" underlies all, the "United States" appeared to me as the states of being or of Man united, all one's states of mind brought together in one governance; and "the Americans of all nations at any time upon the earth" meant clearly that "America" and being "American" was a community that was from the beginning of Man and everywhere in the world. You could tell them by just those virtues of free men that Whitman extols: the free, creative individualist, having and keeping his own inner lawfulness, and the concern for the good of his community—mankind his people—in which that lawfulness has its ground. Is it from Vanzetti's letters or from Whitman's thought?—it will be from both and others too that the lines came to me in writing "The Multiversity":

> Where there is no commune,
>   the individual volition has no ground.
> Where there is no individual freedom, the commune
>   is falsified.

And again:

> There being no common good, no commune,
> no communion, outside the freedom of
>
> individual volition.

Once we read the United States as belonging to the greatest poem, the race of all races, and we hear Whitman speaking of Americans throughout the population of Man—every place and any place and time of Man—then, underlying these United States and this America, comes a mystery of "America" that belongs to dream and desire and the re-awakening of earliest oneness with all peoples—at last, the nation of Mankind at large. It is this that informs Whitman's enthusiasm for America. In the language of Poetry, of "the greatest poem," we rightly read him in the light of Blake's visions of America, direful as they are, the States are seen by the poet as states of Man, and what is happening in the Revolution happens, in Blake's world, not because the colonies are English but because they are colonies of Man. The drama he reads in his figures of fire and outrage and imprisonment and volcanic release is a drama "of all nations at any time upon the earth."

Whitman's politics, like Dante's, is the politics of a polis that is a poem. In both the Preface of 1855 and *Democratic Vistas* Whitman insists that the heart or soul of this matter of America and of democracy is poetic. He comes not to bring a new religion but to bring—more faithful to the truth of things than religion—a poetry. "The time straying toward infidelity and confections and persiflage he withholds by steady faith," Whitman says of the poet in the Preface. "Faith is the antiseptic of the soul—it pervades the common people and preserves them—they never give up believing and expecting and trusting." In the pathos of this resolution, these are the people of a poetry. It is a poetic faith that informs them, a poem, not a nation, they have in common. It is the poet of *Leaves of Grass,* faithful to his mission there, and his readers, faithful followers of the text, and I among them, who "never give up believing and expecting and trusting."

Dante in his *De Monarchia,* seeking the legitimacy of government and the definition of Man's good, finds that the legitimacy of government must lie in "the ultimate goal of human civilization as a whole," in a "civilization of civilizations"—is this not Whitman's "greatest poem"? And he finds that the ultimate goal implies "some function proper to humanity as a whole for which that same totality of men is ordained in so great a multitude, to which function neither one man nor one family, nor one district nor one city-state, nor any individual kingdom may attain." May this not be Whitman's "democracy," a people resonant with the poetry of their common intent? The goal or good of the people, Dante argues, is the fulfillment of their humanity. "The specific potentiality of humanity as such is a potentiality or capacity of intellect"—we would remember here Virgil's words to Dante at Hellgate: "We are come to the place where I told thee thou shouldst see the wretched people, who have lost the good of the intellect"; and, further, this good of the intellect lies in the *ensemble*—it is, we feel, the individual's imagination of the good of the whole population of man. "And since that same potentiality cannot all be reduced to actuality at the same time by one man, or by any of the limited associations distinguished above," Dante continues, "there must needs be multiplicity in the human race, in order for the whole of this potentiality to be actualized thereby." Dante imagines the Empire of One Spirit, a Princedom extending over and preserving the peace and guaranteeing the fulfillment of all beings and things, each free at last, that is, dwelling in the law of its own nature. "Like as there must be a multiplicity of things generable in order that the whole potentiality of first matter may always be in act. . . ."

The monarchy in Dante's *De Monarchia* proves to rest in a mystery, the rule of a Christ-spirit, beyond Christendom, in one Prince who can only be identical with the intent hidden in the true nature of each individual man if he be free to follow his own inner law, the Christ within. The tradition—it is the tradition of a poetry—continues in Whitman's insistence on the poet, the first member of the democratic possibility, as "seer . . . individual . . . complete in himself . . . he president of regulation . . . ." Law is hidden in us, for it—our share of the Law—is what we must create as we create our selves. To be individual is to recognize one's nature, or the Nature in one, to be conscious and conscientious in thought and action. On one hand:

> Whatever comprehends less than that . . . whatever is less than the laws of light and of astronomical motion . . . or less than the laws that follow the thief the liar the glutton and the drunkard through this life and doubtless afterward . . . or less than vast stretches of time or the slow formation of density or the patient upheaving of strata—is of no account.

Self is most intensely experienced in the individual's unique identity as part of the universe at large where the truth of law must comprehend whatever he is to be. Whitman draws upon Lyell in 1855, before Darwin, and before Hegel comes upon his horizon. The logic of earth and of an emerging concept of the physical universe shifts the meaning and imagination of individualities and masses; laws are not imposed upon things, but flowing from things; laws are not of imposed orders but of emerging orders. Today, in the vast democracy in which the events of particles replace the hierarchies of the atomic elements as the creative ground, Whitman's concept of the individual and the mass gains in reality. "These understand the law of perfection in masses and floods . . . that it is profuse and impartial . . . that there is not a minute of the light or dark nor an acre of the earth or sea without it." This idea of the law as a creative entity, creating itself, fires Whitman's imagination wherever he touches upon it.

> He sees health for himself in being one of the mass . . . . he sees the hiatus in singular eminence. To the perfect shape comes common ground. To be under the general law is great for that is to correspond with it.

In all, the very nature of the mass is flowered forth in individualities, new events force new comprehensions of the law. The inner lawfulness of the individual is that he is himself a term of what law is, the critic, the crisis, in the law at large. "The law of laws," Whitman calls it: "the law of successions." What we feel lawful tests the law as it tests our lives.

In *Democratic Vistas* he sees the creative life of politics as a dialectic process in which two forces play: Democracy, "the leveler, the unyielding principle of the average," and "another principle, equally unyielding. . . . the counterpart and offset whereby Nature restrains the deadly original relentlessness of all her first-class laws"—"the individuality, the pride and centripetal isolation of a human being in himself—identity—personalism." Where Dante had written "Intellect" as the potentiality of humanity, Whitman writes "Personality." For both, Intellect and Personality demanded the largest population of human possibilities for its fulfillment; only in the ensemble could they take the ground of ultimate loyalties.

Dante's vision had itself drawn upon the Islamic world outside the European and even the Christian bounds. His Beatrice, the moving spirit of his vision, rimes with a power, angelic and female, the Active Intellect, who belongs to the Sufi revelation. Truth was gathered beyond the bounds of Christendom in the very world of Islam that Christian orthodoxy held most to be the Enemy, as today the dominant orthodoxy of these States holds the Communist world to be the Enemy. For those of us who are *ensemblists* and hold in faith that the Truth of Man is to be found in the resonances of the totality, the truth of democracy lies beyond the bounds of democracy; the truth of "America" is larger, if it be true, than the confines of this nation. Whitman too had come into contact with a world beyond that of Western thought; there had been a passage *from* India as well as the passage to India. The Vedas stood in his mind as part of the greatest poem to which his *Leaves* belonged.

We are in the throes of such an expansion of the imagination in time and space beyond the confines of established policies; a politics beyond cities and nations and civilizations claims our loyalties. For those of us who believe in the unity of mankind, in a new anthropology that no longer thinks of different stages of man, of a progress from primitive to civilized but in terms of different ways of being man; for those of us who further believe in the unity of living beings, the very word "humanity" extends beyond our species to involve us in a largest democracy, in an allegiance to an ecological order: The humanity of man, the difference between the population unaware—the mobocracy—and the population aware of what humanity means—the democracy—extends as far and deep in meaning as his understanding of his relation to his world extends. What we envision as being the well-being of Nature becomes the condition of our humanity. It will never—when will it be settled?

We are, here in the United States of America, the one place where all the peoples of the world are at last gathered together, and we are experiencing what? Of course, we have all the upthroes continually that the world has; old wars between peoples become wars within this one people. The common intent, the contradictions, the world-wide dissensions brought together. Not one religion, but many religions—something larger than religion is needed. Not one race, but many races—something larger than race is needed. America, the melting pot of the world, we saw it as in the thirties. The old orders of races, of ethnic groups, of languages, of religions, of classes to be broken up and mixed, interacting.

Right here in one country. Russia extends between Europe and Asia with many peoples, but they remain ethnically distinct. A visitor from Yugoslavia sees our racial troubles as a symptom of disorder: "We have five races in Yugoslavia," he told me, "and they have learned to live in harmony; they speak their own languages and live in their own parts of the country." He implies that we Americans suffer from some lack of courtesy. Order consists in keeping differences of class and race in order, never speaking out of order or moving into what is not one's place. I said, "I don't think you understand what the term means here." What can they understand where ethnic and even family differences are still thought to be the terms of some individuality? What is at issue in the development of free individuals, men whose identity moves beyond their own origins, beyond race, beyond tribe, beyond class?

Well, let me start here with a passage from my notebooks written along a line that setting out as a path was, as other attempts were, deserted in the field of apprehensions that Whitman's verse called up. "Who learns my lesson complete?" the passage from *Leaves of Grass* begins. So, the promise of an incompleteness led me on in the first place. So many extensions of meaning set my own meanings into motion from themselves, out into the promise of a field of rank growth beyond the projects of city-planning and coordinations, beyond the suburbs, that describe the limits of orderly discourse. The country road rambles and woods take over. In itself this is an experience of Whitman to relate, the multiphasic suggestion of his poetry. He demands ever fresh beginnings, and discountenances conclusions. I called his mode oracular. He himself again and again speaks of the copious, the seminal, the pervasive. He seeks a poetry that will convey his experience of a life that is profusely creative of meanings and in that profusion ever coming forward with diverse hints and potentialities.

We have inherited from Whitman or from our common American spirit an urge that seeks to scatter itself abroad, to send rootlets out into a variety of resources in deriving itself. "No, let me cast aside what begins to take shape and start exploring him afresh," the thought comes ever into the words as I have been writing toward this essay. "Let me start a wandering talk that may come upon some new angle." So, in my talk I did wander from my previous material, and found my concern forming itself along the line of ideas of law and of order in Poetry and the Universe. Just here, my thought returns to the passage from *Leaves of Grass*, from one of the eleven poems which follow "Song of Myself" in the 1855 edition, with which I had thought at first to begin:

Who learns my lesson complete?
Boss and journeyman and apprentice? . . . . churchman and
    atheist?
The stupid and the wise thinker . . . . parents and offspring . . . .
    merchant and clerk and porter and customer . . . . editor,
    author, artist and schoolboy?

Draw nigh and commence,
It is no lesson . . . . it lets down the bars to a good lesson,
And then to another . . . . and every one to another still.
The great laws take and effuse without argument,
I am of the same style, for I am their friend. . . .

As always with Whitman, we will find back of the inspired and enthusiastic phrases the information of a perennial study; his resonances have knowledgeable roots in the ground of the evolution of ideas. The lesson of science in the nineteenth century, in the geology of Lyell, in the biology of Darwin, as in the concept of history after Hegel, was that science was ever to be fruitfully incomplete; and here Whitman proposed a poetry that would be the companion of science. Truth, the grass, was for him the matter of generations, of roots and seedings, in which primary intuitions of the universe are at work to realize themselves.

Back of this Friend of the Great Laws, writing in the same style he saw Life at work in, in the evolution of the poet of *Leaves of Grass*, rightly the name *Friend* will recall Whitman's own Quaker origins and the advent of "the Society of Friends" in America. And we may trace this concept of *Friend* back along the way it has traveled in the evolution of identities from the mystical experience and testimony of George Fox to those Friends of God and the Friends of the Free Spirit, who in the late Middle Ages were Adamites—returning to the conditions of Eden, bearded and naked. We will find there the genetic origins in a Christian tradition of Whitman's recurring themes of nakedness and beardedness; and, today, about us, a century after Whitman, we will recognize his spiritual kin among the new generation of Adamites.

In his essay "George Fox (and Shakespeare)," Whitman sees Shakespeare as "born and bred of similar stock, in much the same surroundings and station in life—from the same England—and at a similar period . . . . fancy's lord, imagination's heir," Shakespeare radiating "a splendor so dazzling that he himself is almost lost in it"—is, indeed, lost in it, for in the dialectics of history, in the development of new spiritual species, it is George Fox who, for Whitman, embodies "something too—a thought—the thought that wakes in silent hours—perhaps the deepest, most eternal thought latent in the human soul." Shakespeare has the splendor of manifest themes that incarnate in its swan-song an historical species—Whitman sees it as the Feudal order. Greatness like that of the Greek dramatists, of Dante, of Shakespeare, can be seen to belong not to the growth and life of the orders they spring from but to the terminal stage. The richness of Shakespeare, "all literature's splendor," "made for the divertisement only of the elite of the castle, and from its point of view," "his infinitely royal, multiform quality"—belongs to an extinct order of life that grows enormous in the period of its extinction, as reptiles at the end of the Age of Reptiles grew into such dragons as have haunted the poetic imagination of Man from his earliest times. "When Feudalism, like a sunset, seem'd to gather all its glories, reminiscences, personalisms, in one last gorgeous effort, before the advance of a new day, a new incipient genius . . . ." The generative orders lie in the common man; it is George Fox who will be the spiritual progenitor of the *Leaves of Grass*. But *Leaves of Grass* in turn is an event in Poetry which today we see, as Whitman saw Shakespeare gathering the glory of Feudalism, gathering the grand sweep of a Democracy, an expanding nationalism, into a great sun that casts its splendors long after its time has past. For surely, no less than Shakespeare's kings and commons and his courtly lovers, Whitman's heroic workers and comrades in love, strong in their individual selves, come to our minds as grandeurs out of perished worlds. Like dragons, they have entered the generative stuff of our humanity.

Back of his coupling of Shakespeare and George Fox in the essay on Fox—"one to radiate all of art's, all literature's splendor" and the other to carry into the community a spiritual latency, yet both "born and bred of similar stock, in much the same surroundings and station in life"—is a genetic drama of alternate potentialities within one nature. Shakespeare in fulfilling his individual genius rises to eminence from the mass; specializing, he is beyond reproduction. The poetic genius too, like the genius of law, works in successions. All grand realizations but clear the way of the urgency toward reality that was all theirs. The achieved is that which is removed from the field of generation or quest of achievement.

"Poetry, largely consider'd, is an evolution," Whitman writes in "A Thought on Shakspere": "sending out improved and ever-expanded types—in one sense, the past, even the best of it, necessarily giving place, and dying out. For our existing world, the bases on which all the grand old poems were built have become vacuums. . . ." *Leaves of Grass* and its poet, the grandly conceived personality Whitman created, are designed "to radiate all of art's, all literature's splendor." But, "born and bred of similar stock, in much the same surroundings," there might be another genius in the work. Within *Leaves of Grass,* more important than its splendors, a seed "latent in the human soul." From the same mass Shakespeare raises the word to an individualized splendor; George Fox returns the word to the anonymity of the mass, to its silent commonality. And readers of *Leaves of Grass* will not only—it is Whitman's dream—find in it the masterpiece that makes Whitman kingly among democrats, but will find in it a common testimony. In the essay on Fox, Whitman might be speaking of this second poet of *Leaves:* "Thus going on, there is something in him that fascinates one or two here, and three or four there, until gradually there were others who went about in the same spirit, and by degrees the Society of Friends took shape, and stood among the thousand religious sects of the world. Women also catch the contagion, and go round, often shamefully misused." Behind these figures of a courageous religious sect to which Whitman's ancestors belonged, we see the figures of the little company who became a Society of Friends for *Leaves of Grass.*

That "deepest most eternal thought latent in the human soul" which George Fox embodies—"that waits in silent hours"—is the seed of a generative silence behind the Word, the seed of latency or intent that informs the ensemble. The ultimate depth belongs, for Whitman, to the revelation of the latent, and the ultimate revelation lies beyond our powers and yet within all powers. It cannot be "realized" by us for we belong to the processes of such realization, it does not belong to us. Whitman is always, then, a compound in his conception, companion of Shakespeare in his grand poetic projection, and companion of Fox, the convert of a mystical experience in poetry. Out of the laws of succession in Poetry, out of the temporal excitement of "improved and ever-expanded types" at work in one, comes a call to Poetry, a call to Order, a call to bear Eternal Witness. The poet then like George Fox must set out to work by faith, beyond belief and beneath contempt.

Setting out in 1855, Whitman had to go on faith. He had the courage of a grand fidelity. But he had no alternative. The poem commanded him. Its reality and truth were imperative. It commands me reading today—the vision of what the Poem is, and within that, *Leaves of Grass* as it has been for me in my own creative life an incarnation of that Presence of a Poetry. This body of words the medium of this spirit. Writing or reading, where words pass into this commanding music, I found a presence of person more commandingly real than what I thought to be my person before; Whitman or Shakespeare presenting more of what I was than I was. And in the course of my own poetry what has drawn me into its depths is this experience of a more intense presence of world and self than I know in myself.

We are just emerging from a period that was long dominated by the idea of a poem as a discipline and a form into which the poet put ideas and feelings, confining them in a literary propriety, giving them the bounds of sound and sense, rime and reason, and the values of a literary—a social—sensibility. Poetry was to be brought to heel, obedient to the criteria of rational discourse, of social realities, of taste. For the New Criticism of the 1930s and 1940s, it was most important that the poet not put on airs. The dominant school of that time thought of form not as a mystery but as a manner of containing ideas and feelings; of content not as the meaning of form but as a commodity packaged in form. It was the grand age of Container Design; and critics became consumer researchers, wary of pretentious claims and seeking solid values. Ideas were thought of as products on the market.

But Whitman's ideas flow as his work flows. He knows that thought is a melody and not something that you manufacture. Poetic thought, Carlyle had proposed, was *musical* thought. And Whitman's verse, as has been amply studied, has form as an aria has form, a pouring forth of thought, not a progression but a medium of thought. The presence belongs to the mass. His imagination of the form at issue, his poetics, moves out from the potentiality he recognized in the aria of the solo singer toward a concept of form to come, of meanings to come. "It poured like a raging river more than any thing else I could compare it to," he writes to a young man in the hospital in Washington in 1863 of an operatic voice: "it is like a miracle—no mocking bird nor the clearest flute can begin with it." But it is a mocking bird or thrush, "solitary, singing in the West," that begins with it for Whitman; and it may be, as it was too in ancient times, poetry began in the music of a flute playing—the forms and meanings that began to flow along the line of another melody. Bird-sound or flute-sound, and words over-heard in their melody by the enraptured ear. That raging river of sound, the aria, becomes in the vision of Whitman a song of the sea, and ever within it, and contrasting, the solitary bird-song of the individual to the Beloved. So too, he found inspiration in throngs—the currents of Broadway within the sea of Manhattan, the throngs upon the ferry boats. The other day, waiting on the steps of the New York Public Library, I found myself giving myself over to contemplate the crowd in the spirit of Whitman, looking at the individual people going about their ways, not watching the individual, but in all, watching the mass of them. Throngs, much as we know the dreadful approaching and already erupting consequences of the swarming and ever-breeding population freed of the information of disease and death, still convey the sense of an exhilaration. There is a thrill about the potentialities of masses of people. So many lives, one feels.

Even the thrill of. . . Well, there was the thrill of all those people walking in that area, of a complicated choreography, unconscious, multiphasic accommodations made to the presences moving each along its own conscious way. It was a fine day, however, and the noontime mood responded to the sunlight and the Spring tide. But even the thrill that whatever we fear out of this monstrous growth of population the future is at work there. This little ensemble and beyond it, the very present, vast ensemble of the City itself—its millions beyond one's comprehension but ever commanding one's apprehensions—calling up for a moment the thrill of the grand ensemble it belongs to.

The element of depth belongs, to Whitman, it has seemed to me, to the revelation of the ensemble in which time moves not toward the end of things but to the fulfillment of things. But now it seems, that word "fulfillment" has too much of the Biblical idea of things fulfilled in the Apocalypse. How far from Whitman's sense of what it means, of filling and fullness, my own poetic apocalyptic sense of signs and meanings fulfilled is. And much has been made of Whitman's alliance with the Vedas, with that endlessness and fullness. And I grow impatient with Whitman's theme of improvement and progress, until I see that theme as one of grander vistas, coming not to the End but into the Full Sea of Time. The crowds upon the Manhattan streets, the throngs of living beings we apprehend, enlarge vividly the impact of "the commonality of all humanity, all time," in which Whitman in his essay on Darwinism sees that the poet "must indeed recast the old metal, the already achiev'd material, into and through new moulds, current forms."

"Who learns my lesson complete?" Nature asks, who learns my lesson complete? History asks, who learns my lesson complete? The Creative Self at work in Creation toward the realization of Self asks, who learns my lesson complete? *Leaves of Grass* was itself a lesson not to be learned complete. The poet returned to his work there in edition after edition. Not addition after addition, but furnishing forth each time a life of the book. What leaf completes the leaves? Each leaf in the ensemble an act of completion. The ensemble, alone the field of the complete, haunts the work of the artist who makes in the poem a fiction of the existence of the whole, a fictional ensemble in which we become aware of the ensemble.

Whitman opens up, beyond Nature and History, an intent and drama of God as Creator at work in the Ensemble to realize his Creative Self. When Whitman thinks of the tradition his vision belongs to, he does not list Heraclitus, but here he is most Heraclitean, for the followers of Heraclitus were most accused of just this heresy, that they believed in a Universe in the process of Its Self-realization. This God does not learn His Self—his lesson—complete except in the totality of Creation, for his learning and his creating are one. The grand Maker or Poet makes his Self come real—realizes Himself—as he makes the field of the Real. We learn who we are by living—we are ourselves the mass of our individualities. Lesson undoes lesson.

"Draw nigh and commence," Whitman continues. Then let's take the contradiction the oracle proposes: "It is no lesson—it lets down the bars to a good lesson, / And that to another, and every one to another still." Hidden in this passage of learning and that in turn a freedom opening upon another learning is the relation of the individual unique undertaking of here and now and the *En Masse*.

God is boss, journeyman, and apprentice, of His own Work, as Whitman, in turn, as poet, creator, is boss, journeyman, and apprentice. Did the editions of 1855, 1860, 1871, 1889, 1891 represent a progress toward completion for him? Or an everlasting command to draw nigh and commence, revealing in the old metal, the already achiev'd material, new demands? As we begin to see evolution as a field in which series of variations, visions, and revisions, and mutations, impulses, and inspirations anew, are at work, these Leaves of Grass are individual reincarnations of a single identity. For my parents, who were theosophical in their religion, Whitman's recurring hints of reincarnation belief were read straight across the board, were taken as the lesson. But draw nigh and commence, the poet asked. This lesson but lets down the bars to another possibility. We see in the course of Whitman's life and works a law of successions, fully achieved versions of *Leaves of Grass* that prove to be given over into the new life of yet another edition.

The line of individual consciousness, of "draw nigh and commence," is the line of an ever-breaking of a wave upon the shore of its sea. Recalling in the close of this essay, the solo of the bird rising in the choral song of the sea, let us, for the moment, take the melody of the bird as identical with the hovering line of the surf-wave, ever about to break, ever drawing nigh and commencing. This configuration I see writing itself again and again in the terms that move through Whitman's work—

the word "En-Masse," that war, that Whitman tells the Muse of War his
poetry wages:

> . . . a longer and greater one than any,
> Waged in my book with varying fortune, with flight, advance
>   and retreat, victory deferr'd and wavering,
>   . . . . . the field the world . . .

at one with the Sea, the all-encompassing "I"; at one with the bird, lonely,
isolate; and, song of the bird heard mingled and commingling with the
surf, the self and the Over-Self at one in the breaking line of the wave
seen. The informing figure is here.

What philosophies, but particularly here rationalist philosophy and
those philosophers of higher mind who would free thought and identity
from the bonds of the sensual, the imaginative, and the passionate, rele-
gate to the realm of illusions and ephemera—the illustrational imme-
diacies of color and sound—are for the artist the deepest ground of the
real. In the poem, the voice given at last its aria, the living pulse and
indwelling resonances, is the true body; and the Incarnation of the Word
is all, that It is embodied in the sound is all, and sound in the stations of a
melody or passionate sequence. The sound incarnates and informs. In
this theology, the Word is identical with its body, having its life in the
interrelating vowels and consonants in which its voice comes. The center
of this reality is what seems the most evanescent of sensual facts, the life
of a man as the center of a universe, the duration of a tone as the cen-
ter of a music, the configuration of sea and the singer as the center of
consciousness moving outward.

"I sing," rings out in the opening Inscription of the *Leaves* in the
1871 edition: "One's-Self I Sing." This is the orphic poet, at one with the
bird outpouring its orisons.

> . . . at dawn the unrivall'd one, the hermit thrush from the swamp-
>   cedars,
> Solitary, singing in the West, I strike up for a New World.

And at one too with the sea:

> . . . the long pulsation, ebb and flow of endless motion,
> The tones of unseen mystery, the vague and vast suggestions
>   of the briny world, the liquid-flowing syllables. . . .

"This is the ocean's poem," he declares in the third inscription of the 1881 edition. "In Cabin'd Ships at Sea," the "ship," his book to be, at once sailing "athwart the imperious waves" and an extension of the deep itself, for these waves are the imperious lines of the verse. The poem is vehicle and actuality of the wave of feeling it rides. "Chant on, sail on," the poet commands; but this chanting that is also a sailing is the wave itself of the sea it sails upon.

In the poem "Eidólons" of 1876, the substance "Of every human life / (The units gather'd, posted, not a thought, emotion, deed, left out,)"

> Ever the ateliers, the factories divine,
> Issuing eidólons

is the surf of a sea upon some shore:

> Ever the dim beginning,
> Ever the growth, the rounding of the circle,
> Ever the summit and the merge at last, (to surely start again,)
> Eidólons! eidólons!

> Ever the mutable,
> Ever materials, changing, crumbling, re-cohering . . . .

at once the very kinetics of Whitman's own line structure within the poem, of poem structure within the *Leaves of Grass*, of edition upon edition of that book, and of his sense of the essential informing motion of the life of Man and of the Universe:

> All space, all time,
> (The stars, the terrible perturbation of the suns,
> Swelling, collapsing, ending, serving their longer, shorter use,) . . .

Here, in Whitman's physics, the vision of the cosmos in process appears as a Sea, and the individual personal Sun, the center of creation for Earth's parochial perspectives and the prototype of God as Father and King, is, in this perspective of "all space, all time," the ensemble, given over to a higher reality of the terrible perturbation of suns, a star now among the throngs of stars, no longer the paradigm of laws but serving a "longer, shorter use" in a source of laws beyond paradigm. Space, time, and the sea of stars, as well as the sea of men to which the

individuality of man belongs, as well as the form of the chant arising in
language—these are expressions of a Sea, a Sea that is itself both cradle
and babe, "endlessly rocking," "swelling, collapsing."

   To our post-Freudian reading, the bird pouring forth its passionate
song from its leafy covert and the poet's "chant of dilation or pride"
betray a sexual configuration, and the "word out of the sea" will be, as it
was for Whitman,

Out of the boy's mother's womb, and from the nipples of her breasts,
Out of the Ninth Month midnight . . .

In the later version, "Out of the Cradle Endlessly Rocking," the direct
image of the boy's mother, womb and nipples, is removed—and yet
insistent enough to intrude at the close of the poem, a line not there in
the earlier "Reminiscence": "(Or like some old crone rocking the cradle,
swathed in sweet garments, bending aside,)" but the Sea remains "with
angry moans the fierce old mother incessantly moaning." Yet we might
go further in our Freudian reading to see that for the poet the genital
reality and the infantile sexuality evoked in the womb and nipples are not
the primary content but lead to the primary content. We might follow
here the Freudian disciple Sandor Ferenczi in *Thalassa* where he pro-
poses that "the mother would, properly, be the symbol of and partial
substitute for the sea, and not the other way about." Yes, the cradle
imitates and restores by man's invention the rocking of the embryo in the
amniotic fluid, but the amniotic fluid in turn recapitulates in the land-
mammal the warmth and surging of the primal Sea in which the seeds of
Life first quickened, the male and female discharging their seed-cells,
spermatozoa and eggs, into the oceanic medium in a pre-genital sexu-
ality. "The amniotic fluid," Ferenczi suggests, "represents a sea 'intro-
jected,' as it were, into the womb of the mother."

   Our reading of the poet then may follow our reading of the psycho-
analyst to see in the ecstasy of the orgasm a return into present feeling,
into consciousness, of the origins, the return of a life (as in death one may
be supposed to recall all of life) going back beyond the boundaries of the
individual, beyond the boundaries of species, to the Primal Scene of
Creation—the Sea of the Universe in which suns pour forth, live, and
die. The more appropriately in that Whitman had been a forerunner of
Freud in this conviction that the whole question of sexuality "strikes far,
very far deeper than most people have supposed." "Is it not really an
intuition of the human race?" he asks in *A Memorandum at a Venture*,

seeing in our sexual consciousness, as in democratic vistas, not something concluded but the promise of something yet to come, an apprehension in the present: "For, old as the world is, and beyond statement as are the countless and splendid results of its culture and evolution, perhaps the best and earliest and purest intuitions of the human race have yet to be develop'd."

The sexual theme is ever-present then as an intuition of the cosmos at large, as in turn the actual bird and the actual sea, once experienced in boyhood, returned to, is an intuition that opens into the feeling of being with a poetry beyond poetry "old as the world is." When, for the poet, the aria "convulses me like the climax of my love-grip," we are not mistaken to recognize in the bird's song pouring forth the pouring forth of semen in orgasmic release. But simile for Whitman is not a mere form of speech, it is a formula of feeling, and that feeling—it is the basis of his poetic understanding—where it arises in the course of the climax of a love-grip or of a poetic seizure, has the authenticity of a primal intuition.

"The oath of procreation I have sworn—my Adamic and fresh daughters," he declares in "Enfans d'Adam," as in the 1860 edition his identification with the Self of the universe and with Man is woven through with another identification with the Adam, male *and* female, and the bisexual ideal, haunting, as it will for the rest of his life, his actual homosexuality. The poet labors to unite the Ideal—and Whitman sees the Ideal not as belonging to the world of high-minded paradigms but to the world of primordial latencies—and the Real, even as his mission is to present a path between the Real and the individual soul. Awkwardly and pathetically, the ideal of bisexuality—not for Whitman of *being* both sexes but of having both sexes as lovers—remains inchoate. He seems not to express but to lay claim to or even boast his sexual love of women. Nowhere is there the physical longing and intensity of loss and gain in feeling that informs the love poems of male lovers. Yet it is a homosexuality in distress, not only in its cry for a mate—there are also the ardent raptures of its fulfillments—but in its generative loss. Mates must be, Whitman sees, "daughters, sons, preluding"; and in the longing for a woman not as lover but as mother to his fathering desire, the intensity of his longing rings true: "I pour the stuff to start sons and daughters fit for These States—I press with rude muscle . . ." "The greed that eats me night and day with hungry gnaw, till I saturate what shall produce boys to fill my place when I am through." But this progeny now must be progeny of his words, the throng of lives invisible in his semen and the throng of readers invisible in his words (or readings invisible in his words) identified; but seminal words never satisfied for the actual semen. In the famous reply to Symonds's enquiry concerning the *Calamus* theme, it is this claim to actual offspring that seems most urgent in answer: "I have had six children—two are dead—One living southern grandchild, fine boy, who writes to me occasionally . . ." As old agony of the heart bursts forth even in his last years.

Urge and urge and urge,
Always the procreant urge of the world . . .

"The song of me rising from bed and meeting the sun" pours forth in *Leaves of Grass* in a rapture and sense of plenitude that mimics the ever present sexual image, the ejaculation of semen, the jetting of a multitude in which one spermatozoa may come to the consummation of its egg, a host jetted forth to live the lifetime of each its own as a sperm. Here again we find the terrible perturbation of the suns, seeds of sons Whitman never fathered, "swelling, collapsing, ending, serving their longer, shorter use." And answering the poet's fathering disappointment, his wisdom extends its sympathetic identification beyond the actual: "You shall possess the good of the earth and sun . . . . there are millions of suns left."

"Urge and urge and urge . . ." "*Agonía, agonía, sueño, fermento y sueño . . . agonía , agonía,*" Lorca will reply, a poet who was himself obsessed with the longing of a woman to give birth, to have a child, and denied fulfillment.

So in Whitman, song is poured forth, love is poured forth, self is poured forth, as semen is jetted, in a life urgency at once triumphant and pathetic. His young friends, his comrades, as he grows older, will be no longer lovers but his boys or sons. And he will be ever aware of the life and death at work in things, the deep coinherence of Eros and Thanatos in the love-act. By the million the seeds find no receptive ground; by the millions the seeds arrive, and Man who is like grass to the beasts of the field springs ever, like grass, anew.

The *souls* moving along . . . . are they invisible while the least atom
   of the stones is visible?
. . . .
What living and buried speech is always vibrating here . . . .
. . . .
I mind them or the resonance of them. . . . I come again and again.

In the moving words "invisible," "visible," "buried," and "vibrating," "the resonance of them," we are reminded of the felt presence of Life beyond our senses—the individual spermatozoa in its life invisible to us, itself in its own life a *soul*. But now the poem speaks of "speech," "living and buried," and the resonance of words become "soul." We begin then to read the poet's "I come again and again" with the common sexual meaning of the word "come."

"Resonance" will give a meaning springing from our sense of the generative orders of life to those principles of music and poetry that many take to be matters of convention and prosody. In the doctrine of resonances rime and meter are no longer thought of as regularities subscribed to or regulations imposed but as Whitman in the 1855 Preface sees rhyme "that it drops the seeds of a sweeter and more luxuriant rhyme, and of uniformity that it conveys itself into its own roots in the ground out of sight."

Poetry and science are close allies for Whitman, for each is ultimately concerned with finding the universe, at once a matter of knowing and a matter of creation. The Real is what we make it out to be. In his time he saw the breakthrough of science as a demand for the breakthrough of poetics. Poetics, physics, politics, all man's serious engagements with life are realms of one Self. A new imagination of the order of the physical universe or of the biological process demands a new imagination of poetic order. So, the political realm "America" will be ultimately "the greatest poetry"; and for its work will demand: "1st, a large variety of character" and "2nd, full play for human nature to expand itself in numberless and even conflicting directions." But this is what the poem also demands; what the origin of species in evolution demands.

The song rises into its melody and pours forth from the passionate throat even as and identical with the rising into the flowing and crumbling melodic line of the breaker of the Sea and poem, line following line to reiterate the urgency of the poem. "Form" and "content" belong to this urgency as the form and content of the wave belong to the very existence at all of the wave.

Taking these two coinherent figures, the bird—the phoebebird, mockingbird, hermit thrush, shy and hidden, crying out "Death's outlet song of life," and the "mysterious ocean where the streams empty," of the 1860 "Proto-leaf"—"prophetic spirit of materials shifting and flickering around me," the lonely, isolate melodic singer pouring forth from its utter individuality and the power *en masse* of the ensemble in which he sings, yield not only poetic meanings, extensions of meaning in terms of

the relations of word, phrase, poem, sequence, and the whole, of reso-
nances throughout, but life meanings, communal meanings, political and
scientific vistas. *Democratic Vistas* are vistas of new poetics and evolution-
ary theory. The singing bird and the surfing sea are images in the sense
that Pound revived in our tradition with his Imagist credo of 1912: "an
intellectual and emotional complex in an instant of time," that brings
"that sense of sudden liberation; that sense of freedom from time limits
and space limits; that sense of sudden growth, which we experience in
the presence of the greatest works of art." Here, for a moment, in the
period of his initial inspiration before the First World War and the
esthetics of the Modernist period, Pound contributes a link in the succes-
sion from Whitman to us as followers of Pound discovering ourselves in
Whitman. In "Psychology and Troubadours," published in *The Quest* in
1916, Pound will still speak in the terms of "our kinship to the vital
universe" and "about us the universe of fluid force, and below us the
germinal universe"; he can refer to certain creative consciousnesses as
"germinal":

> Their thoughts are in them as the thought of the tree is in the seed, or
> in the grass, or the grass in the grain, or the blossom. And these minds are
> the more poetic, and they affect mind about them, and transmute it as the
> seed the earth. And this latter sort of mind is close on the vital uni-
> verse. . . .

But Pound's thought here, with its reflections of the poet of *Leaves
of Grass,* does not go forward with contemporary scientific imagination
to a poetic vision of the Life Process and the Universe but goes back to
Ficino and the Renaissance ideas. *The Cantos* present their own dynamic
life of a universalizing Mind, having, as always, the perturbation of
suns; it seems to us today *The Cantos* even more than *Leaves of Grass*
present "a large variety of character" and expand "in numberless and
even conflicting directions." To Pound's authoritarian superego, or-
der meant the order of totalitarian ideologies and neo-Platonic hierar-
chies, and the creation of his poetic genius seemed to have, like the
music of Bartok or of Beethoven, "the defects inherent in a record of
struggle."

The generation of Pound and Williams, like the critical generation
of the 1930s and 1940s, sought to "objectify" the poem, to free it from
the complex associations of life and history. In the 1950s, Williams ad-
monished us, zealously and even intolerantly, that the poem was written
with words not ideas, *made* with words, as the painting was made with

paints; and the artist in making a poem made a machine or structure of words, freeing language from its contaminations beyond art. Yet for us, Pound's preaching culture and Williams's preaching art belonged to just the process beyond art, the record of struggle, they thought to stand against; and in that, their thought and their work form an antithetical phase in the process in which Whitman appears as our thesis, preparing for a synthesis that begins in their own work in its last phase. Paterson in Williams's *Paterson* is akin, indeed, to Whitman's Myself; and the very word "Cantos," setting out upon the sea and inspired and reinspired by figures of that sea, can recall the word "Chants" of Whitman's *Leaves of Grass,* as well as the Cantos of Dante's *Commedia.* The grand formal courage of Whitman's Personalism in *Leaves of Grass* was to present not argument or rationalization but, as Pound declares his own purpose in writing, "one facet and then another"—an ideogram of Self, a conglomerate Image. Once I returned to Whitman, in the course of writing *The Opening of the Field* when *Leaves of Grass* was kept as a bedside book, Williams's language of objects and Pound's ideogrammatic method were transformed in the light of Whitman's hieroglyphic of the ensemble. So too, the translation-code of Freudian psychoanalysis as, after Whitman, I draw nigh and commence, is both a lesson and "is no lesson . . . it lets down the bars to a good lesson, And then to another."

In the very place where often contemporary individualism finds identity most lost, Whitman takes the ground of his identity and person: in the "particulars and details magnificently moving in vast masses." He saw Democracy not as an intellectual ideal but as an intuition of a grander and deeper reality potential in Man's evolution, beyond the awakening of philosopher-kings and poets, the awakening of the mass. The poet was not individual in his genius, for that genius was the genius of the people; the poet in his poetry an awakening in one of the poetic intent of the mass. "A bard is to be commensurate with a people . . . His spirit responds to his country's spirit." As a dream brings into our consciousness the vision and message of the unconscious mass, so the poet speaks a dream of Man to unawakened men.

As we return to Whitman as a base, we return to just such a poetic courage as the early Pound envisions in those who would "exist close on the vital universe." In Whitman there is no ambiguity about the source of *meaning.* It flows from a "Me myself" that exists in the authenticity of the universe. The poet who exists close on the vital universe then exists close on his Self. All the events of human experience come as words of the poem of poems—the confidence stays with him:

Lilac and star and bird twined with the chant of my soul,
There in the fragrant pines and the cedars dusk and dim.

And in the first pages of *Leaves of Grass* 1855 he had begun, he tells us, to
see the natural world as a text of hieroglyphics:

A child said, What is the grass? fetching it to me with full hands;
How could I answer the child? . . . . I do not know what it is any
   more than he.

I guess it must be the flag of my disposition, out of hopeful green stuff
   woven.

Or I guess it is the handkerchief of the Lord,
A scented gift and remembrancer designedly dropped,
Bearing the owner's name someway in the corners, that we may see
   and remark, and say Whose?

The grass is the very language, embodying as it does the perennial
human spirit and experience, in which the book we are reading is cre-
ated; it is the green blades of words that we call Poetry because the pulse
of that sea of grass enlivens them, common as grass, and having the
mystery of the ultimately *real*, a living word, as Whitman most wanted his
own poetry to have.

Perhaps only James Joyce, in what Ezra Pound saw as his retrograde
work, *Finnegans Wake*, among contemporaries so seizes upon the revela-
tion of the real and of the self as the revelation of the laws of the poem
itself and of its magical authority. "The handkerchief" here that the grass
is, "gift and remembrancer" that is "designedly dropped," "Bearing the
owner's name someway in the corners, that we may see and remark, and
say, Whose?" may be for some readers a passing sentimental figure, but it
may also suggest the concept of creator and creation, of the poet's signa-
ture in his own work in a dropped hint, of the idea of signatures, gift, and
memory (*Mnemosyne*, the Mother of the Muses) that is akin to the letter
that in Joyce's work the Hen has scratched up in the mound of the book,
a scrap presented by the Ensemblist.

Or I guess the grass is itself a child . . . . the produced babe of the
   vegetation.
Or I guess it is a uniform hieroglyphic.

. . . .
To me the converging objects of the universe perpetually flow,
All are written to me, and I must get what the writing means.

That in the cold mad feary father Okeanos of the Sea in *Finnegan* we
may have come at last to some phase of the very Sea that speaks in *Leaves
of Grass* must seem far to have come indeed. Whitman would have found
Joyce's loneliness morbid and his nightmare foreign to the resolution of
Leaves, yet the poet of *Leaves of Grass* had known currents of loneliness
and nightmare. In the poem "The Sleepers," *Leaves* admits such inhabit-
ants. And if the vast populations of man and those words "America," "the
United States," and "Democracy" have been rendered fearful in Joyce's
lifetime by men of his generation, the Sea too darkens.

I would think myself in the very nightmare of it, yet it is Whitman's
Sea that remains primary for me. At the last, evoking that Sea in "With
Husky-Haughty Lips, O Sea!," a poem from *Sands at Seventy:*

. . . a lack from all eternity in thy content,
(Naught but the greatest struggles, wrongs, defeats, could make thee
    greatest—no less could make thee,) . . .

Are we troubled by the threat of sentimentality in the *thy* and *thee?*
George Fox had joined a community of Friends in their courage to bring
back the terms of such a brotherhood in *thee* and *thou.*

Thy lonely state—something thou ever seek'st and seek'st, yet never
    gain'st,
Surely some right withheld—some voice, in huge monotonous rage, of
    freedom-lover pent,
Some vast heart, like a planet's, chain'd and chafing in those breakers,
By lengthen'd swell, and spasm, and panting breath,
And rhythmic rasping of thy sands and waves,
And serpent hiss, and savage peals of laughter,
And undertones of distant lion roar,
(Sounding, appealing to the sky's deaf ear—but now, rapport for once,
A phantom in the night thy confidant for once,)
The first and last confession of the globe,
Outsurging, muttering from thy soul's abysms,
The tale of cosmic elemental passion,
Thou tellest to a kindred soul.

The Lasting Contribution of Ezra Pound

I was eighteen in 1937 when I first opened *A Draft of XXX Cantos:* "And then went down to the ship, Set keel to breaker, forth on the godly sea, and"—set out with Ezra Pound as a master upon the adventure of a poetics to come that is not done with. Today, as passages of *Cantos 110–116* have appeared and the poet speaks "of men seeking good / doing evil," of his errors and wrecks that lie about him and of the sense he has that he cannot make it cohere, as Pound comes into these great Cantos of Contrition, counterparts of the earlier Cantos of Outrage, he remains for me a primary—the master of his craft, yes; but also, in the art at large the creator of a mode, projecting beyond his work new considerations of the meaning of form (as, indeed, our idea of sidereal orders, of cosmos, is no longer that of a creation by paradigm but of a creation in process, and our own experience thereof an ideogram). My concern with the nature of the Law was inspired and continues to be inspired by the poet of *The Cantos* who brought Kung into our studies, tho I derive from the concept that all order proceeds from and depends upon its root in a man's inner order the politics of a lawful anarchism, Vanzetti's voluntarism, opposed to the politics of coercion, be it the "democracy" of majority rule or the "fascism" of Mussolini's dictatorship. What is important here is that I agree with the Pound of *ABC of Economics* that concern for the equities is the key.

As important for me is Pound's role as the carrier of a tradition or lore in poetry, that flowered in the Renaissance after Gemistos Plethon, in the Provence of the 12th century that gave rise to the Albigensian gnosis, the *trobar clus,* and the Kabbalah, in the Hellenistic world that furnished the ground for orientalizing-Greek mystery cults, Christianity, and neo-Platonism. "The tradition is a beauty which we preserve and not a set of fetters to bind us," Pound wrote in 1913. In *The Spirit of Romance* and in the essays "Religio" and "Cavalcanti" he speculates upon this aristocracy of emotion, but in later prose work such as *Kulchur* he is

First appeared in *Agenda*, 4.2 (October–November 1965); reprinted in *America a Prophecy: A New Reading of American Poetry from Pre-Columbian Times to the Present*, ed. George Quasha and Jerome Rothenberg (New York: Random House, 1973).

concerned to qualify if not to dismiss the value of the sublime and the ecstatic. Yet *The Cantos* returns again and again to speak with sublime and ecstatic voice. In his affinity for Plotinus, Proclus, Iamblichus, or the 9th century Erigena, in his poetic cult of the sublime Aphrodite ("crystal body of air") and of Helios, not without Hellenistic hermetic overtones, in his fascination with form in nature ("germinal") having signature, Pound, as does H.D. in her later work, revives in poetry a tradition or kabbalah that would unite Eleusis and the Spirit of Romance, Gassire's lute and the vision of the Spirit Euterpe which came to the Rosicrucian John Heydon on Bulverton Hill. This tradition is an ideogram of the spirit.

That having been summarized, I must note that in his blindness in regard to Lao-tzu Pound diminishes our view of Kung who shares with Lao-tzu the idea of cosmos as Tao, and that in his blindness in regard to Christianity (which he persistently sees in its aspect of the fetter) he diminishes our view of the gods. The Kuanon may enter *The Cantos* but not Mary; Helios, but not Christos.

THE CRAFT: art or skill of rendering a medium (in poetry, the sound and sense of the language) as a force fit for the complex of impression, perception, information, emotion, apprehension, in which the impetus and intent of the work arises. Pound gave us to "compose in the sequence of the musical phrase," thus opening up finer and more complex articulations of feeling and thought, and in rhythmic structure to preserve "the shape of your words, or their natural sound, or their meaning," thus directing our concern to what is happening—shape, sound, and meaning in movement. He found an imperative in poetry when one "must" write in free verse, "when the 'thing' builds up a rhythm more beautiful than that of set meters, or more real, more a part of the 'thing,' more germane, interpretative than the measure of the regular accentual verse." Craft here is not to impose a form upon a force but to find the force, the very movement of shape, sound, and meaning, in which the form of the total process is apprehended.

In "A Retrospect" he speaks of "assonance and alliteration, rhyme immediate and delayed, simple and polyphonic"; in "The Serious Artist" he speaks of "words in a rhythm that preserves some accurate trait of the emotional impression, or of the sheer character of the fostering or parental emotion"; from "The Treatise on Harmony" I have gathered that rhythm is the phrasings in which the time of the composition is created, and that rhyme has to do with time intervals at which similar and dissimilar sounds occur. As early as "A Retrospect," Pound notes that there is "a

sort of residue of sound which remains in the ear of the hearer and acts
more or less as an organ-base."

In 1948, Dallam Simpson in *Four Pages* issued a Manifesto I have
always thought of as Poundian in its origin: "(1) We must understand
what is really happening. (2) If the verse-makers of our time are to
improve on their immediate precursors, we must be vitally aware of the
duration of syllables, of melodic coherence, and of the tone leading of
vowels. (3) The function of poetry is to debunk by lucidity."

In the Norton Lectures of 1939–40 on *The Poetics of Music,* pub-
lished in 1947, Stravinsky defined melody as "the intonation of the melos,
which signifies a fragment, a part of a phrase. It is these parts that strike
the ear in such a way as to mark certain accentuations." From the unit of
the musical phrase, music and poetry too seemed to be turning to the
articulation of the immediate particle—the melos or syllable. In Olson's
"Projective Verse" of 1950, he insists "It is by their syllables that words
juxtapose in beauty, by these particles of sound as clearly as by the sense
of the words which they compose." What, he suggests, if "both rime and
meter, and, in the quantity words, both sense and sound, were less in the
forefront of the mind than the syllable, if the syllable, that fine creature,
were more allowed to lead the harmony on." Then: "With this warning,
to those who would try: to step back here to this place of the elements and
minims of language, is to engage speech where it is least careless—and
least logical. Listening for the syllables must be so constant and so scru-
pulous, the exaction must be so complete, that the assurance of the ear is
purchased at the highest—40 hours a day—price. For from the root out,
from all over the place, the syllable comes, the figures of, the dance."

Pound's craft takes the shape of the phrase as its base; differing here
from the high craft of Williams and Marianne Moore who took the
numbers of syllables as their base. As late as 1954, Williams in "On
Measure" insists "In scanning any piece of verse, you 'count' the syllables.
Let's not speak either of rhythm, an aimless sort of thing without precise
meaning of any sort." Yet certainly by *Paterson II* in 1948, rhythmic
phrasings had begun to take over in Williams's verse, and by 1949 when
the first poems of *The Desert Music* began to appear phrasing is the
dominant base. The line based on the musical phrase is always an articu-
lation arising as the inner shape of feeling and meaning, in contrast to
the line which is determined by count of syllables or stress and usually
functions as a "discipline" imposed like a military drill or court manners
or as a counter-structure to the syntax and to the emotional-intellectual
complex of the poem. In Williams's early verse the line, for instance,

often ends on an article or a preposition, a juncture which originates as an accident of the counting of syllables. But in this "accident" there was the germ of a discovery, for just this juncture, if it be sounded, is the vehicle of a meaningful hesitation in American speech that conveys the pattern of a highly energized emotional-intellectual complex, the movement of a mind that does not take its consciousness for granted but must re-establish it in an immediate instance in relation to a larger field of instances. It is the juncture of the suspension of conclusions at the point of decision, so that all decision moves forward toward a totality that is pending, rather than reinforcing the prejudice of an established totality.

Williams developed this juncture of immediacy as an agency of internal form, so that its origin as an accident of imposed form may be relegated to the study of byways in the evolution of American poetics, such as the expert artifice of Marianne Moore where such terminal junctures are rimed in assonance and consonance in syncopation to the stress system to provide a brilliantly ornamented movement. What is important here is that Williams did not take accident for granted as accident nor did he develop it as a patterned ornament, but he saw it in relation to the shape of words as men use them to communicate "some accurate trait of the emotional impression, or of the sheer character of the fostering or parental emotion," as Pound in the beginning had urged. It was just this "accident," which Williams explored and developed as meaning, that particularly opened the way for a group of younger writers—Charles Olson, Robert Creeley, Denise Levertov, Larry Eigner, Paul Blackburn, Gael Turnbull, Theodore Enslin, Cid Corman, and myself—who were concerned with immediacy and process in the development of their poetics. In *Origin* from 1950 on, a new poetry began to appear deriving its music from the ground Ezra Pound had given us in his theory and practice forty years earlier, from the composition by phrase which Pound had advanced to the high art of *The Pisan Cantos* (1949) and from the finer articulation of immediacies which Williams had brought to that composition by the time of *Paterson II* (1948).

Notes on the Poetics of Marianne Moore

Ezra Pound wrote to Marianne Moore (December 16, 1918): "And as for 'peacock': is it the best word? It means peacock-green??? Or peacock-blue or p.b. green? Peacock has feet and other colors such as brown in its ensemble???" Marianne Moore may be characterized by her ability to respond. In "The Steeple-Jack" we note that Pound's query focused her attentions:

> a sea the purple of the peacock's neck is
>   paled to greenish azure as Dürer changed
> the pine green of the Tyrol to peacock blue and guinea
> gray . . .

She titles an early volume *Observations*. Miss Moore is an ever-ready student—of animals and plants; of objects that from their making bear the imprint of human virtues; of words read and words heard "where there is an effect of thought or pith" to use "the thinking and often the actual phrases"; of the *Illustrated London News* and the *New York Times*. In the poem "Voracities and Verities Sometimes Are Interacting" she acknowledges: "and to a tiger-book I am reading—/ I think you know the one—/ I am under obligation." She has veracity native to the poet who keeps green and alive her ability to respond and has the humility of her affections to remind us, even if *Notes* are necessary, always of her sources. Her work is of a deep-going delight in what is of use that must impart to us its objects and objectives. Of which, Wallace Stevens in his essay "About One of Marianne Moore's Poems" says: "The supreme virtue here is humility, for the humble are they who move about the world with the lure of the real in their hearts." In the root meaning she is an amateur as a student; it is her love of certain qualities that guides her. From this she has constructed a conglomerate form; eschewing connectives, she achieves her unity as it springs from her *genius*, her unsurpassd intuition for coherence.

Written as an introduction to Marianne Moore's reading at The Poetry Center, San Francisco State University, 11 October 1957.

There is that in her temperament that is both quick and deliberate. Her poetry is closer to dance than to song, if I can make the distinction without denying the song that is there. Ezra Pound circa 1928 in *How To Read* defined the mode in which Marianne Moore works as *logopoeia*—"the dance of the intellect among words." In this mode she excels. Excitement (voracity) and discrimination combine in a poetry crowded with particulars that, "free from the smears of mystery as William Carlos Williams commends her work, are at once clearly each itself and intense and at the same time are parts of a total intricate suggestion in design." Eliot notes that "We all have to choose whatever subject-matter allows us the most powerful and most secret release; and that is a personal affair." Well, "voracities and verities sometimes are interacting." In an early poem "To a Chameleon," not reprinted since *Observations*, Marianne Moore has reference to a voracity that might have been the poet's:

> Hid by the august foliage and fruit of the grape vine,
>> twine
>>> your anatomy
>>>> round the pruned and polished stem,
>>>>> Chameleon.
>>>>> Fire laid upon
>>>> an emerald as long as
>>> the Dark King's massy
>> one,
> could not snap the spectrum up for food as you have done.

Upon reflection we realize that the hidden, the twining anatomy, the foliage, fire, spectrum, and chameleon illustrate a feeling of design in life as well as in the art. William Carlos Williams writing on Marianne Moore's poems says: "[Modern work] is a multiplication of impulses that by their several flights, crossing at all eccentric angles, might enlighten. . . . The unessential is put rapidly aside as the eye searches between for illumination," from which I derive: She locates the particular essential for illumination.

In his "Introduction" to Miss Moore's *Selected Poems* (1935) T.S. Eliot wrote: "Of the *light* rhyme Miss Moore is the greatest living master; and indeed she is the first, so far as I know, who has investigated its possibilities. It will be observed that the effect sometimes requires giving a word a slightly more analytical pronunciation, or stressing a syllable more than ordinarily. . . . It is sometimes obtained by the use of articles as rhyme words."

Today, for those of us who are concernd with the articulation of the line in the poem and its notation, Marianne Moore remains a master because she has never ceased to be a student. From a poem like "Style" (in *Like a Bulwark*) we have everything to learn of movement and tempo through the line, where the interplay of regularities (a stanza establishing the pattern of syllabic count by lines, 14–16–9–5–12–7–12, as the basis of repetition in the poem, with the second and third lines having end-rhyme) and spontaneities. The art of the poem here is to establish its pattern even in departing from it, an inner order obeyd the more resolutely because the mind coordinating vowel tones and consonant clusters, duration and number of syllables, the subtle contours of natural stress, and the influences of syntax upon all these, delights in the contrivance—where skill, agility, ingenuity are all displayd—but remains at the same time obedient to the *felt order,* to intimations of coherence that depend not upon the conscious convention or invention but upon the organic complexity in unity of sensibility, emotion, will, and intellect. Yet her objective is not to be profound, it is only to be lively. In her essay "Humility, Concentration, Gusto" Marianne Moore writes: ". . . gusto thrives on freedom, and freedom in art, as in life, is the result of a discipline imposed by ourselves." One thinks of that discipline in her work as springing from a demanding aesthetic (sense of the Beautiful) and a commanding morality (sense of the True). In workmanship the beautiful and the true sometimes are interacting. As Williams notes "the aesthetic pleasure engenderd where pure craftsmanship joins hard surfaces skillfully."

Rites of Participation

The drama of our time is the coming of all men into one fate, "the dream of everyone, everywhere." The fate or dream is the fate of more than mankind. Our secret Adam is written now in the script of the primal cell. We have gone beyond the reality of the incomparable nation or race, the incomparable Jehovah in the shape of a man, the incomparable Book or Vision, the incomparable species, in which identity might hold & defend its boundaries against an alien territory. All things have come now into their comparisons. But these comparisons are the correspondences that haunted Paracelsus, who saw also that the key to man's nature was hidden in the larger nature.

In space this has meant the extension of our "where" into a world ecology. The O.E.D. gives 1873 as the earliest English use of the word in the translation of Haeckel's *History of Creation*—"The great series of phenomena of comparative anatomy and ontogeny . . . oecology." The very form of man has no longer the isolation of a superior paradigm but is involved in its morphology in the cooperative design of all living things, in the life of everything, everywhere. We go now to the once-called primitive—to the bush man, the child, or the ape—not to read what we were but what we are. In the psychoanalysis of the outcast and vagabond, the neurotic and psychotic, we slowly discover the hidden features of our own emotional and mental processes. We hunt for the key to language itself in the dance of the bees or in the chemical code of the chromosomes.

The inspiration of Marx bringing economies into comparison and imagining a world commune, of Darwin bringing species into comparison and imagining a world family of the living in evolution, of Frazer bringing magic, rituals, and gods into comparison and imagining a world cult—the inspiration growing in the nineteenth century of imperialist expansions was towards a larger community of man. In time, this has meant our "when" involves and is involved in an empire that extends into the past and future beyond times and eras, beyond the demarcations of

First appeared in two parts: *Caterpillar* 1 (October 1967), and *Caterpillar* 2 (January 1968). The essay is Chapter 6, Part I, of "The H.D. Book."

history. Not only the boundaries of states or civilizations but also the boundaries of historical periods are inadequate to define the vital figure in which we are involved. "For the intense yearning which each of them has towards the other," Diotima tells Socrates in Plato's *Symposium*, "does not appear to be the desire of lover's intercourse, but of something else which the soul of either evidently desires and cannot tell, and of which she has only a dark and doubtful presentiment."

The *Symposium* of Plato was restricted to a community of Athenians, gathered in the common creation of an *aretê*, an aristocracy of spirit, inspired by the homoEros, taking its stand against lower or foreign orders, not only of men but of nature itself. The intense yearning, the desire for something else, of which we too have only a dark and doubtful presentiment, remains, but our *aretê*, our ideal of vital being, rises not in our identification in a hierarchy of higher forms but in our identification with the universe. To compose such a symposium of the whole, such a totality, all the old excluded orders must be included. The female, the proletariat, the foreign; the animal and vegetative; the unconscious and the unknown; the criminal and failure—all that has been outcast and vagabond must return to be admitted in the creation of what we consider we are.

The dissolving of boundaries of time, as in H.D.'s *Palimpsest,* so that Egyptian or Hellenistic ways invade the contemporary scene—the reorganization of identity to extend the burden of consciousness—this change of mind has been at work in many fields. The thought of primitives, dreamers, children, or the mad—once excluded by the provincial claims of common sense from the domain of the meaningful or significant—has been reclaimed by the comparative psychologies of William James, Freud, Lévy-Bruhl, Piaget, by the comparative linguistics of Sapir or Whorf, brought into the community of a new epistemology.

"Past the danger point, past the point of any logic and of any meaning, and everything has meaning," H.D. writes in *Bid Me to Live:* "Start superimposing, you get odd composites, nation on nation." So, Malraux in his *Psychology of Art* hears "a furtive colloquy in progress between the statuary of the Royal Portals of Chartres and the great fetishes" beginning in museums of the mind where all the arts of man have been brought into the complex of a new idea of Art and Man in their being superimposed. "Our art world is one," he writes in *The Metamorphosis of the Gods,* "in which a Romanesque crucifix and an Egyptian statue of a dead man can both be living presences." "In our imaginary museum the great art of Europe is but one great art among others, just as the history of Europe has come to mean one history among others." "Each civilization had its 'high places,'" he concludes in the Introduction: "All mankind is now discovering its own. And these are not (as the nineteenth century took for granted) regarded as successive landmarks of art's long pilgrimage through time. Just as Cézanne did not see Poussin as Tintoretto's successor, Chartres does not mark an 'advance' on Angkor, or Borobudur, or the Aztec temples, any more than its Kings are an 'advance' on the Kwannon at Nara, on the Plumed Serpents, or on Pheidias' Horsemen."

If, as Pound began to see in *The Spirit of Romance,* "All ages are contemporaneous," our time has always been, and the statement that the great drama of our time is the coming of all men into one fate is the statement of a crisis we may see as ever-present in Man wherever and whenever a man has awakened to the desire for wholeness in being. "The continuous present," Gertrude Stein called this sense of time and history, and she saw the great drama as man's engagement in a composition of the contemporary. Man is always in the process of this composition. "The composition is the thing seen by every one living in the living they are doing," she writes in *Composition As Explanation:* "they are the composing of the composition that at the time they are living is the composition of the time in which they are living. It is that that makes living a thing they are doing."

"Nothing changes from generation to generation," she writes later in her lecture "Portraits and Repetition," "except the composition in which we live and the composition in which we live makes the art which we see and hear." "Once started expressing this thing, expressing any thing there can be no repetition because the essence of that expression is insistence." "Each civilization insisted in its own way before it went away." To enter into "our time," she saw as "a thing that is very troublesome," for life itself was a disturbance of all composition—"a fear a doubt and a judgement and a conviction," troubling the waters toward some needed "quality of distribution and equilibration."

*

The first person plural—the "we," "our," "us"—is a communal consciousness in which the "I" has entered into the company of imagined like minds, a dramatic voice in which the readers and the man writing are gathered into one composition, in which we may find kindred thought and feeling, an insistence, in Plutarch or Dante, Plato or D.H. Lawrence, closer to our inner insistence than the thought and feeling of parents or neighbors. The discovery of self, time, and world, is an entering into or tuning to possibilities of self, time, and world, that are given.

"The single experience lodges in an individual consciousness and is, strictly speaking, incommunicable," Sapir writes in *Language:* "To be communicated it needs to be referred to a class which is tacitly accepted by the community as an identity. Thus, the single impression which I have of a particular house must be identified with all my other impressions of it. Further, my generalized memory or my 'notion' of this house must be merged with the notions that all other individuals who have seen the house have formed of it. The particular experience that we started with has now been widened so as to embrace all possible impressions or images that sentient beings have formed or may form of the house in question. In other words, the speech element 'house' is the symbol, first and foremost, not of a single perception, nor even of the notion of a particular object but of 'a concept,' in other words, of a convenient capsule of thought that embraces thousands of distant experiences and that is ready to take in thousands more. If the single significant elements of speech are the symbols of concepts, the actual flow of speech may be interpreted as a record of the setting of these concepts into mutual relations."

There is no isolate experience of anything then, for to come into "house" or "dog," "bread" or "wine," is to come into a company. Eros and Logos are inextricably mixed, daemons of an initiation in each of our lives into a new being. Every baby is surrounded by elders of a mystery. The first words, the "da-da" and "ma-ma," are keys given in a repeated ritual by parental priest and priestess to a locus for the child in his chaotic babbling, whereby from the oceanic and elemental psychic medium— warmth and cold, calm and storm, the moodiness previous to being— persons, Daddy and Mama, appear. But these very persons are not individual personalities but communal fictions of the family cultus, vicars of Father and Mother, as the Pope is a Vicar of Christ. The Child, the word "child," is himself such a persona, inaccessible to the personality of the individual, as the language of adult personal affairs is inaccessible to the child. To have a child is always a threat to the would-be autonomous personality, for the parent must take leave of himself in order to enter an other impersonation, evoking the powers of Fatherhood or Motherhood, so that the infant may be brought up from the dark of his individuality into a new light, into his Childhood. For the transition to be made at all, to come into the life of the spirit, in which this Kindergarten is a recreated stage set of the mythic Garden, means a poetry then, the making up of an imaginary realm in which the individual parents and infant participate in a community that exists in a time larger than any individual life-time, in a language. For "Father," "Mother," "Child," are living words, deriving their meaning from thousands of distinct experiences, and the actual flow of family life, like the actual flow of speech, "may be interpreted as . . . the setting of these concepts into mutual relations." The toys of the nursery are not trivia but first given instruments of an extension in consciousness, our creative life. There is a travesty made of sacred objects when the building blocks that are also alphabet blocks, the animal and human dolls, the picture books, are rendered cute or babyish.

"The maturity of man—" Nietzsche writes in *Beyond Good and Evil:* "that means, to have reacquired the seriousness that one had as a child at play." In *The Zohar* of Moses of León, God Himself appears as Child-Creator-of-the-World:

> When the Holy One, blessed be He, was about to make the world, all the letters of the Alphabet were still embryonic, and for two thousand years the Holy One, blessed be He, had contemplated them and toyed with them. When He came to create the world, all the letters presented themselves before Him in reversed order. The letter Tau advanced in front and pleaded: May it please Thee, O Lord of the world, to place me first in the creation of the world, seeing that I am the concluding letter of EMeTh (Truth) which is engraved upon Thy seal.

One by one the letters present themselves. At the last, "the Beth then entered and said":

> O Lord of the world, may it please Thee to put me first in the creation of the world, since I represent the benedictions (Berakhoth) offered to Thee on high and below. The Holy One, blessed be He, said to her: Assuredly, with thee I will create the world, and thou shalt form the beginning in the creation of the world. The letter Aleph remained in her place without presenting herself. Said the Holy one, blessed be His name: Aleph, Aleph, wherefore comest thou not before Me like the rest of the letters? She answered: Because I saw all the other letters leaving Thy presence without any success. What, then, could I achieve there? And further, since Thou hast already bestowed on the letter Beth this great gift, it is not meet for the Supreme King to take away the gift which He has made to His servant and give it to another. The Lord said to her: Aleph, Aleph, although I will begin the creation of the world with the Beth, thou wilt remain the first of letters. My unity shall not be expressed except through thee, on thee shall be based

all calculations and operations of the world, and unity shall not be expressed save by the letter Aleph. Then the Holy One, blessed be His name, made higher-world letters of a large pattern and lower-world letters of a small pattern. It is therefore that we have here two words beginning with beth (Bereshith bara) "in-the-beginning He-created" and then two words beginning with aleph (Elohim eth) "God the."

In this primal scene, before the beginning of the world that is also here before the beginning of a writing, the Self contemplates and toys in a rite of play until the letters present themselves and speak; as in another primal scene, in a drama or play of the family, the child contemplates and plays with the sounds of a language in order to enter a world in which Father and Mother present themselves and speak. So too in the fullness of the imagination, blocks and even made-up playmates present themselves. The teddy bear was once in the shaman world of the great northern forests Grandfather or Folk-Father. The figures we play with, the members of our play world, given as they are, like the Katchina dolls of the Zuñi child, are spirit figures. "My unity shall not be expressed except through thee," the Child-Creator promises. It is the first promise of love, "on thee shall be based all calculations and operations of the world."

These powers, the ambience in which all things of our world speak to us and in which we in turn answer, the secret allegiances of the world of play, the psychic depth of time transformed into eternity in which the conceptual persons of Father and Mother, Child and Play-Thing, exist— these are pre-rational. Brother and Sister have such an existence in the unreal that, where actual brother and sister do not exist or are unwilling to play the part, imaginary brother and sister may appear.

For men who declare themselves partisans of the rational mind at war with all other possibilities of being, the pre-rational or the irrational appears as an enemy within. It was not only the Poet, but Mother and Father also, that Plato would exclude from his Republic. In the extreme of the rationalist presumption, the nursery is not the nursery of an eternal child but of a grown-up, a rational man. Common sense and good sense exist in an armed citadel surrounded by the threatening countryside of fantasy, childishness, madness, irrationality, irresponsibility—an exile and despised humanity. In that city where Reason has preserved itself by retreating from the totality of the self, infants must play not with the things of the imagination nor entertain the lies of the poets but play house, government, business, philosophy, or war. Before the guardians of this state the voices and persons of the Child-Creator stand condemned as auditory and visual hallucinations, a dangerous non-sense.

In the world of *The Zohar,* dolls were not permitted. The Child plays with the letters of an alphabet and Logos is the creator of the world. Man is to take his reality from, to express his unity in, the letter. But this letter is, like the doll, alive to the mind. Tau presents herself and speaks, just as the bear in our nursery does. To the extent that once for us too alphabet blocks were animate, all future architectures and worlds are populated, and we are prepared to understand the world-experience of the Kabbalist.

In this world-experience rationality does not exist apart from the whole, but the understanding searches ever to picture the self in the unununderstandable. The human spirit draws its life from a tree larger and more various than knowing, and reason stands in need of a gift, "the gift of the queen to them that wander with her in exile."

There is a return in the imagination to the real, an ascent of the soul to its *"root,"* that Hayyim Vital describes in his life work, *The Tree of Life:*

> The imaginative faculty will turn a man's thoughts to imagine and picture as if it ascended in the higher worlds up to the roots of his soul . . . until the imagined image reaches its highest source and there the images of the supernal lights are imprinted on his mind as if he imagined and saw them in the same way in which his imaginative faculty normally pictures in his mind mental contents deriving from the world.

We seem to be in the description of the process of a poem, for here too the mind imagines, but then enters a real it had not imagined, where the image becomes informed, from above or below, and takes over as an entity in itself, a messenger from a higher real. In his ascent the mystic is irradiated by the light of the tree and in his descent the light finds a medium through which to flow back into the daily world:

> The thought of the prophet expands and rises from one level to another . . . until he arrives at the point where the root of his soul is. Next he concentrates on raising the light of the sefirah to *En Sof* and from there he draws the light down, from high down to his rational soul and from there, by means of the imaginative faculty, down to his animal soul, and there all things are pictured either by the inner senses of the imaginative faculty or by the outer senses.

Returning from *En Sof,* the unknowable, unimaginable God, from beyond sense, the imaginer, no longer imagining but realizing, carries a light from station to station, sefiroth to sefiroth, irradiating the imagined with reality, transforming the sense of the divine—the articulated Tree of Life—the cosmos, the rational soul and the animal soul, in light of a source that is a numinous non-sense or beyond sense.

This Tree, too, we saw each year, for at the birthday of the Child-Christos, we were as children presented with a tree from which or under which gifts appeared—wishes made real. This Christmas tree came, we know, from the tree-cults of the German tribes, ancestral spirits—a burning tree. But it is also a tree of lights, and where, in the time of Jacob Boehme, in the early seventeenth century, the Jewish and the Germanic mystery ways are wedded in one, the Christmas tree may have also been the Divine Tree of the Zohar, lit with the lights of the sefirah.

In this ritual of the imagination of Hayyim Vital, there is not only the ascent by pretending, the *"as if"* of his text, the pretension then, but the mystic is pretender to a throne, a *"source"* or *"root"* in the Divine. In the descent a magic is worked and all the pretended way of the ascent is rendered *"greater than Reality."* Not only the deep dream but the day dream enlightens or enlivens. *"Occasionally,"* Werblowsky relates from Vital, "the imaginative faculty may even externalize or project the effects of this 'light' so that the experience becomes one of external sense impressions such as of the apparition of angelic messengers, the hearing of voices."

This Tree of Life is also the tree of generations, for its branches that are also roots are male and female, and the light or life is a mystery of the Shekinah, the ultimate Spirit-Mother of Israel as well as God's Glory. The root or seed is a quickening source in the immortal or eternal womb, wherein each man is immortal.

*

In his study of Australian tribal rites, the psychoanalyst Geza Roheim draws another configuration of source, dream, and transformation of reality, that may cast further light on our way towards a picture of what is involved in poetry when the images and personae of a dream greater than reality appear as active forces in the poet's world:

Strehlow, who as a missionary living for decades among the Aranda was certainly an authority on their language, tells us that he cannot explain the meaning of the word *altjira,* but it seems that the natives connect to it the concept of something that has no beginning—*erina itja arbmanakala,* him none made. Spencer and Gillen, however, have given another interpretation of the word. In their glossary we find "*altjeringa:* name applied by the Arunta, Kaitish, and Unmatjera tribes to the far past or dream times in which their mythical ancestors lived. The word *altjeri* means dream." Strehlow denies this; he says the word for dream is *altjirerama,* and gives the following etymology: *altjira* (god) *rama* (to see).

For one thing, it is clear that *altjira* means dream and not god or ancestor (as Strehlow indicates) for I found that a folktale, a narrative with a happy end, is also called *altjira.*

It is evident that Strehlow, from his preoccupation with *Altjira* (God) of the Aranda Bible, managed to miss the real meaning of the word. *Altjira* = dream, altjireramaa = *to dream; altjirerinja* = dreaming. This is as near as I could get to Spencer and Gillen's *altjeringa.* Moses thought it must be a mistake for either *altirerindja* or *altjiranga.* There was no name for any mythical period. The time when the ancestors wandered on earth was called *altjiranga nakala,* i.e. "ancestor was," like *ljata nama,* i.e. "now is." Other expressions were noted as equivalents of *altjiranga nakala;* these were *imanka nakala,* "long time ago was," or *kutata nakala,* "eternally was." This led us to the explanation and etymology of the word *altjiranga mitjina. Mitjina* is equivalent to *kutata,* "eternal"; *nga* is the ablative suffix *from;* therefore *altjiranga mitjina* = "the eternal ones from the dream" or "the eternal people who come in dreams." This is not my explanation, but that of the old men, Moses, Renana, and Jirramba. Another Aranda word for dream, ancestor, and story, is *tnankara.* It is not often used, and as far as I could see it means exactly the same as *altjira.*

In story and tribal rite, the Australian native seeks to convert time and space into an expression of his unity, to create a language of acts and things, of devouring and being devoured, of giving birth and being born, in which man and the world about him come into one body. "In an emu myth of the Aranda, Marakuja (Hands Bad), the old man emu, takes his bones out and transforms them into a cave . . . The kangaroo men take the mucus from their noses; it becomes a stone, still visible now. The rocks become black where they urinate." Here the *altjiranga mitjina,* the ones living in a dream of time more real than the mortality of the time past, invade the immediate scene. For the Australian as for Heraclitus, "Immortal mortals, mortal immortals, their being dead is the other's life." The things lost in time return and are kept in the features of the place. "Environment is regarded as if it were derived from human beings," Roheim observes.

In repeated acts—bleeding, pissing, casting mucus, spitting into the ground, or in turn, eating the totemic food and drinking the blood of the fathers—the boy is initiated into the real life of the tribe. "An old man sits beside him and whispers into his ear the totemic name. The boy then calls out the esoteric name as he swallows the food. The emphasis on the place name in myth and ritual can only mean one thing, that both myth and ritual are an attempt to cathect environment with libido. . . . The knowledge of the esoteric name 'aggregates' unites the boy to the place or to the animal species or to anything that was strange before."

The "beast, anus, semen, urine, leg, foot" in the Australian song, chant or enchantment, that is also hill, hole, see, stream, tree, or rock, where "in the Toara ceremony the men dance around the ring shouting the names of male and female genital organs, shady trees, hills, and some of the totems of their tribe," are most familiar to the Freudian convert Roheim. He sees with a sympathy that rises from the analytic cult in which Freud has revived in our time a psychic universe in which dream has given a language where, by a "sexual obsession" (as Jung calls it), the body of man and the body of creation are united.

The "blood" of the Aranda, the "libido" of the Freudian, may also be the "light" of our Kabbalist text. *"En Sof,"* Gershom Scholem tells us in *Major Trends in Jewish Mysticism:* "is not only the hidden Root of all Roots"

> it is also the sap of the tree; every branch representing an attribute, exists not by itself but by virtue of *En Sof,* the hidden God. And this tree of God is also, as it were, the skeleton of the universe; it grows throughout the whole of creation and spreads branches through all its ramifications. All mundane and created things exist only because something of the power of the Sefiroth lives and acts in them.
>
> The simile of man is as often used as that of the Tree. The Biblical word that man was created in the image of God means two things to the Kabbalist: first, that the power of the Sefiroth, the paradigm of divine life, exists and is active also in man. Secondly, that the world of the Sefiroth, that is to say the world of God the Creator, is capable of being visualized under the image of man the created. From this it follows that the limbs of the human body are nothing but images of a certain spiritual node of existence which manifests itself in the symbolic figure of *Adam Kadmon,* the primordial man. The Divine Being Himself cannot be expressed. All that can be expressed are His symbols. The relation between *En Sof* and its mystical qualities, the Sefiroth, is comparable to that between the soul and the body, but with the difference that the human body and soul differ in nature, one being material and the other spiritual, while in the organic whole of God all spheres are substantially the same.

"The world of the Sefiroth is the hidden world of language," Scholem continues, "the world of divine names." "Totemic names," Roheim calls the whispered passwords of the Australian rite. "The creative names which God called into the world," Scholem calls the Sefiroth, "the names which He gave to Himself." It is the alphabet of letters revealed to the initiate as at once the alphabet of what he is and what the universe is and the alphabet of eternal persons.

As Scholem hints, "the conception of the Sefiroth as parts or limbs of the mystical anthropos leads to an anatomical symbolism which does not shrink from the most extravagant conclusions." Man's "secret parts" are secret names or hidden keys to the whole figure of man, charged with magic in their being reserved. In the communal image, the human figure is male and female. Asshole, penis, cunt, navel, were not only taboo but sacred, words to be revealed in initiations of the soul to the divine body, as at Eleusis the cunt of a woman in the throes of birth was shown. In what we call carnal knowledge, in the sexual union of male and female nakedness, God and His creation, the visible and invisible, the above and the below are also united.

Ham, who sees the nakedness of his father, is the prototype of the Egyptian who in an alien or heretic religion knows the secrets of God. To steal a look, like the theft of fire, is a sin, for the individual seeks to know without entering the common language in which things must be seen and not seen.

"At the initiation ceremony the point is to displace libido from the mother to the group of fathers," Roheim writes. In the contemporaneity of our human experience with all it imagines, there may be not a displacement but an extension of libido: the revelation of the mother remains, the revelation of the male body is added.

> Some old men stand in the ring and catching hold of their genitals tell the boys to raise their eyes and take particular notice of those parts. The old men next elevate their arms above their heads and the boys are directed to look at their armpits. Their navels are exhibited in the same way. The men then put their fingers on each side of their mouths and draw their lips outward as wide as possible, lolling out their tongues and inviting the special attention of the novices. They next turn their backs and, stooping down, ask the novices to take particular notice of their posterior parts.

For Roheim, the images and magic of Australian story and rite are one with the images and magic of all dreams:

After having withdrawn cathexis from environment, we fall asleep. But when the cathexis is concentrated in our own bodies we send it out again and form a new world, in our dreams. If we compare dream mechanisms with the narratives of dream-times we find an essential similarity between the two. The endless repetitions of rituals and wanderings and hunting are indeed very different from a dream; but when we probe deeper we find that they are overlaid by ceremony and perhaps also by history. The essential point in the narratives as in the ritual is that man makes the world—as he does in sleep.

These natives do not wander because they like to. . . . Man is naturally attached to the country where he was born because it, more than anything else, is a symbol of his mother. All natives will refer to their "place" as a "great place"; as they say "I was incarnated there" or "born there." Economic necessity, however, compels him time and again to leave his familiar haunts and go in search of food elsewhere. Against this compulsion to repeat *separation,* we have the fantasy embodied in myth and ritual in which he himself creates the world.

Where the nursing woman and the countryside itself are both "Mother," and where in turn the men of the tribe may initiate and reveal maleness as an other Mother, "Mother" means unity, what Gertrude Stein called the Composition. What we experience in dreaming is not a content of ourselves but the track of an inner composition of ourselves. We are in-formed by dreams, as in daily life we experience that which we are able to grasp as information. We see, hear, taste, smell, feel, what can be drawn into a formal relation; to sense at all involves attention and composition. "It is very interesting that nothing inside in them, that is when you consider the very long history of how every one ever acted or has felt, it is very interesting that nothing inside in them in all of them makes it connectedly different," Stein writes in *Composition As Explanation:* "The only thing that is different from one time to another is what is seen and what is seen depends upon how everybody is doing everything. This makes the thing we are looking at very different and this makes what those who describe it make of it, it makes a composition, it confuses, it shows, it is, it looks, it likes it as it is, and this makes what is seen as it is seen." The endless repetitions of rituals and wanderings and hunting as the pattern of life for the Australian is a living inside the Composition; and in their exhibiting the secrets of the male body to the boy, the men of the tribe are making a composition where what is seen depends upon how everybody is doing everything. In the ritual, song, parts of the body, parts of the landscape, man and nature, male and female, are united in a secret composite of magic names.

"One of the main sources of male creative power," Roheim tells us, "is the incantation itself."

> When I asked old Wapiti and the other chiefs what makes the animals grow? the spirits? the ancestors? O, no, they said: *jelindja wara,* the words only. The form of the incantation is an endless, monotonous flow of words, and actually the men urinate very frequently while performing the ceremonies. This parallelism between the words and the fluid is brought out in a description by Lloyd Warner: "The blood runs slowly and the rhythm of the song is conducted with equal slowness. In a second or two the blood spurts and runs in a rapid stream. The beat of the song sung by the old men increases to follow the rhythm of the blood."

We may begin to see, given Stein's concept of insistence that informs composition, and then thinking of the pulse of the living egg-cell itself, that beat, rhythm, underlies every figure of our experience. Life itself is an endless, monotonous flow, wherever the individual cannot enter into it as revealed in dance and melody to give rhythmic pattern; the world about goes inert and dead. The power of the painter in landscape is his revelation of such movement and rhythm in seeing, information, in what otherwise would have been taken for granted.

Gertrude Stein, reflecting upon permanence and change in the artist's vision, sees that "the only thing that is different from one time to another is what is seen and what is seen depends upon how everybody is doing everything." Close to the Cubist Movement in Paris, she had experienced how painting or writing in a new way had revealed coordinations of what was seen and heard towards an otherwise hidden unborn experience of the world, so that one saw and heard with a profound difference. "A new cadence means a new idea," H.D. and Richard Aldington, writing in the Preface to the Imagist anthology of 1916, declared. Here too, cadence is how it is done; to make clear the meaning of cadence they referred to the choral line of Greek poetry that was also the movement of the choral dance, strophe and antistrophe. So too, Roheim, initiate of Freudianism, as Stein was initiate of Cubism, or H.D. of Imagism, sees in the narratives of his Australian informants how "in all of them environment is made out of man's activity," for he had himself experienced a conversion in which a new environment for man had been made out of analytic activity. The "manmade world" in which "environment is regarded as if it were derived from human beings" is the narrative itself; the unity of things in how the story is told.

Parts and operations of the human body, but also parts and operations of the cosmos, are related in a new ground, a story or picture or play, in which feeling and idea of a larger whole may emerge. The flow of sound from the throat and the flow of urine from the bladder, the flow of energy from the dancing feet, the flow of forms in the landscape, the flow of water and of air felt, translated in a rhythmic identity disclose to the would-be initiate what man is but also what the world is—both other and more than he is himself, than the world itself is.

Cézanne working at his vision of Mont Sainte-Victoire and Dali at his paranoiac vision of the Catalonian landscape not only draw but are drawn by what they draw. From body and from world towards an other body and other world, man derives meaning in a third element, the *created*—the rite, the dance, the narrative; the painting, the poem, the book. And in this new medium, in a new light, "man" and "environment" both are made up.

The power of the poet is to translate experience from daily time where the world and ourselves pass away as we go on into the future, from the journalistic record, into a melodic coherence in which words—sounds, meanings, images, voices—do not pass away or exist by themselves but are kept by rime to exist everywhere in the consciousness of the poem. The art of the poem, like the mechanism of the dream or the intent of the tribal myth and dromena, is a cathexis: to keep present and immediate a variety of times and places, persons and events. In the melody we make, the possibility of eternal life is hidden, and experience we thought lost returns to us.

*

"The eternal ones of the dream," Roheim observes, "are those who have no mothers":

> they originated of themselves. Their immortality is a denial of the separation anxiety. Separation from the mother is painful; the child is represented in myth as fully formed, even before it enters the mother. The *tjurunga* from which it is born is both a phallic and a maternal symbol.

The *tjurunga*, like the *cartouche* that encircles the Pharaoh's name as the course of the sun encircles the created world, is a drawing of the spirit being, an enclosure in which we see the primal identity of the person. But all primal identities are Adamic, containing male and female, man and animal, in one. We are each separated from what we feel ourselves to be, from what we essentially *are* but also from the other we *must be.* Wherever we are we are creatures of other places; whenever we are, creatures of other times; whatever our experience, we are creatures of other imagined experiences. Not only the experience of unity but the experience of separation is the mother of man. The very feeling of melody at all depends upon our articulation of the separate parts involved. The movement is experienced as it arises from a constant disequilibrium and ceases when it is integrated.

"Composition is not there, it is going to be there, and we are here," Stein writes. Between *there* and *here* or *then* and *now*, the flame of life, our spirit, leaps. A troubled flame: "The time in composition is a thing that is very troublesome," Stein tells us—"If the time in the composition is very troublesome it is because there must be even if there is no time at all in the composition there must be time in the composition which is in its quality of distribution and equilibration."

An anxious flame: "In totemic magic the destroyed mother is reanimated and in the totemic sacrament, eternal union of the mother and child is effected," Roheim tells us. But the eternal separation of the mother and child is also celebrated therein. "As a religion it represents the genitalization of the separation period and the restitution that follows destructive trends." *War*, Heraclitus called the flame, or *Strife*.

"All men are bringing to birth in their bodies and in their souls," who here speaks as an Eternal One of the Mother, says to Socrates.

> There is a poetry, which, as you know, is complex and manifold. All creation or passage of non-being into being is poetry or making, and the processes of all arts are creative; and the masters of all arts are poets or makers . . . What are they doing who show all this eagerness and heat which is called love? . . . The object which they have in view is birth in beauty.

Beyond beauty—birth in the eternal and universal.

"According to the natives of the Andjamatana tribe," Roheim tells us, "children originate in two mythical women known as *maudlangami*. They live in a place in the sky. Their long hair almost covers them and on their pendulum breasts are swarms of spirit children who gather their sustenance therefrom. These women are the source of all life, each within her tribe producing spirit children of her own moiety." But these women, we realize, are not first sources; they have their origin in turn in the telling of their story. In the communication of the story the narrator and the listeners have their source and all life has its source and draws eternal nourishment.

"Each Aranda or Juritja native has an immortal part or spirit double, whose immortality consists in eternally rejoining the Mother in the sacred totemic cave. From time to time they re-identify themselves with the eternal in them." It seems to Roheim that in the story "they deny their great dependence upon Mother Nature and play the role of Mothers themselves." But Mother Nature in the eternal bond with Man is Herself, as He is, the member of a cast in a drama. In the rites that Roheim sees as denials of dependence, we see the dancers reviving the human reality in all that is disturbing to union, involving themselves in, insisting upon, and taking their identity in, the loss of their identity, keeping the rime of their separation alive in the sound of their unity, rehearsing their exile in the place where they are. The flame springs up in a confusion of elements, times, places.

For the Freudian, it all rests in a "psychical survival of the biologic unity with environment." "This 'oceanic feeling' (Freud) or 'dual unity situation,'" Roheim argues, "is something we all experience in our own lives; it is the bond that unites mother and child." "By taking the *tjurunga* along on his wanderings the native never gives up the original bond of dual unity which ties the infant to his mother."

From the unity once known between Mother and Child, the boy is initiated in a rite in which things once unified in feeling are shown as separated—this is the anatomization of the Australian scene, where parts of the body are exhibited as independent entities; but it is also the anatomization practices in which the poet is born, where words once unified in the flow of speech—the Mother tongue which in turn had been articulated from the flow of sounds in the child's earlier initiation—are shown as articulated—separated into particular sounds, syllables, meanings—in order to be reorganized in an other unity in which the reality of separation is kept as a conscious factor. The "Mother" is now the World, and the "Child" is the Self. The World is revealed as a "Creation" or "Poetry" or "Stage," and the Self, as "Creator" or "Poet." The man or the hero begins his life that demands something of him, a wandering in quest of something known in the unknown. Taking with him the quest itself as his Mother, as the Australian takes the *tjurunga* or the devout Kabbalist the Shekinah, he is to be most at home in his exile.

*

Roheim telling about his Australian natives does not mean to initiate us into the Aranda but through his creation of the Aranda in our minds to initiate us into the psychoanalytic fiction. The old men prancing, bleeding themselves and showing their private parts; the emu ancestors, the eternal ones who come in the dream, the primordial Mother and Child, are people not of the Australian bush but of a creative book, haunted by "the wanderings of human beings from the cradle to the grave in a web of daydream," as the author of this mankind himself wanders in a web of psychoanalytic reverie. "In the eternal ones of the dream it is we who deny decay and aggression and object-loss, and who guard eternal youth and reunion with the mother," Roheim writes in his coda:

> The old and decrepit men of the tribe become young and glorious once more. Covered with birds' down, the life symbol, they are identified with the eternally youthful ancestors. Mankind, the eternal child, *splendide mendax,* rises above reality. . . . The path is Eros, the force that delays disintegration; and hence the promise held forth in the daydream and in its dramatization is no illusion after all. The *tjurunga* which symbolizes both the male and female genital organ, the primal scene and combined parent concept, the father and the mother, separation and reunion . . . represents both the path and the goal.

This *tjurunga* we begin to see not as the secret identity of the Aranda initiate but as our own Freudian identity, the conglomerate consciousness of the mind we share with Roheim. "Above and below, left and right," the Kabbalist would have added in drawing his figure of the primordial man. The whole story is "daydream," a "web," and we are not sure that because the path is Eros, the promise may be "no illusion after all." The hero is the eternal child, but he is also *splendide mendax,* a glorious maker of fictions, in which all the conglomerate of what Man is might be contained. The simple *tjurunga* now appears to be no longer simple but the complex mobile, that Giedion on *Mechanization Takes Command* saw as most embodying our contemporary experience: "the whole construction is aerial and hovering as the nest of an insect"—a suspended system, so contrived that "a draft of air or push of a hand will change the state of equilibrium and the interrelations of suspended elements . . . forming unpredictable, ever-changing constellations and so imparting to them the aspect of space-time."

If, as in Malraux's *Psychology of Art,* we see painting and sculpture not only as discrete works but also as participants in a drama of forms playing throughout the time of man, so that what were once thought of as masterpieces of their time and place are now seen anew as moving expressions of—but more than expressions, creations and creators of—spiritual life, as acts of a drama of what Man is that has not come to its completion, but which we imagine as a changing totality called Art; so poems too begin to appear as members of a hovering system called Poetry. The draft of air or the touch of a hand reappears now as the inspiration or impulse of mind that will change states and interrelations—"time in the composition comes now," Gertrude Stein puts it, "and this what is troubling everyone the time in the composition is now a part of distribution and equilibration"—"past the danger point"—throughout the history of Man. History itself, no longer kept within the boundaries of periods or nations, appears as a mobile structure in which events may move in time in ever-changing constellations. The effort of Toynbee's *Study of History,* beyond Spengler's comparison of civilizations, is towards an interpenetration of what before seemed discrete even alien areas of the life of man. Present, past, future may then appear anywhere in changing constellations, giving life and depth to time. The Eternal Return, no longer conceived of as bound to revolutions of a wheel—the mandala of a Ptolemaic universe or of a Jungian Self—beyond the "organic" concept Toynbee derives from Vico's life cycles, we begin to see now as an insistence of figure in an expanding universe of many relations. The Composition is there, we are here. But now the Composition and we too are never finished, centered, perfected. We are in motion and our meaning lies not in some last or lasting judgment, in some evolution or dialectic toward a higher force or consciousness, but in the content of the whole of us as Adam—the totality of mankind's experience in which our moment, this vision of a universal possibility, plays its part; and beyond, the totality of life experience in which Man plays His part, not central, but in every living moment creating a new crisis in the equilibration of the whole. The whole seen as a mobile is a passionate impermanence in which Time and Eternity are revealed as One.

Elie Faure in *The Spirit of Forms* (from which, as from Spengler's *The Decline of the West,* Malraux's thought, we take it, develops) writes:

> We have reached a critical point in history when it becomes impossible for us to think profoundly—or to create, I imagine—if we isolate ourselves in the adventure of our race, if we refuse to demand a confirmation of our own presentiments from the expression in words or in the arts that other races have given themselves. . . . One of the miracles of this time is that an increasing number of spirits should become capable not only of tasting the delicate or violent savor of these reputedly contradictory works and finding them equally intoxicating

(he speaks here of those fetishes and cathedral statues that Malraux in his work is to find "sinister" in their colloquy)

> even more than that, they can grasp, in the seemingly opposed characters, the inner accords that lead us back to man and show him to us everywhere animated by analogous passions, as witnessed by all the idols, for all of them are marked by the accent of these passions. . . . The critical spirit has become a universal poet. It is necessary to enlarge inordinately, and unceasingly, the circle of its horizon.

This "we" was "an increasing number," but it was also, Faure saw, a few, an élite—a cult, then, of "the mobility of the spirit, favored by the exigencies of environment and the mixture of the species," projecting "a limitless visible field of emotion and activity," towards a cathexis of all that was known of man and the word, in terms of an open and expanding consciousness, as our Aranda initiates project their field of emotion and activity in terms of a tribal consciousness as an enclosure of time and space. For the Australian, the hardness of Nature herself drives him out from his home-place. The Aranda is a man of an actual wasteland where he is again and again forced to wander in times of drought and famine when a man in want of water often opens a vein in his arm to drink the blood, and the brotherhood of the tribe must be kept in a constant imagination against the hunger in which men eat each other. Here the "we" is a term of survival itself. The creative fiction—the tribal narrative, the eternal ones of the dream, the spirit doubles, and the immortal sky-mothers—has its intensity of realization in the traumatic experience of the actual environment.

The esoteric tradition in Jewish mysticism again had its intensity in the loss of the home-land and in the long wandering in exile as children of a spirit-Mother, the Shekinah. She was the Glory, but She was also the Queen or Mother or Lady, and She might appear, as She does in *The Zohar,* as a great bird under whose celestial wings the immortal spirit-children of Israel nestled. The Jews, like the Aranda, lived in a threatening environment that called forth, if they were to survive, an insistent creation, the tenacity of a daydream to outlast the reality principle.

For the Imagists in London in 1912 there had already been exile. Pound, Eliot, and H.D. had sought a new spiritual home among eternal ones of the European dream, among Troubadors or the Melic poets, in refuge from the squalor and stupidity of the American mercantile, industrial, and capitalist world—"the American dream," it was called. Joyce had chosen a voluntary exile from Ireland, "dear dirty Dublin"; and Law-

rence had fled from his environment in the industrial working-class vil-
lage to wander in exile in search of his own Kingdom of the Sun.

It was the World War that provided the traumatic crisis—it was the
very face of the civilization showing through at last, the triumph of
squalor and stupidity where the cult of profits and the cult of empire
combined to exact their tribute, and the other cult-world of the poetic
vision was challenged as a reality. Only in the imagination would beauty
survive. "I would bid them live," Pound sings in his Envoi to "Mauberley"
in 1919—

> As roses might, in magic amber laid,
> Red overwrought with orange and all made
> One substance and one colour
> Braving time . . .

He addresses in the "Envoi" a "her," whose "graces give/Life to the
moment"—a Lady "that sang me once that song of Lawes," but also a
Mother that the Imagist poets had taken—Beauty. To survive in spirit
men must be reborn in Beauty's magic amber, for the rest were revealed
by War where

> Died some pro patria,
>   non "dulce" non "et decor"
> walked eye-deep in hell
> believing old men's lies, then unbelieving
> came home, home to a lie,
> home to many deceits,
> home to old lies and new infamy. . . .

"Wrong from the start—" Pound describes himself: *"No,"*—

> . . . hardly, but, seeing he had been born
> In a half savage country, out of date . . .

They did not "belong." In that feeling their exile was not voluntary,
but a recognition of necessity. In the poem "Cities" published in *The Egoist*
in 1914, H.D.'s sense of a "we," a lonely few, isolated by their common
devotion to beauty, and to the goods of the intellect, in the midst of a city
of "them" who worship squalor, profit, and war, as the "one god," is not a

fantastic attitude assumed but a feeling rooted in the social reality. "Can we believe," she proposes, "by an effort"

> comfort our hearts:
> it is not waste all this,
> not placed here in disgust,
> street after street,
> each patterned alike,
> no grace to lighten
> a single house of the hundred
> crowded into one garden-space.

Two ways of life—the one realized by the Protestant-Capitalist cult in its terms of usury, real estate, production for profit, and profitable work, and the other realized by the Military cult, in which old orders of Mithraic and Wotanic cult survived, in terms of Fatherland, death in battle, holocaust, and the hero's reward in the Valhalla orgy and the memorial days—these two had combined forces in 1914 to make a new world. War was to become, as it is in our own day, the most profitable business, the foundation of the economy, and the economy was to become the cause of the soldier. Not "Light," as it had been for the Zoroastrian Mithraist, against "Darkness"; but the right of private property in the sense of capitalism against socialism or communism.

H.D. sees wartime London of the First World War in terms of the Platonic myth of the Golden Age and the Iron Age, and also, as in her War Trilogy London of the Second World War, in terms of the gnostic myth of souls from a creation of Light surviving in a second creation of Darkness. In "Cities," the maker of cities has made a second city and a second people—this is the hive of the modern metropolis, crowded with cells

> hideous first, hideous now—
> spread larvae across them,
> not honey but seething life
>
> And in these dark cells,
> packed street after street,
> souls live, hideous yet—
> O disfigured, defaced,

> with no trace of the beauty
> men once held so light.

Back of this world is the memory of another, first, city:

> with the beauty of temple
> and space before temple,
> arch upon perfect arch,
> of pillars and corridors that led out
> to strange court-yards and porches
> where sun-light stamped
> hyacinth-shadows
> black on the pavement.

It is the Poictiers or Verona of the first *Cantos,* and thirty years later in *The Pisan Cantos* it is "the city of Dioce whose terraces are the colour of stars" and also the *Wagadu,* the Mother-City of the Fasa, that four times in their wandering has been lost—"gone to sleep" the epic tale *Gassir's Lute* puts it, as given by Frobenius in the sixth volume of *Atlantis,* his collection of African folk tales and poetry. In the prison camp at Pisa the memory of Wagadu, four times fallen asleep—"once through vanity, once through breach of faith, once through greed, and once through dissension"—with the chorus naming the cities of its four incarnations— "Hoooh! Dierra, Agada, Ganna, Silla!—Hoooh! Fasa!"—returned to Pound as the lost city that is also the strength of those who live in the thought of her. "For in herself Wagadu is not of stone, nor of wood, nor of earth. Wagadu is the strength that lives in the hearts of men and that one time can be seen because eyes let her be seen, because ears hear the strike of sword and the clang of shield, and one time is invisible because worn out and beset by the untameable nature of men she has gone fast asleep." "Now in the mind indestructible," Pound sings in Canto LXXIV, and in Canto LXXVII: "now in the heart indestructible." Wagadu may then be the first city of H.D.'s "Cities," the Mother that those who are devoted to Beauty remember. "For each man will salvage Wagadu in his heart," the African epic promises—"*bergen*"—the German translates, which means to salvage or rescue and also to give shelter to, to hold or to hide: "and each woman will keep hidden a Wagadu in her womb."

The people of that city, the people of a dream of a kind of human life once known that perished as the dominant way and is yet carried forward in the minds and hearts of certain devotees, this people remains, like the "we" of H.D.'s poem, intensely aware of themselves in their allegiance to an invisible city more real than the city in which they are:

> Can we think a few old cells
> were left—we are left—
> grains of honey,
> old dust of stray pollen
> dull on our torn wings,
> we are left to recall the old streets?

To be a poet was to be disowned in terms of the reality values of the new city, to be outcast from the true motherland. In "The Tribute," published in *The Egoist* in 1916, the First World War and the city of London are again seen in terms of an evil state that has taken the place of a good:

> Squalor spreads its hideous length
> through the carts and the asses' feet,
> squalor coils and reopens
> and creeps under barrow
> and heap of refuse

"Don't use such an expression as 'dim lands of peace,'" Pound had commanded: "It dulls the image. It mixes an abstraction with the concrete." For a moment the word "squalor," if we take it as an abstraction, may abstract us from the immediacy of the poem, but the squalor of the city is itself the presentation of a person of the poem. A "personification" it is called by those who believe such things are mere devices of a poetic grammar. But this squalor is the face or mask of an actual entity:

> it lengthens and coils
> and uncoils and draws back
> and recoils
> through the crooked streets

the Evil One Himself, the old serpent or worm, seen by the poet in the seizure of the poem as He has been seen in the vision of saints and satanists or in the clairvoyance of seers, an astral shape pervading the ways of the city, so that the streets are "crooked," as in *The Mills of the Kavanaughs* Robert Lowell sees a path "snake" up its hill. Where He wounds us there are "our old hatreds," and in victory He may blacken the song upon singing lips. The dragon is Neschek as He appears in Pound's fragment of Canto C or Jormungand, the Midgard Serpent, whose scales are the corpses of men and whose venom is a corrupting greed and ambition, in whose likeness is the squalor of the slums, the coils of usury, and the murderous arrogance of modern war. In "The Tribute," the tribute seems first to be the draft of young men into the armies of America and England, and the dragon has triumphed:

> with no voice to rebuke—
> for the boys have gone out of the city,
> the songs withered black on their lips.

The "larvae," the unawakened people of the poem "Cities," are now the people of the dragon, their "one god":

> They have banished the gods
> and the half-gods
> from the city streets,
> they have turned from the god
> of the cross roads,
> the god of the hearth,
> the god of the sunken well
> and the fountain source

and now they show their enmity openly towards those who do not hold their values and would oppose the tribute to their war:

> Though not one of the city turned,
> not one girl but to glance
> with contempt toward us . . .

The few with convictions against the war really did face social ostracism. "The world of men is dreaming," Lawrence wrote to Lady Ottoline Morrell in 1915: "it has gone mad in its sleep, and a snake is strangling it, but it can't wake up." Two years later, driven out of Cornwall where they had been raided by the police, the Lawrences took refuge with H.D. at 44, Mecklenburgh Square. "London is really very bad: gone mad, in fact," he wrote Cecil Gray: "People are not people any more; they are factors, really ghastly, like lemures, evil spirits of the dead." And young men who had already begun their work for beauty's sake had died, "the songs withered black on their lips"—"non 'dulce' non 'et decor.'" In the pages of *The Egoist* war lists, first of young French and German artists and writers, then of English, had begun to appear.

The "we" of "The Tribute" is a remnant few very like the pitiful group that in Aristophanes's antiwar *Lysistrata* hold the decimated city:

> A few old men rose up
> with a few sad women to greet and hail us,
> a few lads crept to welcome . . .

And the song was *"withered black"* upon the lips in another sense. For Pound, Lawrence, Joyce, H.D., Eliot, have a black voice when speaking of the contemporary scene, an enduring memory from this First World War that had revealed the deep-going falsehood and evil of the modern state. These had from their early years as writers a burning sense of the "they" that ran the war and that accepted its premises and of the "we" whose allegiance belonged to a Wagadu hidden in their hearts, among whom now many ghosts or specters—Wilfred Owen had come as the first great English loss among poets, but Gaudier-Brzeska and Hulme from the immediate circle of *The Egoist* had followed.

At the close of "The Tribute," a prayer for deliverance begins:

> May we know that our spirits at last
> will be cleansed of all bitterness—
> that no one god may trample the earth,
> but the others still dwell apart
> in a high place
> with our dead and our lost.

Now the Wagadu no longer appears as an earlier city back of or surviving within the squalor of the contemporary city as in the poem "Cities," where those "who recall the old splendour,/await the new beauty of cities," but as a city in an other world evoked by a wish:

> That the boys our city has lost
> and the gods still dwell apart
> in a city set fairer than this
> with column and porch.

They appear here, the banished gods and lost boys, as the eternal ones who come in dreams, to whom the poet's tribute is offered:

> That the lads of that city apart
> may know of our love and keep
> remembrance and speak of us—
> may lift their hands that the gods
> revisit earth.
>
> That the lads of the cities
> may yet remember us,
> we spread shaft of privet and sweet
> lily from meadow and forest. . . .

"And this we will say for remembrance," the poet continues: "speak this with their names"—

> Could beauty be caught and hurt
> they had done her to death with their sneers
> in ages and ages past,
> could beauty be sacrificed
> for a thrust of a sword,
> for a piece of thin money
> tossed up to fall half alloy—
> then beauty were dead
> long, long before we saw her face.

"The Tribute" is not an easy poem to appreciate in terms of what came to be accepted as H.D.'s virtues in the modern aesthetic of the twenties—the ardor kept in restraint, the Hellenic remove, the hard-wrought art, the spare statement. The Imagist rules will not fit. But once we turn from "Cities" and "The Tribute," keeping the context of these poems, the seemingly "removed" Hellenism of "Adonis," "Pallas," or "Sea Heroes," written in the same period, proves to be a screen image in which another level of feeling is present.

> Akroneos, Oknolos, Elatreus,
> helm-of-boat, loosener of helm, dweller-by-sea,
> Natueus, sea-man,

are lists of the war dead and lost from Homer. And now from our own sense of the experience of the War—and here her rites of remembrance have quickened in us the impact of what happened before we were born—we understand anew and in depth the agony of

> But to name you,
> we reverent are breathless,
> weak with pain and old loss,
> and exile and despair—

Since the dark, bitter, impassioned days of the First World War, even the words themselves—"beauty," "lad," or "boy"—have become uneasy words, smacking of the idealistic or the sentimental before what we call the Real, the pervading triumph of mercantile utilitarianism: the display aesthetic of packaging and advertising art to put over shoddy goods, repeated in the display aesthetic of the new architecture, where a wealth of glass or cellophane, aluminum, copper, or gold paper facing takes over the city, presented in a poverty of imagination, housing the same old shoddy operations of whiskey, cigarette, or paper companies; and back of the sell, the demand for profit and increase, the exploitation of mind and spirit to keep the rackets going, the economy of wage-slavery and armed forces, and over all, the threat of impending collapse or disastrous war. We too, in a hostile environment, taking our faith and home in our exile, live in creative crisis.

*

There is this sense, then, in which the Imagists—that group of poets printing in the pages of *The Egoist* between 1914 and 1917—stand at the beginning of a phase in poetry that has not ended. Pound, writing in 1914, felt that a break was necessary with the preceding generation in poetry: "Surely there was never a time when the English 'elder generation as a whole' mattered less or had less claim to be taken seriously by 'those on the threshold.'" For my own generation, our elders—for me, specifically Pound, H.D., Williams, and Lawrence—remain primary generative forces. Their threshold remains ours. The time of war and exploitation, the infamy and lies of the new capitalist war-state, continue. And the answering intensity of the imagination to hold its own values must continue. The work of our elders in poetry was to make—"a Dream greater than Reality"—a time-space continuum in which their concern for quality and spirit, for romance and beauty, could survive. Estranged from all but a few about them, they made a new dimension in which eternal companions appeared. As to the Aranda the ancestors came, or to the Kabbalist mystics dreams and even immediate presences of Elijah or of a *maggid* or angel came, so to Pound Plotinus appears, to H.D., in the orders of the new poetry, the Christos or the Lady.

In 1919 Pound published in "Quia Pauper Amavi" a first draft for the opening three cantos of a new poem, addressing Robert Browning:

Hang it all, there can be but one *Sordello*,
But say I want to, say I take your whole bag of tricks,
Let in your quirks and tweeks, and say the thing's an art-form. . . .

It was to be a realm in which Robert Browning and Arnault, Brancusi and Kung could coexist; where Eleanor and Cunizza come and go; and

Gods float in the azure air,
Bright gods and Tuscan, back before dew was shed.

For the banished gods and for the heroes. And those lost. But not now, as in Dante, appearing each in his place in a set scene or architecture of Hell, Purgatory, and Paradise. For here in *The Cantos*, the dead gather in as at a séance.

Ghosts move about me
patched with histories

it seems to the poet. But there are not only voices speaking, *personae,* in this *"catch"* of time as Pound called it, there are also scenes—images of the poem, moving pictures. Where Dante had back of *The Divine Comedy* his magics to call upon: the magic of the poetic and of the mystic descent or ascent to the eternal world, drawing upon the practice of the dream-vision in not only Medieval Christian but in classical Roman tradition, but also upon the practice of the *Mi'raj,* the spiritual transportations of the Sufi Recital; Pound had these and other magics: the séance tables of London mediums, the discourse of voices in which the rivers of many traditions came into a sea of humanity, but also, a new clairvoyance, the photo montage of times and places in the movies of Griffith.

In the three masterworks of this period—Pound's early *Cantos,* Eliot's *The Waste Land,* and Joyce's *Ulysses*—the contemporary opens upon eternity in the interpenetration of times. The literate public objected to or made fun of what they called their "references" or "quotes." "Say that I dump my catch," Pound had put it in the first draft of the *Cantos*—

> shiny and silvery
> As fresh sardines flapping and slipping on the marginal cobbles?

and the image stands, for he was "fishing" and in it all working to catch something being said, about to be said, fishing along lines of metamorphoses in the beginning. Surely, knowing Mead and Yeats, Pound was aware of Eisler's *Orpheus the Fisher*, where the god appeared as a fisher of souls who was also the divine poet—the lyre was also a net or the poem a net of words. In the early "Canto I," the poem itself appears as a fish-monger's booth:

> (I stand before the booth, the speech; but the truth
> Is inside this discourse—this booth is full of the marrow of wisdom.)

It may also be then the medium's cabinet. Our own net casts wider than Pound would, and we see that the shaman's tent is also such a booth. But Pound's intuition moves out, back of his evocation of Robert Browning's magic practice of the dramatic monologue, and So-shu churns in the sea,

> So-shu also,
> using the long moon for a churn-stick . . .

So Pound will give up the intaglio method and in the flux of a cinematographic art call in the swarming fish of the sea, where Robert Browning, Peire Cardinal, Catullus, gods, oak-girls and maelids, Metastasio, Ficino, Kuanon, Guido Cavalcanti, Botticelli, Mantegna are drawn into the nets of the first haul. These persons, like the place names of Wagadu— Dierra, Agada, Ganna, Silla—are loci of a virtu moving through time. Frobenius traces the wandering of the Fasa from Djerma of the Garama which he equates with Dierra, mentioned by Herodotus five hundred years before Christ, from the Fezzan of North Africa, to Tagadda on the ancient route through the Sahara, to Ganna and then to Silla of the Sahel. But the Wagadu of *The Cantos* is the lost city not of a tribe but of a kindred among all men, "an aristocracy of emotion" Pound called it.

It was the mixture of times and places, and especially the breakdown of all nationalistic distinctions that most angered the hostile critics and readers. Renaissance English or medieval Italian or modern French could enter into an American poem: not only Dante but Kung and even Gassir were to be our heroes in the new legend. The new practice was most concentrated in the famous coda of *The Waste Land* in 1922:

London Bridge is falling down falling down falling down
Poi s'ascose nel foco che gli affina
Quando fiam uti chelidon—O swallow swallow
Le Prince d'Aquitaine à la tour abolie
These fragments I have shored against my ruins
Why then Ile fit you. Hieronymo's mad againe.
Datta. Dayadhvam. Damyata.

Children singing a round dance; Dante in Purgatory telling of Arnaut Daniel, master of the *trobar clus*, "Then he hid himself in the fire which refines them"; and the voices of the poet of the *Pervigilium Veneris*, of Gerard de Nerval, of Kyd in the person of Hieronimo, and of the thunder out of the Upanishads, speak one after another, taking over from Eliot's "own" voice. Or speaking for Eliot, meeting through Eliot as through a medium. "Tiresias, although a mere spectator and not indeed a 'character,'" Eliot notes, "is yet the most important personage in the poem, uniting all the rest. Just as the one-eyed merchant, seller of currants, melts into the Phoenician Sailor, and the latter is not wholly distinct from Ferdinand Prince of Naples, so all the women are one woman, and the two sexes meet in Tiresias."

For William Carlos Williams it was "the great catastrophe to our letters." "There was heat in us, a core and a drive that was gathering headway upon the theme of a rediscovery of a primary impetus, the elementary principle of all art, in the local conditions," he writes in his *Autobiography:* "Our work staggered to a halt for a moment under the blast of Eliot's genius which gave the poem back to the academics." Picturing himself as defending something betrayed by Eliot, and by Pound in his admiration of Eliot, Williams posed against the internationalism of *The Waste Land* the authenticism of the American speech. "Nothing from abroad would have the reality for me that native writing of the same quality would have," he resolves as an editor of *Contact* in 1922: "Eliot or Pound might say to me today—'Read Laforgue!' I might even be tempted to read because I had respect for their intelligence. But their words could not tempt me, force me, accompany me into the reading." Against the cinematographic time-flux, he meant to take with a vengeance the camera eye of still photography, the locality in time.

There was the studied disdain of silence on Eliot's part for Williams's work. It meant that Williams was never taken up in England; no influence could move Eliot who came to rule the informed taste abroad as Pound never did. And there was the increasing grievance on Williams's part. Not only Eliot but Pound and H.D. came to be seen as betrayers of the American thing in their exile, their "foreign" work. "When one's friends hate each other," the old man Pound would write in "Canto 115":

how can there be peace in the world?
Their asperities diverted me in my green time.

At heart, Williams's genius as a poet lay not in the local condition, in the isolated percept, the "American" thing or speech, but in the heritage Eliot—Jacob to his Esau—had stolen from him, in the world-poem where the wives of an African chief, a red basalt grasshopper recalling Chapultepec, Toulouse Lautrec, Madam Curie working the pitchblende, Sappho, and Peter Brueghel were to enter in. *The Waste Land* had stolen a march on *Paterson,* but by the time the first volume of *Paterson* appeared twenty-four years later Williams had brought his early poem into a fullness that was to be a challenge to the poets to come as *The Waste Land* was not.

In his Preface to *Selected Essays* in 1954 Williams tells us: "Poetry is a dangerous subject for a boy to fool with, for the dreams of the race are involved in it." He sought, he writes of *Paterson* in his *Autobiography* in 1951, "to find an image large enough to embody the whole knowable world about me." Between "the dream of the race" and "the knowable world," between the "idea" and the "thing" his river was to flow, the Passaic, yes, but also in the realized poem "the thunder of the waters filling his dreams!"

"The *subject matter* of the poem," he said in his lecture at the University of Washington in 1948, calling upon Freud's theory of the dream, "is always phantasy—what is wished for, realized in the 'dream' of the poem—but the structure confronts something else." "The Poem as a Field of Action," he titles that lecture, anticipating Charles Olson's "Projective Verse" with its composition by field. "The only reality we can know," he continues, "is MEASURE. . . . How can we accept Einstein's theory of relativity, affecting our very conception of the heavens about us of which poets write so much, without incorporating its essential fact—the relativity of measurements—into our own category of activity: the poem. Do we think we stand outside the universe? Or that the Church of England does? Relativity applies to everything, like love, if it applies to anything in the world."

Williams's local condition and his "no ideas but in things" must ring true, find their resonance, in "the dreams of the race" and in a relativity of measurements that applies to everything, as H.D.'s elect, the lovers or the writers, must somehow in their vision prove to keep the dream of "everyone, everywhere." The very heightened sense of the relatedness of everything set poets apart. The very secret of the impulse in poetry is the troubled awareness the poet has of meanings in the common language everywhere that those about him do not see or do not consider so important. "We," H.D. writes in *The Walls Do Not Fall*, "bearers of the secret wisdom," and then:

> but if you do not even understand what words say

> how can you expect to pass judgement
> on what words conceal?

The ancient instruction "As above, so below" from the Smaragdine Tablet may be "the secret wisdom," but H.D. was initiate of Freud where she had learned in analysis that for the good of her soul she must bear the wisdom of "what words conceal." She tells us Freud said to her, "My discoveries are a basis for a very grave philosophy. There are very few who understand this, there are very few who are capable of understanding this." But he might also have said "very few who are willing to understand," for the crisis of the new psychoanalytic wisdom lay in the resistance men have against knowing what is above or below, the strange refusal to see what they are doing or to hear what they are saying just when they are most engaged in their own self-destruction—"the untameable nature of men," the epic of *Gassir's Lute* says. So, Oedipus cannot and will not understand the vatic warnings of Tiresias or the fears of Jocasta but must pursue his blind course in order to expose the conflict within only at the cost of catastrophe for all. He seems to seek in the drama a compelling reason to make his blindness actual.

The great compulsion of our own states with their war economies and compulsory military servitude, the history that is now all written upon verges of a war to come, about which we can do nothing and which we can imagine only in terms of total destruction, bears a curious resemblance to the hubris and fate of the Greek drama. The People of the Truth and the People of the Lie, the Zoroastrians called the adherents of peaceful agricultural ways and the adherents of war; but Ahura Mazda, the Lord of Truth, was to become a War-Lord, for His was the *One* Truth, and all other truths were lies. "And now just look at what is happening in this wartime," Freud writes in a letter to Van Eeden in 1914: "at the cruelties and injustices for which the most civilized nations are responsible, at the different way in which they judge of their own lies, their own wrong-doings, and those of their enemies." "The individual in any given nation has in this war," he writes in *Thoughts on War and Death* in 1915, "a terrible opportunity to convince himself of what would occasionally strike him in peace time—that the State has forbidden to the individual the practice of wrong-doing, not because it desired to abolish it, but because it desires to have the monopoly of it, like salt and tobacco."

For Freud, as for Lawrence, H.D., Pound, Joyce, or Eliot, the immediate experience of the First World War brought an intensified experience of the "we" and the "they." "The individual who is not himself a combatant—and so a wheel in the gigantic machinery of war," Freud writes, "feels conscious of disorientation, and of an inhibition in his powers and activities." So, in "Cities" H.D. in 1914 could still imagine the task of the "we" to be to awaken the "they" from their hideous larval life, to "recall the old splendor" towards a "new beauty of cities." In an essay on the work of Marianne Moore in August 1916, she speaks of Marianne Moore's work as if it were under question: "these curiously wrought patterns, these quaint turns of thought and concealed, half-playful ironies" that readers "have puzzled over . . . and asked—what is this all about?" This poetry might be her own as well with its curiously wrought patterns. Even among the literate, the few who made any pretense at all of being concerned with poetry, the Imagists were ridiculed and reviled. And among the less than few who appreciated, appreciation was not the same as understanding. In the conclusion of that essay, H.D. breaks out and the "they" that had been readers appear as the other "they" of "Cities," and likewise, the identification of herself with Marianne Moore in a "we" is outright: "She is fighting in her country a battle against squalor and commercialism. We are all fighting the same battle. And we must strengthen each other in this one absolute bond—our devotion to the beautiful English language."

The war experience had revealed a division in which one side could no longer communicate with the other. "It rends all bonds of fellowship between the contending peoples," Freud writes in *Thoughts on War and Death,* "and threatens to leave such a legacy of embitterment as will make any renewal of such bonds impossible for a long time to come. Moreover, it has brought to light the almost unbelievable phenomenon of a mutual comprehension between the civilized nations so slight that one can turn with hate and loathing upon the other." But this abyss of incomprehension appeared not only between opposing states, but within each state between the few antipathetic to the war itself and those obedient to or sympathetic with the war. In the poem "The Tribute," H.D. sees the "we" and the "they" divided by a will on the part of the "they" not to hear, not to see—a resistance against beauty and any hope of peace, but also a compulsion towards ugliness and war, a conspiracy that these shall be the terms of the real. The City of the Gods, "set fairer than this/with column and porch," no longer what once was or what will be, the city of an historical task, is now a dwelling place of youths and gods "apart."

Augustine, when Rome fell to the Vandals in the fifth century and the Christians were accused of betraying the empire in their disaffiliation from the war, answered in *The City of God* with the ringing affirmation of an eternity more real than historical time, a life eternal or supreme good more real than the good life of the philosopher. "And thus it is written," Augustine tells us: "The just lives by faith, for we do not as yet see our good, and must therefore live by faith." For Augustine—as for Freud there was the incomprehension between nations, or for poets the incomprehension between writers and readers, or for Sapir the incomprehension between the individual happenings and the language as communication itself—for Augustine too in the world beyond the household and the city, the world of human society at large "man is separated from man by the difference of languages. For if two men, each ignorant of the other's language, meet, and are not compelled to pass, but, on the contrary, to remain in company, dumb animals, though of different species, would more easily hold intercourse than they, human beings though they be."

> But the imperial city has endeavoured to impose on subject nations, not only her yoke, but her language, as a bond of peace, so that interpreters, far from being scarce, are numberless. This is true; but how many great wars, how much slaughter and bloodshed, have provided this unity! And though these are past, the end of these miseries has not yet come. For though there have never been wanting, nor are yet wanting, hostile nations beyond the empire, against whom wars have been and are waged, yet, supposing there were no such nations, the very extent of the empire itself has produced wars of a more obnoxious description—and with these the whole race has been agitated either by the actual conflict or the fear of a renewed outbreak.

For Augustine, convert of the Christian cult, Latin words themselves had a difference of meaning, and in that difference there was a disillusionment with all the values of the Roman world. Only in a total conversion could the "they," the would-be good and just men of the empire, understand the "we," the little company of would-be saints. The rest— the whole "realistic" approach—meant utter misery.

But, say they, the wise man will wage just wars. As if he would not all the rather lament the necessity of just wars, if he remembers that he is a man; for if they were not just he would wage them, and would therefore be delivered from all wars. For it is the wrong-doing of the opposing party which compels the wise man to wage just wars; and this wrong-doing, even though it gave rise to no war, would still be a matter of grief to man because it is man's wrong-doing. Let everyone, then, who thinks with pain on all these great evils, so horrible, so ruthless, acknowledge that this is misery. And if any one either endures or thinks of them without mental pain, this is a more miserable plight still, for he thinks himself happy because he has lost human feeling.

*

To write at all is to dwell in the illusion of language, the rapture of communication that comes as we surrender our troubled individual isolated experiences to the communal consciousness. But this "commune" is not, even in the broadest sense, the language of the human society at large. To write in English is not only to belong to a language-world different from French or Aranda but also to belong to a language-world different from though within the English-speaking world other national literatures. Writing and reading is itself an initiation as special as the totem-dance of the Aranda, and just as the Aranda learns to read his own parts in the parts of the landscape about him, so that the body of the world becomes one with his own consciousness, so we learn to find our life in a literature, and, in turn, literature itself is valued as it seems true to life.

But once we would derive our life not in terms of tribe or nation but in terms of a larger humanity, we find our company in Euripides, Plato, Moses of León, Faure, or Freud, searching out keys to our inner being in the rites of the Aranda and in the painting processes of Cézanne. We must move throughout the history of man to find many of our own kin, for here and now those who think and feel in the terms we seek are few indeed. But from each of these the cry goes up—to whom other than us, their spiritual kin—from an intense solitude. Not only Freud's "There are very few who understand this," but Stein's "Do you know because I tell you so, or do you know, do you know. (Silence) My long life, my long life," or Joyce's "Thinking always if I go all goes. A hundred cares, a tithe of troubles and is there one who understands me? One in a thousand of years of the nights?" or Pound's plea from "Canto 116":

> I have brought the great ball of crystal,
>   who can lift it?
> Can you enter the great acorn of light?
>   But the beauty is not the madness
> Tho' my errors and wrecks lie about me
> And I cannot make it cohere.

Before war and death the whole world of the higher culture seems to be an illusion indeed. For Freud, the war evoked a powerful disillusionment. The cosmopolitan man, as Freud portrays himself in *Thoughts on War and Death,* in peacetime dwelt in an "other" world, leaving the mother-land or father-land of the national state and entering a new Mother-land of an international dream:

> Relying on this union among the civilized races, countless people have exchanged their native home for a foreign dwelling place, and made their existence dependent on the conditions of intercourse between friendly nations. But he who was not by stress of circumstances confined to one spot, could also confer upon himself, through all the advantages and attractions of these civilized countries, a new, a wider fatherland, wherein he moved unhindered and unsuspected.

The generation of Joyce, Eliot, Pound, and H.D., living in the dream of European culture, or of Lawrence living in the dream of Western Indian culture, is the last to live abroad so. The generation of the twenties—the "lost" generation, as Stein called it—Hemingway, Fitzgerald, Mary Butts, Henry Miller, Katherine Anne Porter, Kay Boyle, Robert MacAlmon, live in Europe or Mexico as if in limbo, forerunners of the jet set and the new wave. The cosmopolitan son of an imaginary world-father pictured by Freud had his roots in a time "before the War," in an illusion of peace, and thought of the achievement of the past as his spiritual heritage.

"This new fatherland was for him a museum also, filled with all the treasures which the artists among civilized communities had in successive centuries created and left behind," Freud continues: "As he wandered from one gallery to another in this museum, he could appreciate impartially the varied types of perfection that miscegenation, the course of historical events, and the special characteristics of their mother-earth had produced among his more remote compatriots."

This dream of European Culture must recall the Palace of Eros. But Freud's heir of the ages and of the earth finds his reality not in daydream but in an actual sea and actual mountains, in the treasure store of men's actual works. "Property is not capital. The increment of association is not usury," Ezra Pound insists in *Social Credit: An Impact* (1935) and prefaces his pamphlet with Jefferson's saying—"The earth belongs to the living." In the rites whereby man became cosmopolitan man he came into an increment, an environment enhanced by his realization of the work and experience of others involved, into an increase that was not taken from things but taken in them. In the cult-life of Freud's cosmopolitan man, as in the life of the Imagists, the gods and the heroes, the imagined beings and the men who in their creative work have increased the store of the imagination, are ancestral, Eternal Ones of the Dream. A new father-land is taken in the image of a world-father of mankind. And a new kin is found in the ancestors—those who have contributed to the association of man "any and all of the qualities which have made mankind the lords of the earth."

"Nor must we forget," Freud concludes his picture of this illusion of the civilized man: "that each of these citizens of culture had created for himself a personal 'Parnassus' and 'School of Athens.' From among the great thinkers and artists of all nations he had chosen those to whom he conceived himself most deeply indebted for what he had achieved in enjoyment and comprehension of life, and in his veneration had associ-ated them with the immortals of old as well as with the more familiar masters of his own tongue."

*

It is not the world of nature from which the poet feels himself alienated. One of the primaries of the poet is his magic identification with the natural world—"the pathetic fallacy" the rationalist-minded critics and versifiers call it. Freud's cosmopolitan man is a poet and a primitive mind, for in his pathetic union with the world, he "enjoyed the blue sea, and the grey; the beauty of the snow-clad mountains and of the green pasture-lands; the magic of the northern forests and the splendor of the southern vegetation . . . the silence of nature in her inviolate places." Where the rationalist will be quick to see that to find joy in the blue sea or beauty in mountains, magic in forests, splendor and silence in nature, is to live in an environment transformed by human sentiments; for these qualities are just that increment that would make man a lord. The joy and the splendor exist in a magic reciprocity—a property that is not capital; an increment that is not usury. Joy, magic, splendor, beauty, and the silence of "inviolate places" are pathetically present too in the language of the Aranda sexual organs and orifices, the "secret" organs of joy, magic, and splendor in the flow of blood and urine, the excitement and release of orgasm.

So too, the nature poems of H.D.—the early poems of sea and orchard, shell and tree in full blossom or fruit—betray in their troubled ardor processes of psychological and even sexual identification, and those critics who have rebuked her for these poems may be disturbed by content in the poem they do not want to recognize. In "Orchard," she writes: "and I fell prostrate / crying: / you have flayed us with your blossoms." This flowering tree—it is the flowering half-burnt-out tree of *The Flowering of the Rod*—may also be emotional tree of a sexual encounter; for this poem addresses the "rough-hewn / god of the orchard," "alone unbeautiful," "son of the god," and in its first publication in *The Egoist* was titled "Priapus (Keeper of Orchards)," and the *"you"* was then *"thou,"* the too-intimate almost forbidden second-person pronoun in English. The first pear falling, the thundering air, and the honey-questing bees of the poem appear then in a poetic magic in which the natural environment and the sexual experience are fused. The intensity belongs neither to the tree as object nor to the priapic penis as object but to the evocation of the image in which they are fused.

Nor is it from the world of the ancestors that the poet feels alienated. The ultimate reality that the eternal ones of the dream have for the Aranda—the ultimate reality that our toys and imaginary playmates had for us in childhood—Moses, Michelangelo, Leonardo da Vinci, Hannibal have for Freud; and Sappho, Euripides, Shakespeare or Browning have for H.D. They are forefathers of the work, but they seem also at times previous reincarnations of the spirit at work.

These poems where many persons from many times and many places begin to appear—as in *The Cantos, The Waste Land, Finnegans Wake, The War Trilogy,* and *Paterson*—are poems of a world-mind in process. The seemingly triumphant reality of the War and State disorient the poet who is partisan to a free and worldwide possibility, so that his creative task becomes the more imperative. The challenge increases the insistence of the imagination to renew the reality of its own. It is not insignificant that these "poems containing history" are all products of a movement in literature that was identified in the beginning as free verse. *The Egoist,* where Pound, Eliot, Joyce, Williams, Marianne Moore, H.D., Lawrence, and Aldington first appeared together, had formerly been *The New Freewoman;* free verse went along in its publication with articles on free love and free thought. And the "new" we find also as a demand. In his quarrel with Eliot, Williams could oppose the "new" to the "past"—as if all of the past were what Eliot meant by his "tradition." But the definition of the "new" was given by Ezra Pound from Confucius in *Make It New,* and in *The Spirit of Romance* and the essay "Cavalcanti" he turns to the late Medieval reawakening of poetic genius not with the antiquarian's concerns but in search of enduring terms for the renewal of poetry in his own time. The study of literature, he wrote then, was "hero-worship"—"It is a refinement, or, if you will, a perversion of that primitive religion."

The image, for the Imagists, was something actually seen. "At least H.D. has lived with these things since childhood," Pound writes to Harriet Monroe in 1912, "and knew them before she had any book-knowledge of them." In *ABC of Reading* he argues for a statement of Dante's as a starting point "because it starts the reader or hearer from what he actually sees or hears, instead of distracting his mind from that actuality to something which can only be approximately deduced or conjectured FROM the actuality, and for which the evidence can be nothing save the particular and limited extent of the actuality." In the major phase of his last years William Carlos Williams, the poet who was to have "no ideas but in things," would relate poetry to dream and to fantasy, as H.D. would in *Good Frend* project the fictional life of Claribel who had no more actuality than her being mentioned in passing in Shakespeare's *The Tempest*—itself a drama of the poet's powers to enchant—and in *Helen in Egypt* she would weave another fiction of persons who belong not to actuality but to an eternal dream. But the bias for what Williams called "the local conditions" as the primary impetus is strong and continues to haunt my own generation.

The immediate persuasion of Imagist poets was against the fantastic and fictional as it was for the clear-seeing, even the clairvoyant, and the actual, for percept against concept. The Image as "that which presents an intellectual and emotional complex in time" or "the local conditions" could open out along lines of the poet's actual feeling. The poem could be erotic and contain evocations of actual sexual experience as I have suggested in the poem "Orchards." And then, the image was also something actually seen in the process of the poem, not something pretended or made up. It was the particular image evoked in the magic operation of the poet itself—whatever its source, and it usually had many sources. In reviewing Fletcher's poetry in 1916, H.D. may be speaking too of her own art: "He uses the direct image, it is true, but he seems to use it as a means to evoke other and vaguer images—a pebble, as it were, dropped in a quiet pool, in order to start across the silent water, wave on wave of light, of colour, of sound."

There was in the image a presentation that gave, Pound writes in "A Stray Document," "that sense of sudden liberation; that sense of freedom from time limits and space limits; that sense of sudden growth, which we experience in the presence of the greatest works of art." When he tells us that the total plan of Dante's *Commedia* is itself an image, there is a possibility that the image is something seen of or in the "other" world, a clairvoyance. Works of art here are works of a magic comparable to the imaginative practices of Vital or Ficino in which the imagination is thought of not as creative but as a higher vision. In Pound's *Aux Etuves de Wiesbaden*, Poggio says: "We are fortunate to live in the wink; the eye of mankind is open, for an instant, hardly more than an instant."

The *personae* of the Imagists had derived from the *dramatis personae* of Robert Browning. Pound and H.D. wrote not in the tradition of the personal lyric, but they drew upon the dramatic choral lyric and the trance-voice of religious evocation to charge the actual with meaning. In this making the actual the condition of the true and the real, there was a curious consequence. For those elements of the imagination that are usually distinguished from what is actual—the impersonations, the projections, the creations of worlds, and the speculations in ideas—return now in their higher truth and reality to be identified with the actual. In such an operation, H.D. suggests in her notes to *Ion*, for the devotee of Euripides, the actor of Hermes is indeed Hermes:

> Roughly speaking, there were two types of theatre-goers in ancient Greece, as there are to-day. Those who are on time and those who are late. The prologue is the argument or libretto; it outlines the plot. The ardent lover of the drama will doubtless be strung up to a fine pitch of intensity and discrimination from the first. The presence of this actor, who impersonates the god Hermes, will actually be that god. Religion and art still go hand in hand.

If poetry has to do with enchantment and the imagination has traffic with what is not actual but a made-up world, if indeed these would-be serious poets wove a romance of the actual itself, then religion and art may both be fictional and the intensity of their truth and reality the intensity needed to make what is not actual real. The crux for the poet is to make real what is only real in a heightened sense. Call it his personal feeling, or the communal reality, it exists only in its dance, only to its dancers. Outside the created excitement, what we call the inspiration of art, the things done—the bleeding, the exhibition of private parts, the reiterated correspondences of the human world to the great world of nature and the eternal world of the dream—do not communicate. The reader of the poem must be just such an ardent lover as the communicant of the Mass, or the magic of the sacrament is all superstition and vanity. Christ is not actually there, even where He is most real.

The poet and the reader, who if he is intent in reading becomes a new poet of the poem, come to write or to read in order to participate through the work in a consciousness that moves freely in time and space and can entertain reality upon reality. "He has to begin as a cloud of all the other poets he ever read," Robert Frost says, comparing the poet to a water-spout at sea: "and first the cloud reaches down! toward the water from above, and then the water reaches up! toward the cloud from below—and finally cloud and water join together to roll as one pillar between heaven and earth: the base of water he picks from below, all the life he lived outside of books." But, in eternity, there is a cloud below, a sea above, as well: books are real and also imagined, and they must be included if we would draw upon all the life we have lived; life, a dream or a stage on which we act, is also larger than the life we have lived, for its reality is extended in all the poets we have read.

In this great poetry, "Today shalt thou be with me in Paradise" may have its resonance with "Tomorrow, and tomorrow and tomorrow, / Creepes in this petty pace from day to day, / To the last Syllable of Recorded time," for we have come in the comparison of languages to imagine one human drama in many tongues. If the language of Matthew be inspired, so is the language of Shakespeare. Christ and Macbeth have become *personae* of a world-poem. Not only this is true, but if it is, then also this is true. It has come to pass, anyway, that only in the imagination are Christ and Macbeth surely real.

As Testimony: Reading Zukofsky These Forty Years

When Jess and I went to Mallorca in 1955, I brought with me, along with some twenty books, Zukofsky's *Anew* and typed copies of other poems I had gatherd. He stood in my mind, as he remains for me, the master of a salutary art, a call to order along my way, as from the beginning I took the functionalism of the modern style to be, to seek the essential in the working articulation of the poem. In "Letters for Denise Levertov: An A Muse Ment" ["For A Muse Meant"] which had appeard in *Black Mountain Review* 3 (Fall 1954) Zukofsky had appeard among my Masters:

> 11 the addition of the un
>   plannd for interruption;
>   a flavor stinking coffee
>   (how to brew another cup
>   in that Marianne Moore—
>   E.P.—Williams—H.D.—Stein—
>   Zukofsky—Stevens—Perse
>   surrealist—dada staind
>   pot by yrs. R.D.

I had brought into the "Black Mountain" nexus a polar force to the force of Olson. Though in 1953 Zukofsky still appeard to me to belong to my inheritance from the past, as Creeley, following my first visit, wrote for work to publish in *Black Mountain Review*, Zukofsky himself was in the midst of the creative uprise of his work in *"A"* ["A-11" had appeard in *Botteghe Oscure* 8 in 1951; and part of "A-12" had appeard in *The Beloit Poetry Journal* in 1954]. He was now, for me, with Charles Olson, one of two contemporary poets whose work I knew to be clearly directive of my own attentions. In relation to each I was to be heretical—for in the face of Zukofsky's process of stripping to essentials, I was working toward a proliferation of meanings; and in the face of Olson's drive toward the primordial roots, I was working from interpretations of the text. The two

First appeared in *Paideuma*, 7, 3 (Winter 1978).

could not read each other; but it was my sense early in the 1950s that the test of our sources in Poetry must be in the reading of them both as primaries.

But here, in some kind of memorial to Zukofsky 1904–1978, I would give some sense of what it was like to begin reading him in 1937. I may be the only one of my generation who carried his work at heart from the very first reading into my enduring sense of what Poetry must be—I know of no other. Robert Creeley was to be the first convert I made to Zukofsky (unless it be Jonathan Williams the previous year in San Francisco).

1937—that spring—I was just eighteen—Stravinsky's *Histoire du Soldat* and his *Ragtime for Eleven Instruments* and *Les Noces* and Picasso's synthetic Cubist *Musicians* had the year before initiated the breakthrough into the idea of the modern, and now *The Cantos* of Ezra Pound, Stein's *Portraits and Prayers*, e.e. cummings's *W(ViVa)*, and installments of Joyce's *Work in Progress*, opened up a world of what writing could mean and, indeed, of a life way, outside the bounds of my college courses and the discussion groups of my fellow students, where only *Ulysses* and *The Waste Land* gave any hint of what the "modern" might be, of the shift from the idea of writing, and especially poetry, as an expression or cultivation of sensibility as such, to that of writing as meaning realized as it was "made" or "discovered" in the process of invention and experiment—of a kind of industrial revolution in the production, the function, and distribution of meanings. "Make it new" was the call to order of the day for one who took Pound as his mentor as I did, and, from Pound too, one got the idea that what was involved was not only a spiritual commandment from Confucius but also a technical revolution. I was to be a Romantic, but it was to be no simple Romanticism, such as courses in college portrayd and, despised in the portrayal, for in the Romantic too there was to be now no element that was not seen as a function at once of the poem and of the mind; and no element of poem or mind that was not to be seen as a function of a social and historical consciousness.

In the Imagist revolution, there had been the announcement that "a new cadence means a new idea"—how a thing was made and what a thing was were inextricably one. Now, in the wake of Vorticism and then of the "Machine" style of Paris 1925, from the period 1925–33—the *art moderne,* sans serif, streamline "look" that took over in the commercial publicity of the Chicago World's Fair of 1933—there was a kind of futurism, a drive forward, a world-of-tomorrow fever presented in the "new." How you made it was the new idea; but one saw pushed forward "how it looks is the new idea."

Pursuing the idea of the "modern," I read entire the files of *The Little Review,* of Pound's magazine, *Exile,* and *transition* in 1937, and I carried in hand *New Directions* (1936). I had to research the world-of-tomorrow, for it was already the passing style of my older cousins who had grown up before the War and been members of the Jazz Age youth, but I was searching too for a deeper sense of form as action and process that I sensed was there. Zukofsky's "Poem Beginning 'The,'" which I found in reading *Exile,* was part of the modern "tradition" for me; and "Mantis," which appeared in that first issue of Laughlin's *New Directions,* which I read over and over, along with Stein and Pound, cummings and Cocteau, I saw as belonging to this challenge of "experimental" writing, of making writing do things, of writing as a process of an engaged consciousness. There was an idea of the writing back of the writing.

"Poem Beginning 'The'" in *Exile* 3 (Spring 1928; the writing of the poem, as one learns from Celia Zukofsky's *Bibliography,* is dated 1926) took its place as an exemplar of the "new," lasting, along with Stein and Pound, as the line of inheritance and challenge for writing yet to come in 1937, even as cummings would begin to wear and his flair would emerge as a stunning period piece. Pound's *Draft of XXX Cantos, Eleven New Cantos XXXI–XLI,* and, that year, *The Fifth Decad of Cantos,* could be read as a stream-of-consciousness, as I did read them and as I continue to read them, along the line of William James's *Principles of Psychology,* which had appeard in 1890 and which in 1937 I had also read for the first time. The underlying figures in Pound's poetry and in his essays on poetics of light and water, of radiations, magnetic fields and electric currents, of fountains and waves, welling-up, streaming, flowing, in Pound's ever returning World-Mind-Image, were not for me modern then. I saw them in the light of James's pluralism and vitalism, recalling too the chapter "The Dynamo and the Virgin (1900)" in *The Education of Henry Adams* which we had read in our undergraduate survey course. *The Cantos* were engendered in the passing of the Art Nouveau energy-stream concept, even as the stream of *The Cantos* was engendered in the company of Yeats's neo-Platonic emanations of divine powers and of theosophical lectures of G.R.S. Mead; and their modern cast was the result of Pound's organization of the forces of *The Cantos,* even as he "modernized" the impact of Eliot's *The Waste Land.* But the dual concept of flow and radiation remains (as it would appear in William Carlos Williams's *Paterson* and in his last phase)—in the drafts and fragments. Pound sees the condition of the modern mind as a fractured stream, not as a construct. In *Canto XXIX* (*c.* 1928) "The wail of the phonograph has penetrated

their marrow / (Let us . . . / The wail of the pornograph. . . .),"
then "The djassban has hammered and hammered" come forward
in the time-flow as if they were already passed, currencies, into that
flow.

In contrast, Zukofsky's proposition in "Poem Beginning 'The,'" with
its lines presented by the number, its constructed line-movement events,
not as a stream but as a sequence of line-shots or frames making up a
motion-picture film strip, proposed neither tradition nor past but imme-
diate presentation. If, as I have pointed out in "The H.D. Book," the
movies of Griffith, particularly the reincarnations of the theme in a series
of historical times co-existing in the film medium in *Intolerance*, had
prepared for the time reincarnations, the "all times are contempora-
neous," of Pound's scenario in *The Cantos*, the art of Eisenstein must have
been a conscious resource for Zukofsky, for by the 1920s the films had
made their critique of the stream-of-consciousness. But there was also
the art of the comic strip. "A refined sensibility for appreciating love,
war, death, El Greco, Krazy Kat, Negro spirituals and relativity," so
Zukofsky describes "our present," the modern current of 1928. Part of
this "advanced" American culture was due every day to the creative
intelligence of George Herriman in his *Krazy Kat* with its changes of
points of view and of meaning from frame to frame. Later Zukofsky
would seem to come "home" to Wittgenstein. In "Poem Beginning
'The,'" the youthfulness of the twenty-two-year-old poet's showing off
and deliting in his inventions and ingenuities on the theme of the Jewish
son and his mother in U.S. 1926, even as he kept potential the Hymn to
the Sun with which the poem closes (where the "Jewish" and the post-
Freudian themes—"Residue of Oedipus-faced wrecks / Creating out of
the dead,—" parallel, one would note, Joyce's "Irish" theme as Stephen
Daedalus goes forth to "forge" the conscience of his race in English
Literature in *A Portrait of the Artist as a Young Man* and the son and
mother theme of *Ulysses*) recalls too, in its quick sense of the play of ideas
as a humorous sequence, the comic strip. This articulation of the time of
the poem, this "animation" of the sentence, remains today a striking
feature that charges the flow of impulse and vitality with the counter-
check or tension of a mental cutting-room, a double-take on one's frame
of mind. If a neo-Platonism presides over the poetics of Pound, and it
does, then we have broken with Plato in Zukofsky and a neo-Aristote-
lianism takes its place. Where Pound in the flow of his vitalities was being
drawn to see a Vortex in the power politics of "The Boss" (it must be
noted that Mussolini in the 1920s proposes himself as a ruthless func-

tionalist in the social realm and that fascism is not far from the world-of-tomorrow technocratic dreams of U.S.A. 1933 that would come to their fruition in the development of world corporations), Zukofsky in "Poem Beginning 'The'" in 1926 checks out Mussolini in lines which one saw, reading in 1937, as proofreading Pound's growing enthusiasm, even craze:

74   "Il Duce: I feel God deeply."
75   Black shirts—black shirts—some power is so funereal.

Pound was to print that in 1933 in *Exile* without, it would seem, further checking out Zukofsky's point.

The other Zukofsky work that first year was "'Mantis'" and "'Mantis' An Interpretation," which had appeard in *New Directions*, where the placing of the title in quotes spoke of a Henry Jamesian rectitude (though I was not to read James until 1943). A kind of self-consciousness in which not the poet but the act of writing itself was this "self"—an active conscience in making—enters in that is an extension of the counter-check of the line-by-line construction of idea and feeling in movement. Going back today to reread Zukofsky's 1931 Preface to *An "Objectivist" Anthology*, I find that he points to his use of quotes as having to do with the particularity of the context and with what he calls "philosophical etiquette." After reading my poem "After Reading *Barely and Widely*," Louis Zukofsky in an answering poem askt: "How will his praise sound back to him?" There is a proofreading again, a re-proof, in hearing how ones line sounds back to oneself. It might be noted that Pound's uncheckt course through the 1930s and 1940s had produced, for those who followd his lead, a crisis of etiquette for the poem itself. "Pound again—Emotion is the organizer of poetic form," Zukofsky observes approvingly in his 1931 Preface; but then, of the stream-of-consciousness he is moved to dissent: "not following Mr. Pound in his case, one might just as well not mention the streaming consciousness," and Zukofsky proposes an *"attained"* emotion, the product of a work, a poem as a piece of work like a desk "as a piece of work, the parts, the process of making it"—the prospect of constructing and attaining an object built up of parts of "emotion" in process. He draws his analogy from the art of woodworking:

> Or put the job of explanation up to cabinet-making again: certain joints show the carpentry not to advantage, certain joints are a fine evidence; some are with necessary craftsmanship in the object.

Then:

> The transitions cut are implicit in the work, 3 or 4 things occur at a time making the difference between Aristotelian expansive unities and the concentrated locus which is the mind acting creatively upon the facts.

The "Poem Beginning 'The'" presented few problems for the youthful reader. But "'Mantis'" means to present "The actual twisting/of many and diverse thoughts" wherein "the feeling of the original which is a permanence." For me in 1937 it presented the very promise of what a poetry might come to, a poem in which the fittings of rime and of sense were more and more wonderful as one sounded the poem and found them more and more exact. Its art was beyond me yet somehow available in my sounding the poem—the presence of the thought being so immediate a thing proceeding in the very feel of the lines. The idea came into existence through the working of the poem. Wasn't there too, as I remember, an identification of the appearance of the mantis with Joyce's idea of an epiphany necessary in the work of art?

Not until I caught up with a serious reading of Williams, and that was with *The Wedge* (1944) and *Paterson I* (1946), when I regaind the ground of his early work (for all of *The Descent of Winter* being there, intact, in the issues of *Exile* I had read through years ago), not until that emergence of Williams along with Pound as a major source of my consciousness in Poetry, was I prepared to read "'Mantis'" as I do today, where Zukofsky's art reflects his affinities with the art of Williams.

It was with the appearance of "A-8" in *New Directions 37* that the first phase of reading Zukofsky was fully there. In the midst of the Moscow trials, coming to consciousness in the transition from Roosevelt's W.P.A. and Depression programs to the Permanent War Economy which still presides, and in the period too of what we read to be a betrayal of the anarcho-syndicalist Left in Spain by the Stalinists, and then of the Berlin-Moscow pact (though we heard too from Trotskyite sources that the pact was only a strategy), in the midst of a growing antitotalitarian reaction, reading "A-8" with its praise of Stalin was hard to explain. What I did know was that the two ongoing poems that meant most to me when I was eighteen had as contemporary heroes Mussolini and Stalin. Whatever a poem meant in its truth of particulars it was not a political directive. The truth of a poem was the truth of what was felt in the course of the poem, not the truth of a proposition in whatever political or religious persuasion outside the poem. The particulars of the poem were in process.

What matterd was that this poet Zukofsky had indeed read his Pound and his Williams and in the course of his reading derived a new art, an art that has anticipated problems of the poems that I have found essential in my own work as it has developed. In the work of poets from Creeley to Michael Palmer I see the implications of Zukofsky carried further than I know in my own work. Not to praise or to appraise, but to bear testimony to the enduring resource: his work in *All,* in *"A,"* in *Bottom: On Shakespeare,* and *Catullus* stand as primaries for all of us at work in the closing decades of the twentieth century.

As an Introduction: Charles Olson's *Additional Prose*

The two decades from 1950 to 1970 were, for some of us, the Age of Olson. It was the experience of a conversion in Poetry, for me in a poetry that had already declared itself, of a conversion, that is, in the Imagination, a breakthru into a deeper going and intending Imagination. And he set large for us our "subject"—not the personal or the cultural, but the Nature and Identity (Id-Entity) of the species "Man."

The proposition of a new history of Man was there in 1947 with his *Call Me Ishmael*, with its vision of what we were as "Americans," a vision out of Melville, in which Olson saw the New World as, in truth, the Primordial, and men returning to this continent—a proposition of Man that extended "from Folsom cave to now"—the waves of pre-glacial and post-glacial migrations out of Asia, the adventuring voyages out from the Phoenician world, the Norse world, and then the Renaissance, as coming "home," "back" to their origins. "SPACE": "I spell it large because it comes large here," he wrote: "Large, and without mercy."

In 1950, the essay "Projective Verse;" in 1951, in *Origin* I, "I, Maximus" and "The Gate & the Center"—the opening up of great spaces in consciousness had begun, and in the very beginning, in its origins, he moves in, as he knows he must, to redirect the ideas of language and of the body, of Man, of commune, and of history; and this drive remains throughout his creative life. Sometimes it must have seemed hopeless. Every passionate and eloquent pouring forth of his vision goes on in those *Letters for Origin* to convert the editor of *Origin* from the literary concerns to revelationary fervor. He finds himself at last (as in "A Work" in this little volume) clearing away all the literature of the Indo-European epic , coming to the Hesiod of the *Theogony* as "one of its gates": "a total placement of man and things among all possibilities of creation."

"My purpose is only to wake up the time spans and materials lying behind Hesiod, so that they can seem freer than they have. . . ." It had been his purpose in the beginning, in his own conversion-experience. The awakening of Purpose. That so moves the phantasmal Kultur thing

Written in 1972; appeared first in *Sulfur*, no. 35 (1994).

from the generative meaning of Ezra Pound's work; and so removes the phantasmal blood-thinking thing from the generative meaning of D.H. Lawrence, to form a tradition, a line of inheritance, incorporating long separated elements in a new force.

He saw the Westward movement of scouting, exploration, traffic with the natives, first settlements, raids and massacres, exploitations, scientific observations as a great psychic happening, a drive into the mythopoeic; and then the Ur-History does come back, not as it is in Europe, as a depth in memory, but as it is, for us, as an immediate disorder in the mind. We have no where else to be than here, in this first history, in which vast extensions of meaning, trance, and fantasy, alchemistries of language, take over. He goes "back," back home, to come into the depths of the immediate, going over the documents and old maps, the texts of sciences and the historical diggings, as data of what our species is, read in the light and dark of a Divine Intention. He wants to establish us, to re-establish us in the Ideal, to redeem all idealism from the commitments that claim prior authority there. "Otherwise the present will lose what America is the inheritor of: a secularization which not only loses nothing of the divine but by seeing process in reality redeems all idealism from theocracy or mobocracy, whether it is rational or superstitious, whether it is democratic or socialism."

To redeem Idealism as Primordial Thought, as a driving force. Charles Olson is a frontiersman in thought, grand and noble as the broad plains, the commanding mountains and the ocean depths and masses instruct him to be in certain measures of his poetry. He has no peers in this sweep of his imagination, in which every intention in him is ancient, and none are current or contemporary. He has the range of the continental drift or of the geological era he took his thought in. He can also be, as the continent was for those who first tackled it, as it remains for those who realize what is going on, a hard taskmaster. He *is* hard—hard going, hard to get at, hard to come by, hard driving, hard to read through; and he can go wild—shoot wild, talk wild, read wild. He was, after all, almost a man who might have been an eminent scholar in American studies, except for an ungovernable enthusiasm in which Idea went out of bounds. Except he went wild. He saw America as a dark and vast Fate to which Man returned, the Indians first, and then, since 1500, all the races of the species, Man Entire in His various cultures, HERE in one place, in one people. And there I am with Olson. He saw the power of a wilderness, not conquered, but invading Man, in which a crisis gathers. "The trouble is, it is very difficult, to be both a poet and an historian," he writes in his closing note to *Mayan Letters* in 1953. More and more, he came to mistrust the propriety of history.

The Creative Will, the urgency to make or name a "world," to make history or name history oneself ["man as himself a universe," Olson insists in "A Work"] is haunted by the Identity, the Id-Entity, with God the Creator, which we can take now as an Idea, belonging to that Idealism freed from the authoritative limitations that Idea has been under from Plato on, in the philosophical "disciplines," the theological logics, the political dialectics, etc. that have sought to circumscribe Idea and make it subject to their uses. Idea, as it comes to us, as it comes to Man, as an immediate seeing, as seeing it that way. Straight on. The Creative Will is there, and where we are at all aware of ourselves, we immediately know it is there. This is the heart of Poetry in its proper sense, of Poetry as Making, as distinguished from voice or song, from the melic verse-record or the commemorative monument. The distinction is not absolute. The melodic is itself essential to the creative power. It *is* song that moves; song enters the world and makes it a singing environment of physical events. But what is important for the Maker is the direct charge of his making, a poetry that raises a crisis in What Is, a crisis in our Idea of the world and of what we are, a crisis in the body-idea—that is the crux of "Proprioception"—and in the identity of Man idea—that is the crux of "A Plausable 'Entry' for, like, man."

Charles Olson drives deep. He wanted not only a crisis in consciousness but a crisis in the unconscious. That word too he spelled large: "ex., Lawrence, preface, FANTASIA OF THE UNCONSCIOUS, where he imagines states of being & geography divers from the modern." "For those who have the wit to tell the Unconscious when they see one," he writes again in *Mayan Letters*. He is to be read by men who have their wits about them, the wit to tell the Unconscious "when they see one." And often, Olson is not only telling it from the Unconscious, or letting the Unconscious tell, but telling the Unconscious a thing or two. He means to instruct the Unconscious, and to do that he must stir such a trouble in all the structures of what he has known as Consciousness, all the established structures of what we take ourselves to be, that his instruction drives deep. "Neither the Unconscious nor Projection (here used to remove the false opposition of 'Conscious'; 'consciousness' is self) have a home unless the DEPTH implicit in physical being . . . is asserted, or found-out as such." Consciousness is God, the occult tradition says. "Consciousness is self," Olson puts it. In this vision, it is Consciousness that contains the Unconscious.

Move the verse-line out of the reach of our predilections of con-
sciousness, especially hit at obstinate rationalizations of experience with
the obdurate and the obscure task, drive the expert mind into that des-
peration in which it must struggle once more in wildness with the Old
Man of the Sea, Proteus—this was the hope Olson had in Poetry. He
hadn't a hope. It was the desperation he had. "To have a third term, so
that *movement* or *action* is 'home.'"

And he did bring it home. He brought to focus in a driving will and
intellect a tradition. And that we have our roots, not in the old family
farm plot, or in the tribal smokehouse, or in the national convention, but
in a moving Idea of Man. The continent where we are is where that Idea
is moving. As much the idea of Man moving in the Indian, as much the
idea of Man moving in the European, we must gather to find ourselves.
That is all the archaeology to gather ourselves from out of time and space
into what we truly are, the archaeology of morning.

In "Bridge-Work" he names again a team as he sees it (1961) of
challengers to the accepted idea that places any of us short of the busi-
ness of Man. It is his essential reading list to undo our minds from the
modern. Why? He insists upon just those carriers of a knowledge that has
been systematically excluded from our education. We all know that
Dante is a pre-eminent force of European civilization and that his *Com-
media* is an essential event of Man's spirit in Poetry. But the entire system
of public education excludes from our picture of European civilization
any reference at all to the Jewish contribution to that world; hence it is
viewed as an obscure reference to speak of Moses of León, a master of
the same order as Dante in the Imagination, and as a peculiar and exotic
"private mythology" to have to do with *The Zohar,* a work of the Imagina-
tion as far-reaching and deep-going in its influence in the thought and
spirit of Europe as is Dante's Vision. Our generation has had the duty to
carry in our work the content of an excluded knowledge, to work at a
"bridge-work" between the repressed content and the Consciousness
that is Self. Charles Olson must work at ground work as an educator
against a massive and repressive construct in which all the sciences of
Man outside of the post-Christian rationalizing science of "EUROPE"
have been declared to be out-of-bounds. Blasting at indoctrination,
Olson blasts with a thunderous indoctrination. He insists that it must be
dogmatic. A Roman Catholic in origin, he transforms the meaning of
Catholicity to mean just that—*katha holos,* having to do with the whole of
Mankind, to be the idea of Man in the whole of Man. Where he waxes
most dogmatic, speaking *ex cathedra,* the Protestant in me rises, and,

deeper than Protestant, the heretic in me protests. But heretically, I see his dogmatic mode, as I read, as one aspect of Olson's genius that works in formulae, his mappings out of territories, his lists and topographies of the soul, his "Logography" as it appears in this collection. As he was dying of terminal cancer that had come into his liver and was eating away each day, Olson was writing out, as if to unlock in a logographic magic the secret message or to break the code of that event, *"LIVE- HER."* He is trying words, to find in the body of the language he loved and worked in and incarnated himself in, this event that was eating at him. He had to know it in words, what he knew in flesh.

The great drive West was for Olson toward the Idea of Man, toward the vision of what each of us as Man is. Proprioception then, how we get the appropriate idea of what we are (who we are) in the feel of what the body is, how the body knows itself, is the ground work of any right language of what Man is. In "Projective Verse," the knowledge of the art of Poetry is to be driven back there, to its own proprioception: "RIGHT HERE WHERE THE LINE IS BORN"—"the HEAD, by way of the EAR, to the SYLLABLE/the HEART, by way of the BREATH, to the LINE." He is mapping out there in 1950 circuits and establishing the art in the reality of the body that intends that art. Here again Olson is profoundly Roman Catholic, and I am with him and with the Catholic doctrine in this: the Word is incarnate, living, suffering in the flesh, is Man, then. The Ideal has no other ground in which to be but our passional life in historical time. I know of no Ideal outside of that realm. The Incarnation is a physical event. "The 'soul' then is equally 'physical,'" Olson writes in "Proprioception."

Forcing our recognition of the crisis, the crisis of our times or of our state or of our psyche, as the crisis of our physical body, the good doctor I see Charles Olson to be as poet-critic attends his patient and strives to bring him through to the moment of truth beyond the matter of life or death, up to the necessary test, beyond his strength to an other strength he has, to confront his living or dying. In the new medicine he is not to seek to escape what is happening but to go into it. Health here lies in the body of the total life, in the soul as a life-time, and self as a consciousness of where that is, toward which the creative will and from which the creative will moves. He would not relieve us of this confrontation.

Sensibility, as I read it, Olson insists is not "ours" but "its own" [within the organism by movement of tissues "its own"]. We've to realize the cosmic intent or event that the physical body we call "ours" is "as object which spontaneously or of its own order produces experience";

and that depth is "asserted, or found out as such . . . implicit in physical being." The thing is we have just this physical event we are, an incarnation, a body, a locality of cosmos having in that locality an experience of "confronting" cosmos, in which our life, our experience of the actual, springs alive. Metaphysics then is the mind's proprioception of its physical condition—a local and immediate event imagining the totality that comes to crisis in that event. And metaphysics only proves true as it is imagined as physics. The problems of metapsychology are ultimately to be read in a physics we have not come to. Hence, Olson's persistent interest in alchemical terms. Body, logos, society, history, as I read him, must be brought to this door of the physical fact, of Incarnation.

He forces us, if we are to read at all—as once in the Hellenistic period men were forced to such business and, the best they could tell us, saw action as *agon*—to be involved, if we are to participate at all at the level of self-consciousness, with finding ourselves in such primaries. In his early essay "The Gate & the Center" he argues that men once had in Sumer such a "home" as later Olson is to tell us we must take in movement; that the City was the action, the incarnate body of man's action in history, the one center. What we enact comes into being in the act itself, has no other place to be. I've not to be right or wrong here, I've to move forward to the way it appears to me. We are creatures of the physical world and in that creature nature are impelled to create. We have no other "consciousness" except the consciousness of the act. Hence the making in words, the enactment of laws or poems.

In "The hinges of civilization to be put back on the door" or in "A Plausible 'Entry'" Olson is not making an historical outline of what happened in the past but is making a diagram of what we Are, a morphological anatomy of our body in time. What we have to do, our body in time, carries with it crises. "We" are the body of man that remains unsatisfied, unrealized, of impending disasters or creative breakthrus then, redemptions of form, we're still that much involved with the impetus. In the earliest traces of man we find, we find that imperative that will not let us go. To uncover city, man, trace, being that involvement that will not let the past go but must bring all into the present demand for consciousness in action. And action, the truth of action, brings us into the Primordial, into the place where the New is yet to happen. The "past" is all that has not happened. We are, where we are, at the threshold of the First Things, the as yet to begin. "God is the organ of novelty," we find in Olson's "Theory of Society." In all of this thought, Olson is close indeed to his reading of Whitehead's *Process and Reality* in 1956–57.

Grammar again is not a system but a formulization toward involvement in what impends. It must be moving or not at all. Sapir and Whorf (I know of no others of this order in linguistics) are kindred to Olson in this stance toward language as being poetic, creative, a matter of process, as a way in moving. This "way" is for Olson an imperative.

Then, last, to say that these essays are not to be taken as summaries or notes of something known, but as the push, from knowing, toward such action. I would like to escape that inner alliance I have made in taking what I have of Olson's thought—the urgency of his directive renders it impossible to read his poetry or prose in the mode, still the dominant literary mode of our time, of disinterested discourse. Since the early fifties when what Olson was about gradually began to dawn for me, what I am about myself has been seen in a new way in that light, in the light of his thought and in the dark of that thought. And I read it today, as I read it when I first got it, as a call to order. The only alternative has sometimes seemed to be at home in that waste called Tiamat. "Superstition & idolatry also rampant: anything can happen" (BS Olson warns).

"Costly in loss of something the 1st, as later the 15th & 16th still held, a sense of the divine" and later—we have cited this before—"a secularization which not only loses nothing of the divine but by seeing process in reality redeems all idealism." The crisis we face seems to be there—or else to flounder in psychology, sociology, and what Olson points out as the greatest danger, "the area of pseudo-sensibility," the disengagement of entertaining the idea of the world, as if we had no consequence in that entertainment.

After *For Love:* Robert Creeley

And there to discourse of love . . .

"E quivi ragionar sempre d'amore," the line goes in Dante's sixth sonnet. To which Robert Creeley in an early poem, not included in the canon of the book *For Love*, refers directly, taking his title from Dante's first line— *"Guido, vorrei che tu e Lapo ed io,"* which he translates in the opening of the poem:

> Guido
> I would that you, me & Lapo
>
> > (So a song sung:
> > *sempre d'amore* . . .)

There is the common usage of "me" in the nominative series, evidence of Creeley's care or ear for the natural eloquence of the vernacular, a primary in his aesthetic which he shares with Dante. "Instinctive feeling," so Jespersen in his *Modern English Grammar on Historical Principles* tells us, seizes upon the similarity or rime of the nominatives *we, ye, he, she,* so that *me* and *thee* follow where the influence of sound governs: "likeness in form has in part led to likeness in function." So, "Guido" leads to "me" to form a phonic link and reinforces the vernacular tendency. For the poet form and function are always at play as one, and Creeley can delight to catch in a jargon the peculiar syncopation of feeling as a song. So, in the poem "The Man," he will invert a syntax too in order to sing:

> He toes is broken
> all he foot go
> rotten
> now. He look

First published in *New Mexico Quarterly,* 32, 3/4 (Autumn/Winter 1962-63), and reprinted in *Boundary 2,* 6 no. 3/7 no. 1 (Spring/Fall 1978).

I don't have to establish the excellence of Creeley's art in poetry here.
Others over the past decade have given clear testimony. "The subtlest
feeling for measure that I encounter anywhere except in the verses of
Ezra Pound," William Carlos Williams writes. Donald Hall more care-
fully remarks "colloquial speech with accuracy and a fine sense of pro-
portion."

Williams' superlative does not clarify. Not only Pound, but Williams
himself in *The Wedge* (1944) and *The Clouds* (1948) gives the young
Creeley his challenge of what form and measure in poetry must be and
defines, more certainly than Pound, the particular mode or convention
of the common-speech song with a persisting convention of two, three,
or four line stanzas, highly articulated to provide close interplay and
variation, which Creeley is to specialize in and to develop toward his own
poetic voice. Yet in the opening passage of the poem "For Love," as late
as 1960, Creeley's voice is close indeed to its modal base in Williams's
music:

> Yesterday I wanted to
> speak of it, that sense above
> the others to me
> important because all
> that I know derives
> from what it teaches me.
> Today, what is it that
> is finally so helpless

His articulation of the line here follows Williams in its phrasing,
counter to the facilities of statement, a structure ready to register minute
shifts in confidence, emotionally telling in its hesitations. The juncture
between "to" and "speak," defined by the line, expresses in the raised
pitch of the terminal "to" and in the increased stress of the word "speak"
the exact contour of a searching consciousness, an exacting conscience
in the course of the poem, that will not take "to speak" for granted in
its ready formation but must find its exact way. So, Creeley speaking at
once of instances of love and instances of form (poems) in his Preface
to the book *For Love* has his sense "the misdirected intentions come
right . . . wherewith a man who also contrives a world (of his own
mind)." Williams is, in this, Creeley's master—not his superior, but his
teacher. Given the invention or development of the articulated line (ap-
pearing in Williams' work as early as 1916 in the poem "March"), a

variety of lyric and dramatic forms have been derived. Louis Zukofsky, Charles Olson, Denise Levertov, Paul Blackburn, Larry Eigner, Cid Corman, and myself, as well as Creeley, have all taken over directly from Williams the operative juncture, the phrasing of a composition in which the crisis of the form is everywhere immediate. "It is the LINE," so Olson relays the dogma in his essay "Projective Verse" of 1950: "that's the baby that gets, as the poem is getting made, the attention, the control, that it is right here, in the line, that the shaping takes place, each moment of the going." It is the fact that no pattern can be taken for granted as a given procedure[1] but that every measure means decision, immediately carries the crux of the form, that demands the subtle feeling for measure, the accuracy and fine sense of proportion characteristic of Creeley's art.

Given the decade 1950–60 defined by the book *For Love* and the specific form of the speech song with its highly articulated line and its set stanzas, Creeley has no superior but he has peers. Williams in this period no longer writes in stanzas but develops a three-phase line in *The Desert Music* and in *Journey to Love* that can be compared to Creeley's more traditional three-line stanzas. Zukofsky in *Some Time* and in *Barely and Widely* or Olson in certain poems like "O'Ryan" and in the "Variations Done for Gerald van de Wiele" have surely equaled Creeley's achievement in *For Love*.

Then there are poems of Creeley's—"The Warning," "The Hero," "The Flower," "The Hill," "The Cracks," "The Rose"—that take their place in my mind with poems of Denise Levertov's—"The Absence," "With Eyes at the Back of Our Heads," "The Goddess," or "The Park"— where moving images of a psychological process appear. We have to do in our appreciation of Creeley's art not with a lonely excellence or an idiosyncratic style but with the flowering of a mode, a community of feeling in poetry. Just as Dante's art has company in Guido Cavalcanti's and Lapo Gianni's (in *De Vulgare Eloquentia* Dante relates his art also to that of Cino of Pistoja), so Creeley's art belongs to a movement in poetry redefining the ground of feeling.

It was not only in order to trace Creeley's style that I referred to his concern with Dante's sonnet addressing Guido. I had in mind also Creeley's continued association of the poet with the Tuscan tradition and, further, his ever-returning subjects, the hero and love, with the cult of Amor, and back of that with a line of poet love-heroes.

---

[1] Creeley's adherence to the set convention of the stanza should modify this disallowance of the given procedure.

"The Spirit of Romance" Pound called the tradition, tracing it from *The Golden Ass* of Apuleius and from the *Pervigilium Veneris* of the second century A.D. through to Dante and Guido. One of the key reiterations of the tradition in our time is Pound's rendering of Cavalcanti's great "Donna Mi Prega" in "Canto XXXVI":

> A Lady asks me
> I speak in season
> She seeks reason for an affect, wild often
> That is so proud he hath Love for a name

which Creeley echoes in the poem "Lady Bird":

> A Lady asks me
> and I would tell
>
> what it is
> she has found the burden of.

The "Lady" then of the poem "Air: 'Cat Bird Singing,'" even of the rueful "Ballad of the Despairing Husband," and certainly of later poems—"The Door," "Kore," "Lady in Black," "The Cracks," "The Gift," or "The Wife"—is a power in women that Dante once knew in his Beatrice, and that, before Dante, troubadors of Provence addressed their love songs and petitions. "The lover stands ever in unintermittent imagination of his lady (co-amantis)," Pound quotes from a chivalric code of the Courts of Love. For the poets of the Provençal movement that made the matter of Love paramount as once the matter of war had been, romantic love was adulterous love, the Lady was not to be the Wife. Dante, who was married, as a poet has no wife but adores a lady, virginal in his mind, though she was actually the wife of Simone de' Bardi. And Rossetti, who revives the tradition in English poetry in the nineteenth century, adores the woman he is married to as a lady, not as a wife. But at the turn of the century, Hardy addresses the woman as both lady and wife in one, and D.H. Lawrence continues. The pathos and strength of Williams's later work, the personal immediacy and the communal voice, springs from his concern with these powers a woman can come to have in a man's feelings. For Creeley too, the Lady is both archetypical and specific.

Thus, the wife's part in marriage in the poem "Wait for Me" is also to "give a man his/manliness," a function of the Lady, and in the later poem "The Wife" Creeley tells us:

> I know two women
>   and the one
> is tangible substance,
>   flesh and bone.
>
> The other in my mind
>   occurs.
> She keeps her strict
>   proportion there.

"*La gloriosa donna della mia mente*"—the glorious lady of my mind—Dante calls Beatrice in *La Vita Nuova*. But for Creeley what is held in the mind is what is realized in the act, and a poetry arises in the constant working of tangible substance and idea at tension.

It is the perplexity of a life, as in the poem "The Whip," where the husband lies by his sleeping wife, unable to sleep himself because there is this *other* on his mind. In the scene we see two levels of the poem itself illustrated:

> above us on
> the roof, there was another woman I
>
> also loved, had
> addressed myself to in
>
> a fit she
> returned. That
>
> encompasses it. . . .

As, in the terms of the language, the vulgar and the noble are involved, and Creeley resolves an eloquent vulgate of his own, a vernacular elegance. It is a synthesis of a moral demand and an esthetic demand, her "strict proportion," where song must take command over what had otherwise been a moral or esthetic mandate. The song itself, the vent of the poem, is "for Love" and is given over to "her tired/mind's keeping," to Her who is this woman, wife and lady, and who is also beyond her the Lady—the Muse or Divine Being of the poem "The Door":

> I will never get there.
> Oh Lady, remember he
> who in Your service grows older
> not wiser, no more than before.

The common speech, the immediate expression, the contemporary style, the poetic tradition, take on new resonance in each other. Graves's book *The White Goddess* and Jung's theories of the Anima and feminine archetypes play their part here, perhaps. But Creeley, unlike Graves or Jung, insists there is no system: "one stumbles (to get to wherever) at least some way will exist." The faith of this poetry is not dogmatic but pragmatic, in a world where lessons are not learned, though we may derive our selves from them.

The serious reader may relate the reference to Campion in the poem "Air: 'Cat Bird Singing'" to Creeley's awareness of what the song has been in itself as a tradition and to his recall of Pound's dedication of the "Donna Mi Prega" translation (in the book *Make It New*): "To Thomas Campion his ghost, and to the ghost of Henry Lawes, as prayer for the revival of music." He may find the ghost of Dante haunting the poem "Heroes" when Creeley recalls Virgil:

> That was the Cumaean Sibyl speaking.
> This is Robert Creeley, and Virgil
> is dead now two thousand years, yet Hercules
> and the *Aeneid,* yet all that industrious wis-
>
> dom lives in the way the mountains
> and the desert are waiting
> for the heroes, and death also
> can still propose the old labors.

He may note Creeley's returning the image to the great thematic constants of Romance—the dark forest, the wind, the candle "lit of its own free will," the lady, the traveler the poet is, the company strangely come upon

in a dream, in shapes
of all this: faces and hands,
and things to say, too.

It is in the quest not of some *Divine Comedy* that Creeley follows the
lead of Dante but in the quest of the primaries back of the tradition, of
depths of self that are also depths of Time, as in the poem "A Form of
Women":

My face is my own, I thought.
But you have seen it
turn into a thousand years.
I watched you cry.

So that the old orders of feeling are brought into his own new orders, so
that the immediate moment opens upon other worlds. He turns to the
world of story as he turns to the world of dream or of daily life, to find a
door leading to a self he is that is not his, to a revelation that is beyond
"The Rose":

And all about a rosy
mark discloses
her nature
to him, vague and unsure

There roses, here roses,
flowers, a pose of
nature, her
nature has disclosed to him. . . .

on them there is a mark
of her nature, her flowers,
and his room, his nature,
to come home to.

"For the revival of music," but it is also "for Love": "Form is never
more than the extension of content." As in the spoken song, what we
would say finds itself only in the emerging melody, the rime, the moving
numbers. Feeling, unborn were it not for the art of the poet, coming to
life in a magic then. *"Mighty magic is a mother,"* Creeley says in the poem

"The Door": *"in her there is another issue."* In his craft he may have peers; but here, in the music itself, in the magic, he is unique; we are mistaken to compare. This art can go to the heart of things, the melody of this voice is, most rare, in love with song—

> *Into the company of love*
> *it all returns.*

Introductory Notes: Denise Levertov

Sometime in the fall of 1952 is the date of my upon first reading Denise Levertov. A poem, "The Shifting," which appeared in *Origin* 6, came like a key turnd in a lock to release a fresh sense of poetry—

> The shifting, the shaded
> change of pleasure
>
> soft warm ashes in place of fire
> —out, irremediably
>
> and a door blown open:
>
> > planes tilt, interact, objects
> > fuse, disperse,
>
> this chair further from that table—hold it!

Music, the care of the word, and the immediacy of the movement of the poem to the movement of the image, these awakend an awe and a certainty that have increased with study. She had mastery, but she was not a Master, she was a Servant of the Language, a guardian of inner orders— not self-expressive but self-informing.

Poets must *use* the language; it is at once their material and their genius. The powers of poetry are an increment of association in which all the inhabitants of a language have participated, whose morphology discloses an All Souls' Night of meanings breaking upon the edge, the brink of morning realities. Yet the poets who serve the language in turn are rare. Of such, T.S. Eliot wrote: "Living, the poet is carrying on that struggle for the maintenance of a living language, for the maintenance of its strength, its subtlety, for the preservation of quality of feeling, which must be kept up in every generation." In the course of

Written as an introduction to Denise Levertov's reading at The Poetry Center, San Francisco State University, 19 January 1958.

Origin's publication three poets of this order emerged—Charles Olson, Robert Creeley, and Denise Levertov; and they have become leaders for those of us who seek to serve the language, mediators anew of its forms.

But back of reality there is the coming into tune; previous to the service there is mastery. To focus the eye, to grasp the fact, to advance the foot. Measure (mastery) in poetry is kinesthetic—in folk verse and barrack ballad a steady force of the foot; in narrative ballad and villanella a graceful alternation of simple conventional measures moves from march into dance. In verse as subtly balanced as Denise Levertov's there is increased articulation. More than the foot comes into play. The art springs from a body tone in which a variety of pulsations and movements are discriminated and interrelated. Dance then is significant; and it is interesting to note that Denise Levertov had training in Russian ballet between the ages of twelve and sixteen, for there is the further sense in her work that a dancer has among a group of dancers within a choreography, the sense of a unity that involves more than self. Complex movements in the scene represent a community of movements. Traffic, winds, shifting light, children's games, the sea—question and answer inner felt movement. Objects are not static but conceived as part of a moving world, verifications of emotion. Form then cannot be taken for granted. Conventions of the 18th and 19th centuries that viewd the object as decor or commodity, the regular quatrain as form given by Reason, and God as the Supreme Poet, will not serve. "Here" and "now" demands an open composition for a fine adjustment of the changing elements of the poem to grasp a reality always coming into existence. Here the object is imminent event, form emerges from process ("a living language"), and God is the Supreme Poetry. The genius is in the poem, not in the poet, who is only the vehicle for its realization.

There is a strain of perception where process is paramount in an art, a strain that holds within the poetic order a disorder of the scene at the moment of its entering the order by which it is known. There is an epiphany then, a showing forth of reality, containd, at the boundaries of the primordial. We may return to it in reading, to an experience that is charged with immediacy.

In range her poetry moves between this impending reality—what we call the objective world—(in this she is close to William Carlos Williams) and another world, equally objective, of the imagination that springs into life and voice from the ground of common things. "And for God's sake" she can cry in "The Departure"

> don't let's leave in the end
> without the ocean! Put it
> in there among the shoes, and
> tie the moon on behind. It's time!

Like Rilke, she is devoted to the sounds and apparitions of the City—I'm thinking of the old scavenger in her poem "An Innocent (II)" with his hook projecting "beyond the hand," "an aid / to delicate poking"

> for I'd seen on the old man's face
> only the calm intense look of a craftsman . . .

Yes, she is closest to Rilke. "Poetry" for her is dream, magic or unconscious sympathy that informs everything—not the "dream" of the psychoanalytic cult with its self-ish preoccupation, but that crossing of the psyche and the outer realm of spirit that is one event, where we have our wholeness of feeling in the universe. She catches it as only the craftsman devoted to the language can catch it and revives meaning. With invention, with a hook for a hand if need be!

Preface: Jack Spicer's *One Night Stand & Other Poems*

With his first publisht poems in *Occident* (the student literary magazine of the University of California at Berkeley) in 1946 and in *Contour 1* in 1947, Jack Spicer's voice, at once humorous and painful, in which his delight in nonsense and his fear of nonsense meld, is already there. "The Bridge Game" and "The Chess Game" project his governing poetic fate; that is to say he took them seriously and he would follow through to the end of their series. He read language as he read cards or the plays in baseball as signs. Robin Blaser tells us in his terminal essay to *The Collected Books of Jack Spicer* that Spicer's last words were "My vocabulary did this to me"—words out of the misery of a terminal alcoholic coma. It seems true indeed that he died of a disease of the language game. Bridge, Chess, Pinball, the great American spectator sports Football and Baseball, and language, produced messages: sportscasts relayd binds and double-binds. In this sense of the death-throes underlying life, of the rules of the game, he was throughout an original of such power in my own imagination as a poet that whole areas of my creative consciousness still seem to me to have to do with a matter that was ultimately from him. His wit and his fine critical intelligence from the beginning are sharpend and exercised in a never-ending battle against the autistic drive of the poem for him. And as with all autistic systems, his work haunts surrounding poetries. Those of us who knew him, and "we" must include all readers, for what he askt of us again and again was that we read him, carry with us his sting—the sting of the gadfly he so often in early days claimd to be—his wry dissent in the midst of sweetness, for again and again he knew the honey of Apollo to be bitter. In the end the fury could break loose, and the tyranny he sufferd in the courses of the poem would be inflicted upon his followers and readers. When I first met him in the summer of 1946, he wanted to know first of all what I might know of the German poet Stefan George and his circle. The volume *Poems* with its introductory essay by Ernst Morwitz had been publisht in 1943, where— Spicer was right—I too had read the legend of the cult of Maximin,

First published in Jack Spicer, *One Night Stand & Other Poems*, ed. Donald Allen (San Francisco: Grey Fox Press, 1980).

where a young boy in his death is enshrined in poetry that is also the heart of the poet. But there were also stories one heard of George's tyrannical hold on his followers. "To find an adequate expression for the pain of loneliness, is the problem of this book," Morwitz tells us of George's *Hymns*, "in which the poet turns his disappointment over a friendship that did not mature into rhythms of torment and regret." What is striking in Spicer's searching for what lay back of George's legend is not that George would ever be, as Rilke was, a model of the poet for Spicer, but that he was searching for his own self in poetry yet to be. The art was to be Orphic. Orpheus would be the tutelary daemon of Spicer's poetry: Orpheus, the Singer, yes. "The proudest boast made about Orpheus," Spicer wrote in a symposium on "The Poet and Poetry" in *Occident* in 1949:

> was not that his poems were beautiful in and of themselves. There were no New Critics then. The proudest boast was that he, the singer with the songs, moved impossible audiences—trees, wild animals, the king of hell himself.

And it was Orpheus, the bereft Lover: the Spicer of these early poems was at war with the doctrines of the New Criticism that would see the poem as a thing in itself. In the course of *After Lorca* he would himself come to face the specter of the text in Poetry, and in the book *Language*, which I read as I read all Spicer's work in the spirit of his poems from the beginning, a new generation of poets after his death would read the crisis of an old poetry of reference and passion in which the directive to a New Criticism and its Poetry, again demanding that reference be stript away, is given. But the Spicer of 1949 was determined that the poem was voice:

> They have taken poetry (already removed from its main source of interest—the human voice) and have completed the job of denuding it of any remaining connection with person, place and time. What is left is proudly exhibited in their essays—the dull horror of naked, pure poetry.

A Singer of Love Song. At the end in 1965 there will be that song: "The dark / forest of words lets in some light from its branches. / Mocking them, the deep leaves / That time leaves us / Words, loves." (*Language*) and (*Book of Magazine Verse*) "What is important is what we don't kill each other with / And a loving hand reaches a loving hand." "Words, loves" the despairing of words, the dis-pairing of loves: in those last "words" after "My vocabulary did this to me," he said, so Robin Blaser remembers his legacy: "Your love will let you go on." That "you" is beautiful, for it is not only immediate and personal, so that Blaser emerges as the chosen disciple as John (Jack's baptismal name) emerges in the gnostic *Acts of John;* but it is also plural—it blesses all who answer to its declaration. For the Orpheus-Poet that Spicer came to be was not only the Singer of Love but the Hero who entering Hell returns and in the rite of passage loses his Beloved to sing of unrequited love, of Love in Search: he is the Leader of a Circle of those who follow his Song—"impossible audiences."

It makes us wonder, this Master of Song's Magic whom we heard of long ago in childhood fairy tale, where Persephone may have been also the Queen Under the Hill, and Eurydice, a changeling sylph, a shadowy love slipping back from the light of day and our wakening search, back into the shadow-world, her own element. In these early poems, "Orpheus After Eurydice," "Orpheus in Hell," "Orpheus' Song to Apollo," "A Night in Four Parts," and "The Song of the Bird in the Loins" speak from this mask—Spicer in the period of these poems immersed in the study of Yeats would have so used the word "mask": it would verge upon the Hallowe'en mask—he could identify with Jack Pumpkinhead in *The Land of Oz.* Just as the Orphic mystery Master of Song was always in part the story hero of a Wonder Tale, so mystery cult and wonder story were stage figures. It is part of the travesty of theater that we find Eurydice out to be a young man (as in high poetry, Maximin for George was a counterpart of Dante's Beatrice): Eurydice will be "the alley-cat of Hell" or she is banisht and a young man takes her place "in streams too deep for love." Spicer's wit is quick to present emotion in grimace. In "Orpheus in Hell": "Later he would remember all those dead voices / And call them Eurydice."

That vocabulary had begun for Spicer in 1946 with the second part of my poem "Heavenly City, Earthly City" in which I had projected such a confusion in the figures of Orpheus:

> Sweep, then, Orpheus, the wild music from your lyre
> as if you sang lost love, but remember
> the beauty and charm are hate's machineries,
> demonic art that catches the damnation into its disk
> and lends to hell its immortal strain.

and of Eurydice:

Sweep, then, Orpheus, the wild love from your lips
and when from the far room your forgiven lover
cries out from the rejection that forgiving is,
remember Eurydice's face because you turnd
is turnd toward her death . . .

remember his face as your Eurydice
that was the woman's face in the lunar gleam of sleep.

*

In the Berkeley period 1946–50 we dreamd—Jack Spicer, Robin Blaser, and I—on the seashores of Bohemia of a Berkeley Renaissance and projected Orphic mysteries and magics in poetry. "Among my friends love is a great sorrow" was written in 1946 before I met Jack Spicer I think. He did not originate bitterness for me, but he deepend my recognition of it. By the last months of that year, when I was in the throes of writing "Heavenly City, Earthly City," even as I was in the throes of a sexual psychodrama, Spicer was in attendance every day to witness the events or hear the aftermath of the love affair or the poem, to commiserate with the friend's suffering and to hear in rapt attention the installments of the poet's rhapsody that went so far beyond the bounds of the decorum establisht for the art. If later he was to draw upon the poem, what seems most important here is that his intensity in audience drew me on into reaches, wooing his listening, where over-riding/over-writing the actual events and relationships I raise figures of another realm of feeling in which visionary ejaculation and nightmare fantasy are confused.

In "Chinoiserie" Spicer seems to be referring directly to the impact of "Heavenly City, Earthly City" as he affirms his "share of that desiring / And that aching, slapping sound of a hundred waves." And in "An Arcadia for Dick Brown" he writes his own turbulent rhapsody in which "the pull of a Rococo wildness / aching full of fauns takes shape" and a Chinaman who dances "the Pan, the Wandering Jew, the little dream the analyst forgot" and holds the key to this poetry may be the poet of that preceding poem he draws upon. I was, anyway, the first poet Spicer took to be of his order, and the obsession remains, more than a quarrel, more than a contention, a war against the figure I was for him—that's but the half of it. In the other half, I am also the one who betrayd again and again the figure I was for him. From the beginning my rhetorical mode must have been difficult for him, for he was puritan in his ethos of the poem and hostile to the "poetic," the charm or luxury of the poem. Increasingly his work would take on an apotropaic magic against the seduction of words. "Words, loves."

It was the difference between ideas of God. Had we been atheists the difference would have remaind between the ideas of God we refused. In the beginning the difference must have been one of temperament. It seems to me that we seek ideas of God because they are necessary to some picture of our own nature and world. Both of us were homosexual in orientation; but for me my homosexuality was a potentiality, a creative promise for love; for Spicer his homosexuality was a curse, a trick in the game of a God who predestined such love of man for man to damnation. Poetry was then the second brand of Cain he was condemned to carry: "My vocabulary led me to this." He was addicted to Poetry as he was to alcohol, sick unto death with it. In a letter of 1954 to Graham Macintosh, Poetry appears to be as invasive and tyrannical as the Army is for a draftee: "When we return to the chessboard there will be no more marching and making beds for you, no more losing and finding of poetry for me, we will be human beings again moving our selves across a board that has definite limits and allows for laughter." But in the 1946 poem "The Chess Game," the board is hostile to us as human beings.

*

So in his twenty-first year, Spicer sees projected—"in the cards"—the fortunes and misfortunes of a dual curse in "The Bridge Game" and "The Chess Game," as if he were reading his own palm, but significantly it is not given in the palm but in the trap of playing in the riggd game. In "The Bridge Game" the rebus of twenty years to come—he will die in his forty-first year—is given. Is it this that is his "vocabulary"? The poem declares the issue to be given in Hart Crane's tragic life and in his poem *The Bridge:* in his doomed search for homosexual love and in his adherence to the poetic quest in which his personal life and his American vision will be brought into one language. "The Bridge / Two Hearts" I read to mean here the game in which the heart devoted to love and the heart devoted to poetry are bridged to be broken (as in "An Apocalypse for Two Voices" later "the aching chord is broken"). "Everything echoes" is from the first the condition of poetry for Jack Spicer. The first words announce themselves as they fall as members of a fateful vocabulary he must follow through to the end. Not only the words one writes but the words one reads that "get to" one. Hart Crane's vocabulary as Spicer reads it to be primary becomes his own where he will in his own art echo back now plaintively, now derisively to the resounding sea—the sea of Duncan's "Heavenly City, Earthly City" rememberd, yes, but back of that the sea of Crane's "Voyages." "Two hearts," but the bid calls attention to the magic of a doubling: in writing "Crane of Hearts" is Spicer catching "Knave of Hearts," some hint of Crane's disorderd sexual adventuring.

That bid is followd by three spades and Dashiell Hammett of *The Maltese Falcon* ("The Bird") leads to a bid of two spades, "The Sam" and the "Queen." The Bird too as it becomes an eternal member of the cast of this poetry to be will double and redouble. Is it already, as it will strikingly be in "The Song of the Bird in the Loins," in the "gamecock" of "Five Words for Joe Dunn," in "A poem to the reader of the poem," or the Holy Ghost in "Song for Bird and Myself," the phallus as angel? The fraud of the bird in Hammett's mystery story is bitter then in reference. Sam Spade like Hart Crane is a prototype of the poet, but now not the victim but the hard-hearted detective who answers Brigid O'Shaughnessy when she challenges him that he knows if he loves her or not:

> "I don't. It's easy enough to be nuts about you. [This thematic stand will be taken by Spicer again and again in his life and his work and in the voice of Sam Spade.] But I don't know what that amounts to. Does anybody ever? But suppose I do? What of it? Maybe next month I won't. I've been through it before—when it lasted that long. Then what? Then I'll think I played the sap. I won't play the sap for you."

In "Some Notes on Whitman for Allen Joyce" this handing over of Whitman not to be taken in by the promise of love is the Sam Spade voice of the poet. "At least we both know how shitty the world is," he addresses Allen Ginsberg in the last poem of *Book of Magazine Verse*. "You wearing a beard as a mask to disguise it. I wearing my tired smile. I don't see how you do it." In a lasting sense Spicer does not reject life, he simply refuses to be taken in by it. He turns it over to the judgment that falls on it— predestined—as he turns himself over to judgment.

Brigid in *The Maltese Falcon* is, anyway, the Queen of Spades, the Black Maria, Bad Luck: *pique dame* in French which even as I may overreach Spicer's intended meaning is all the more telling a reading, for "pique" doubles in English as "offense taken by one slighted or disdaind, a fit of resentment" which is a pervasive mode in Spicer's feeling.

"Pass, Pass, Pass." The bird, the Maltese Falcon, passes for real. In the early years 1946–48 Spicer was not sure whether or not he was passing sexually. A poem from that period reads "My chastities express the hermit's act / To go and bar the door." He might yet pass. Yet not escape, for the lot in this game is built in in the rules. As the cards are revealed to be Tarot, this bridge proves to be the casting, the laying on, of a fortune. "Madam Alice" will recall "Madam Sosostris" from *The Waste Land,* but now as "Alice, Alice, Miserere" the cry goes up, we realize it is Alice of those "Adventures Under Ground," and the King of Hearts, the Queen of Spades, may be Hades and Persephone, even as the Bi-cycle Playing Cards are the host of the dead:

> "Now for the evidence," said the King, "and then the sentence."
> "No!" said the Queen, "first the sentence, and then the evidence!"
> "Nonsense!" cried Alice, so loudly that everyone jumped, "the idea of having the sentence first!"

But, just so, in this poem predicting the poetry to come it has yet to come to, it is the sentence that comes first. On the evidence of the sentence we begin to read. It is the world of Calvin's God and of Predestination that is back of this nightmare.

*

In the Pleasure Dome of Kublai Khan, in the realm of the poem, the cards as they fall in the game are "fortunes told by Madam Alice."

The conjunctions of Hermes Trismegistus, Marco Polo, and Kublai's Palace have their origins, I would venture, in John Livingston Lowes's *Road to Xanadu,* and—is it an accidental strike?—when I turn to where Hermes Trismegistus occurs in that text I find it lies in the chapter "The Bird and the Demon" on "Wingy Mysteries":

> And with the new wonders of the air which science was disclosing merged the immemorial beliefs in its invisible inhabitants, whether vouched for by Iamblichus, or Hermes Trismegistus, or Captain Cook.

What I do know is that Lowes' book in 1946 was already a key work for Spicer, where he had surely found beautifully researcht and glowingly projected the idea of a ground of lore, an intricate network of associations and informing minds beyond the poet's at work in the poem: it suggested more than sources upon which the poet drew in his inspiration; it suggested "invisible inhabitants" coming in to the poem like spirits to a medium's table. Madam Alice as she lays out the cards, like Madame

Sososotris in Eliot's *The Waste Land,* is not only the reader of fortunes, so that we see the poem itself as a casting of fortunes, but she is a medium reading what the spirits tell her is in the cards. In the text she reads another text, so that we see the poem also as a medium of messages. What John Livingston Lowes taught us was that no poem was an isolated or insulated product but drew upon and led in return to all that the poet or the reader of the poem had known, even what he but subconsciously rememberd, what he knew not he knew, from the world of Mind and Imagination at work in all he had experienced:

> Nobody who knows the period can dream of isolating its poetry from the ferment of its thought or of detaching Samuel Taylor Coleridge from that ferment. And when Wordsworth suggested his "spectral persecution," all this accumulated lore, held in solution in Coleridge's brain was precipitated in the strange vengeance which overtook in haunted seas the slayer of a solitary albatross. What the fortunate bird acquired, in fact, along with immortality, was the efficient, if belated, championship of a fully accredited Neoplatonic daemon.

As the reader of the "Books" of Spicer will be aware, Spicer was to come to a doctrine of poetry as dictation, as "spectral persecution." For a moment in "The Bridge Game" one might have passed, but Buddha's Wheel turns round into "Rod and Creel," the Father's punishing rod and the Son's fishing net. Once the wedding guest is caught by the Ancient Mariner, he will not get past. The net of the poem takes over and leads into a spell binding lives to lives—into a community of the poem. This compounding of texts belonging to the poem: *The Bridge, The Maltese Falcon, The Road to Xanadu,* "The Pleasure Dome of Kublai Khan," *Alice in Wonderland,* and, with the Ace of Cups revealed as the Holy Grail, the Grail legends, but also the lore in which Tarot and Grail legends are confused, proposes the mode Lowes found in Coleridge's imagination, of a host of energies "at work behind these fabrics of its weaving."

The movement from the Tarot cards, which Spicer knew at work in the poetry of Yeats and Eliot, to the "Courtesy Bi-cycle Playing Cards," from fortune or occult text (as the Tarot was also the Book of Thoth) to "Playing" Cards is a movement toward greater terror: once we are "playing," we have entered the trap itself. So too in the movement from Crane's *The Bridge* with its idealizing stand heroic to the "hard-boiled" realism of Hammett's novel. The Queen of Spades trumps the King of Hearts: when Brigid calls upon Sam Spade's heart he turns her over to the Black Maria. But it remains, the sinister woman trumps the man: can Bi-cycle Playing Cards mean not only the two Wheels—the Tarot rota, and Buddha's—but also bring to mind bi-sexual, the two sexes turning upon each other. "Bi-" as the fortune goes. The Hanged Man on the Wheel of sexuality. The omens of this poem forecast long shadows.

Does the "Miserere" of "The Bridge Game" go back to Psalm 51 with its prayer for mercy and its confession of rebellious spirit against the Father? back to Spicer's pursuit of Christian doctrine that so continues in his later work? We may rightly hear among these voices informing the word "Miserere" the confession: "My rebellious acts that face me I know too well, and my sin is ever before me" and the plea "in your kindness, in your immense compassion delete my rebellious acts." For the homosexual, whose very making love is bound with a desire for the Father's love, even as it is bound with the love of man for man, that if it be sexual is abominated by Jahweh, there can be no evidence of His kindness, of His compassion. The Bird here is the bird of *The Maltese Falcon,* and Brigid pleads in vain with Spade: "If the bird had been real, would you have handed me over?" Unremittingly the God of Judgment in Spicer predestines without kindness or compassion. The Game is designd to defeat kindness. In "The Chess Game" the Lord's Prayer appears in a sinister cast: "And forgive us our love as we forgive thy hatred."

*

Among my mementos of Jack Spicer is an early gift from him, his Junior Department Promotion Certificate to the Intermediate Department of the Wilshire Presbyterian Sunday School, dated June 14, 1936. In Robin Blaser's cautionary note regarding the depth of Spicer's Calvinist background, he writes: "His mother tells me that during his first college year, 1944, at the University of Redlands, he joined a Baptist or Methodist group." The God who appears in Spicer's poetry is that Creator—the Designer of the Game and of the Rules and of our Winning or Losing—who has projected upon Man the predestination of a Hell along with the agony of a sexual compulsion, a poetic compulsion, an alcoholic compulsion, a gaming compulsion, a psychodramatic compulsion that leads him deep into the defeat rooted in his given nature. Spicer, strikingly, in a period when Man's biological and cultural origins have been an important poetic research, is not a poet of origins. The Fall,

even in its ecological guise, is not a leading theme with him. It is the
Cheat, the Trap, designd from the beginning as the condition of the
world and of our being that goads him. But back of the predominant
theme, from the earliest poems to the last, of Love itself's being predes-
tined to defeat, the Father's hatred is unremitting, and the poet, as son of
his father, is eaten at the core with an abhorrence of life's conditions.
Blaser is more than right that Spicer by 1946 was no longer a Calvinist.
But what made for his seeking out Presbyterian schooling? There must
have been first of all, I think, the search for a Jesus: the Jesus we find in
Spicer's "Mr. J. Josephson, on a Friday Afternoon" who says "Reject
reflected light," seeing the light's broken reflection in the glass, and "gave
the world his throat to break / And made the glass opaque and real with
blood"; or the Jesus we find in "The Inheritance—Palm Sunday" "a
precious scarecrow, bound and crucified," Man's victim; or the Eros of
"Five Words for Joe Dunn" "Who will cling to you every birth-
night / Bringing your heart substance" so that "Whomever you touch will
love you, / Will feel the cling of His touch upon you / Like sunlight scat-
tered over an ancient mirror." There is a special poignancy for the ho-
mosexual lover both in his being just in his love crucified by the scorn, the
disgust, and the laws of the Judaeo-Christian society he belongs to and
also in his finding his ultimate beloved in this Bridegroom. In the late
1950s when I was reading the theosophical works of Jacob Boehme,
Spicer urged me, Don't neglect the most important, *The Way to Christ.*
And in his late work, in the set of "Four Poems for *Ramparts*" in *Book of
Magazine Verse,* his allegiance is reaffirmed:

> And yet it's there. Accepting divinity as Jesus accepted
>   humanness. Grudgingly, without passion, but the most
>   important point to see in the world.

Here the voice passes from the mode of poetry into credo.

By 1945–46 when he came up from Redlands to the University at
Berkeley, he was seeking in Buddhist readings and in universalizing and
rationalizing philosophies for a belief that would supplant the religion in
which he had known the misery of his soul as it confronted what it could
not but see as the impossibility and prohibition of the love it needed.
Robin Blaser tells us that when he first knew him, Spicer was expounding
the universe of Leibnitz with its monads. Spicer in the summer of 1946
when I met him sounded me out with the doctrines of Buddhism in

which heavens and hells were but part of the fabric of illusions the mind projected. But he also asked about what I knew of the Albigensians and back of them about gnostic doctrines of the Hellenistic world, in which the Creator of this World, the Father of the Old Testament, was revealed to be Ignorant of Truth or the very Enemy of Truth, and we were his creatures only as we had been enslaved or drawn down from our true heritage. In "An Answer to a Jew" he writes:

> When asked if I am an enemy of your people,
> I would reply that I am of a somewhat older people:
> The Gay, who are neither Jew nor Goyim,
> Who were cut down in your Lord God Jehovah's first pogrom
> Out at Sodom.

Both God and Man are to blame: "None of the nations ever protested about it" he adds. But the issue is deeper going than the matter of Sodom, for in the very order of the Creation, God's vengeful nature, his hatred, is felt.

In "Chess Game," the companion poem to "Bridge Game," the hopelessness of the cry "Miserere" in "Bridge Game" becomes clear. Here the universe appears where "the king is dead and the queen is mad" and Alice is locked in a dementia. "Yes, we are curved now and all the arcs/Are round with envy./We move counterclockwise toward another Wonderland"—it is a vision of a creation that is a game where terrible angels move men like pawns toward absolute zero. Bishops, knights, and rooks look down "on the brave little pawns/that march in solemn column toward the curve/That leads below the chessboard." "Where are the players?" the poet asks. "Perhaps they pray"; then there follows a Hell's version of the Lord's prayer. "Give us this day our daily doubt/And forgive us our love as we forgive thy hatred." It is strange indeed to come from this diabolical chess game seen so in 1946 to the chessboard of the letter to Macintosh in 1954 where the pattern is made to fit human beings. Yet it is of the essential nature of Spicer's poetics that they co-exist: the board where men are moved by God like pawns and the other where "we will be human beings again moving our selves across a board that has definite limits and allows for laughter." Robin Blaser in his "The Practice of Outside" remembers him "full of laughter," saying "We [Blaser, Spicer, and I] were the three immortals," for some moment standing in the Taoist world of Tu Fu. I can only see deeper as I read in his work, no laughter, unless it be mocking, a resolve that holds to the promise of Jesus but, even as the travesty of "as we forgive thy hatred" sounds, will not give up the curse for it so needs the accusation against Creation itself. In this he comes close to Baudelaire and close indeed to Artaud. Jehovah is the other person of Jesus.

In "Four Poems for *Ramparts*" the sentence "God is palpably untrue" might be read at first take to mean that the proposition of God is false; but the statement remains that God is Himself untrue, as a lover is untrue. He is untrue to us who are His creatures as a poet is untrue to his poems, untrue in love. Then there follows what I can barely keep at the level of belonging to the poem but it breaches that understanding and sounds to be a confession of a rueful faith:

> But Jesus dies and comes back again with holes in his hands.
>   Like the weather,
> And is, I hope, to be reached, and is something to pray to
> And is the Son of God.

In the fourth poem of that set—"(in a dark forest between grace and hatred)"—there is the confession of a need not only for grace "Like almost, without grace, a computer center," but also for hatred:

> Without his hatred
> A barren world.

In his later poetry, the bridge game and the chess game of the early poems become "Baseball or the name game" and the Calvinist God, or the Gnostic Lord of This World, the Demiurge, Spicer proposes now "is a big white baseball that has nothing to do but go in a curve or a straight line." If it is a conceit, it is as serious as John Donne's propositions leading as it does to the sudden revelation of a needed depth of feeling:

> Off seasons
> I often thought of praying to him but could not stand the
>   thought of that big, white, round, omnipotent bastard.

If "a curve or a straight line" might stand in a sexual level of meaning, in "the little dream that the analyst forgot," for *bent* and *straight* sexual orientation, remembering the "curve"—the curve thrown—in "Chess Game," the "him" of the passage at hand may be read anew to mean the

omnipotent aroused penis in erection. At every level the suffering pro-
test against compulsion becomes itself in a double-bind compulsive.

> Yet he's there. As the game follows rules he makes them.
> I know.
> I was not the only one who felt these things.

*

It is throughout the authenticity of feeling that informs Spicer's
poetry: the need, the mistrust, the spite, the longing, the tenderness, the
playful glee, the cunning manipulation, the profound underlying
depressions—whatever they are untrue to, are true to feeling. What he
sought in Calvinist and gnostic theologies was an ideogram in which
God's betrayal and Man's love would never change but co-exist. And in
the declarations of love, the pathos of Spicer's love feeling and the cha-
grin, the poignancy of his remaining a love poet in the midst of what
appears to be overwhelming evidence of hatred increases.

"To pierce the darkness you need a clock that tells good time," he
writes in *Book of Magazine Verse:*

> Something in the morning to hold on to
> As one gets craftier in poetry one sees the obvious messages
> (cocks for clocks) but one forgets the love that gave them Time.

*

"Your play," our Fate says. Meeting with his fellows of the bridge
game was as important for Jack Spicer as meeting with his fellows of the
poetry game at Gino and Carlos or meeting with his fellow watchers of
the baseball game. "North, the partner vulnerable—West, the opponent
vulnerable—East, the opponent vulnerable—South, the dealer vulner-
able," the table reads. And we must play the hand out.

In the bi-cycle of that word "play," the child long ago knew how
playing that he was Hart Crane or Sam Spade or Alice led into his losing
himself in his play—rapt, seized: to pretend as to imagine was to be
transfixt, transformd. If the "Arcadia" for Dick Brown is made-up, "in-
tentioned," a "chinoiserie," Spicer writes, it is no sooner proposed so that
it is immediately "real," and Dick Brown, the actual Dick Brown, is re-
vealed to be Nijinsky, the faun Nijinsky "playd," Beauty's very self, more

true than real. What the poem creates in actual life at the time overtook
Spicer himself and he was in love with Dick Brown—the poem created it in
him—or is it the other way round? the poem revealed to him what other-
wise he would not know he felt so? In the order of this play, Spicer's calling
up of this "aching" Rococo Dresden landscape, all artifice—first cousin of
Yeats' Symbolist Byzantine "gong-tormented sea"—once Dick Brown is
seen to be the faun, "startling, young, streaming with beauty," the evoca-
tion itself "breaks like dawn," revealing itself to be the poet's being in love,
a falling-in-love real beyond the bounds in this pretended world.

The poem in this early period was conceived as an entertainment, a
serious amusement. The listener is, even as the poet is, drawn in once the
play begins, distracted, bemused, and the world turns out to be funny.
Not funny ha ha, but the other sense of humor, of darker humors: funny
strange. Estranged. "There is more of Orpheus in Sophie Tucker than in
R. P. Blackmur," Spicer says in the 1949 Symposium. Poetry was to be a
vaudeville act. Vachel Lindsay, Spicer proposes as the model. The per-
forming voice of "The Congo" and "The Chinese Nightingale" is back of
Spicer's proposition. When we remember what contempt Pound had for
Harriet Monroe's prize awarded to "The Chinese Nightingale" we may
appreciate something of the declaration of independence in Spicer's
stand.

It is this insistence upon the primary, the primitive magic reality
taken in a staged magic, the deadly play-earnest working in the mask
behind the face, that is Spicer's creative forte—more significantly, that is
his creative task. And the act is to be American and popular. "One needs
no Virgil, but an Alice, a Dorothy, a Washington horsecar conductor,
to lead one," he writes in "Some Notes on Whitman for Allen Joyce":
"Calamus is like Oz." This is a poetry that has common roots, or a com-
mon Road to Oz, with much of contemporary science fiction, yet it ex-
ceeds the common sense of being "fantasy," for his fantasies are taken to
be not escapes from reality but descents into reality.

Spicer is not only the *miglior fabbro* of this fiction, but also creature
through and through of the auto-fabrication, for the very making-
believe is reveald at every stage to be not "his" but his Creator's. If
Nijinsky dancing the faun presents the Beloved, the lover Spicer has his
likeness presented in Nijinsky's Petrushka. The Joker in the deck of Bi-
cycle Playing Cards is wild, somehow funny-not-funny. We don't laugh.
The heart for Spicer in these poems is Hart Crane, is resisting, besieged,
a dead weight—"the blood's weight under the heart's alleys pressing,"
falling, jagged and half-awake, twisting,

Heart so monstrous naked that the world recoils,
Shakes like a ladder,
Spits like a cat.

Spicer is a master of humors, but he is never "light"-hearted. I see him as playful always, but it is the play of the moth-soul's wings caught in the meshes of the spider, the soul somehow also is in its art: "Arachne . . . twisted deep like thread upon a spoiled / sewing machine" portrays the poet who is caught in the "Rags, bottles, and old beauty, bones." There is no facility, nothing facile, about Spicer's amazing and cunning wit, about his feints and strategies—for they are struggles in earnest.

Sing from the heart! Sophie Tucker's song is belted out from the heart. Love songs, blues songs. "Spook singer, hold your tongue," Spicer writes in "A Postscript to the Berkeley Renaissance"—he is funny then like a spook at Hallowe'en, a ghost dancer at the door of the heart to trick or treat.

"I sing a newer song no ghost-bird sings," he tells us: "My tongue is sharpened on the iron's edge."

Iconographical Extensions: On Jess

The whole sequence is a picture book, belonging then to the great primary tradition that extends from the illustrated walls of the Cro-Magnon man's galleries to the emblematic and magical art of the Renaissance and the revival of enigma and visionary painting in the Romantic Movement. Its original may have been a child's coloring book, for each painting is a picture translated from a drawing, an engraving, a lithograph, or a photograph, in sepia or in black and white, into the density and color of oils. Still again, its original may have been a child's scrapbook or paste-up book, for the variety and readiness of its recognitions of what belongs. Paste-up or coloring book, the original the painter presents to us is just now coming into being in our mind out of whatever was—it is the primer of a new need in vision aroused in him by the demand of a missing beginning hidden in the disclosures of what he comes to see as his tradition.

*

His series of copies presented here belong to a larger constellation again of works in progress—romantic paintings, paste-ups, drawings and illustrations, constructions in studious play with playthings rescued from throw-aways of the world about him—in which he works to transform our household, our way of living, and beyond, to illustrate, with all the glow and depth of color, the interplay of possible forms and boundaries, and the mysteries of light and dark, our being. As, in turn, he sees his Translations as, in Translation 11, *Fig. 2—A Field of Pumpkins Grown for Seed* (even as he has come to see the paintings of his beloved Renaissance and Romantic Movement) "grown for seed," scattered abroad in the imaginations of men to give rise to new visionary generations. Our *being*, here, is ultimately generative in picture, in continual imaginative reproduction.

Published privately by Robert Duncan with the title "Notes on Jess's Translation Series: Preface for the Catalog" (San Francisco, 1971), and reprinted in *Translations* (New York: Odyssia Gallery, 1971).

*

It is important that they are copies, redundancies or visible *ideas* (where we must remember that the word *idea* comes from the verb *idein*, meaning *to see*), making visible what the painter comes to see in the process of making it visible. His relation to the visible is as immediate as he draws from what he sees in an 1895 engraving from a painting by Dvorak as Cézanne's is as he draws from Mont-Sainte-Victoire. Each is painstakingly faithful in translating what he sees into his own world of paint and color. It is important that their work is fictional; what their eyes see they translate out of sight into factors of the picture they are creating. The painting by Cézanne becomes a primer to the eye seeing the mountain. The painting by Jess becomes primary to his originals.

*

Translation 3, *Ex. 2—Crito's Socrates,* rightly suggests to us the lead of Plato's theory of the work of art as a copy of a copy of the original; and we might recall Ben Jonson's: "It was excellently said of Plutarch, poetry was a speaking picture, and picture a mute poesy," and from his *De pictura:* "Picture is the invention of Heaven, the most ancient, and most akin to Nature. It is itself a silent work, and always of one and the same habit." Like the surrealists, Jess surrounds his pictures with texts and undermines our taking them for granted with titles that disturb any easy sense of what we see as apparent. The Translations in the visible world have their "originals," and their accompanying "Imagist Texts," as Max Ernst's *Visible Poems* are introduced by poetic propositions; and visible signs, handwriting, passages of printed texts enter into the paintings themselves, as in the paintings of Magritte words come into play. All the operations of the visual field are admitted into the intelligence of the painting. The eye that sees the printed word reads the image. Puns, tricks of translations, abound. In Translation 5, *Ex. 4—Trinity's Trine,* the picture of the Truth—at once of Science and of Religion— as seen in the laboratory trompe, suggests the rebus of the trompe in *trompe-l'oeil.*

In Translation 6, *The Enamord Mage* (related in the series 3-6-9 to *Ex. 2* above) the fantasy and the glamor of the painter's color takes over the real of his world. In Translation 9 in this series, *The Nonsense School,* whatever can be pictured comes into the picture. The "rules" of this universe are entirely pictorial, beyond what is visually sensible. For Jess,

as for Jack Spicer, as Jess's evocation of Burgess and of Edward Lear and
Lewis Carroll means to bring to our mind, fantasy and the humors of
creative play beyond the boundaries of our senses—here his concern
with the astral world portrayed in Lloyd's strange American novel
Etidorhpa comes into the picture—carry important intuitions of the Real.
The Real? the Irreal? the Surreal? the Subreal? The Nature of the World
the Artist is at work to realize in his Creation.

*

 Pli selon pli, translation leads to and from translation. But there are
no established orders here, every order in the order of another order
appears significantly disordered. In order that we see what *Crito's Soc-
rates* comes to mean, we must follow the lead of the god, that will bring us
along our way to the picture of the Beatles as the Jumblies, copied from
the Bubblegum card. Fold according to fold, we must hold in one habit a
conglomerate of ideations: the recognition of a divine informing world
of images that moves the picturing artist, the recognition of the creation
emerging as he works as a world to which he is faithful, the free play of
fictions potential in each realization in which each work of art is a seed of
art.

*

 The "abstract expressionists" or "action" painters—particularly here
Clyfford Still, Edward Corbett, and Hassel Smith, who were his teachers
in the West in his school days—created a new iconography that continues
to be relevant to the language of the later painting. The vocabulary of
color and mass, of texture and of the actual activity of painting, became
paramount in the intention of the painter; he sought to picture in the
painting the process of the painting's realization. A picture of painting
itself emerged, no longer to be taken merely as the medium of images but
as an immediate presentation. The eye disturbed began to see that be-
yond representational meanings, beyond symbolic figures, beyond the
psychological readings of the organization of the canvas, the very process
of painting was itself a primary meaning from which structures of vari-
ous meaning were built up. What had been taken before to be an "effect"
was seen now to be an "event."

*

So, in Jess's painting, we are led to see, permeating the world of representations that meet our eyes, the primary world of actual paint and of the painter's work in painting out of which his representations rise. We are immediately aware of the underlying layers of paint. At the interstices minute flickers of earlier periods in the painting are active where between continents, states, localities of surface areas, they are exposed. Under the skin of surface paint, globs of thickened pigment are brought into the play of the process, so that everywhere in the layers of illusion and illustration arising from the visual syntax of color and mass, of boundary and reference, the painter pictures the painting itself.

*

"Abstract" for the American movement in the late 1940s was a misnomer, for the terms were not so much *drawn from* a reality as *creative of* a reality. "Action" painting, a field of creative activity, working *with* what happened and *in* its happening, an art of recognitions and participation—the force of the great painting of the generation preceding Jess's work was to present the experience of the immediate act of the painting itself.

"Expressionist" intentions in which the techniques of the artist, his architectures and equilibrations of the picture, are still media of something behind the painting to be communicated, passed into initiatory intentions in which the painting became itself the ground of a primary revelation. The painting as the medium of the painter's experience of the world, either then *impressionistic* (conveying how he saw the world) or *expressionistic* (conveying how he felt about the world) remained; but now the painting as an immediate event of a world comes into play. A Still or a Corbett in the fanaticism of their turning against a representational play, striving to banish from the field as they worked every activity in which the potentiality of images arose to their eye, found themselves confronted by the image of the painting itself. Whatever else it might succeed in avoiding—the world of angels or of men, of mountains or of blue—the painting represented the world of paint. For some—indeed, for many— the world of paint was less real than the world of angels or of men, of flowers or of mountains. For such too, it seems outrageous that a poem should have to do with the very process of its own creation. Sing love, sing ocean, sing peace or war, but do not sing of Song!

But in the complex world of vision, when we are looking at a painting, though a two-fold, a three-fold, a four-fold field of realities may emerge, extensions of visual language in which the full range of man's experience may come into play, there is but one ground of that play and that is the primary ground of the action painters, the properties of the canvas and the oils as they give rise to recognitions in the creative will. In the master generation of the action painters, the creative will had returned to affirm the primacy of that creativity itself over all representations. And, acknowledged in the ever-active presence of the paint in the picture, that primacy remains an important principle in Jess's work.

PUNS, RHYMES, AND MULTIPHASIC ORGANIZATIONS

A pun is an element that sets into motion more than one possibility of statement. This brush stroke at once appears as a member of the painter's language of painting—we see it as a statement of the act of painting, or as a statement of paint—and as a member of the image of a foot. In Celtic design, ground is everywhere possibly figure; figure, ground. In a field of interacting melodies a single note may belong to both ascending and descending figures, and, yet again, to a sustaining chord or discord. A rhyme is a member in whose force of identity we remark—remember or anticipate the presence of another member. In composition by field, a color does not glow in itself or grow dim, but has its glow by rhyme—a resonance that arises in the total field of the painting as it comes into that totality. The "completion" of the painting is the realization of its elements as "puns" or "rhymes." The painter works not to conclude the elements of the painting but to set them into motion, not to bind the colors but to free them, to release the force of their interrelationships.

*

What was once thought of as a tradition, a doctrine of images handed across from Egypt, Babylonia, the Semitic and Grecian world, into the Hellenistic, and from the Hellenistic revived in the Renaissance as its treasury; or what in our time has been proposed as a dialectic of styles—as Picasso, for instance, presented a mimesis of historical styles and destruction of styles as the drama of his work—in Jess's imagination is neither linear nor directional but pervasive. Each element is present in and informs every other element—in the time of Man, as in the individual canvas. To see the face rightly, one must see the skull in the face; to see the skull rightly, one must see the face. Likewise texts and images are members of one operation: the picture is "translation," the word is "imagist," for the mind that addresses the whole of human meanings toward which the arts point. The word imagines; the painting speaks. And in turn, the word refers to a series of texts, as the painting refers to a series of visual events in time.

*

The immediately apparent series of Figures 1 thru 8 with the propositional Figure 202 and Examples 1 thru 7 should suggest that Jess's Translations series is built up of cross-series. "Fig." may mean Figment as well as Figure or, mindful of the insistence upon pun and upon nonsense, it may mean that the artist does or does not give a *fig* to or for art; as "Ex." may mean "X" or "Ex-" as well as Example. In the sequences of the paintings chronologically arranged, the serial relationships become more complex, cross-patternings appear where we begin to realize we have to do in seeing with the play of visual humors. In painting we see by the tricking of a surface in lights and darks that arise entirely in the interplay of colors, depths, and heights that float upon the skin of the canvas, and Jess brings into this interplay a wide range of dictions and contradictions to keep us aware of the world of paint alive in the world of image, a grammar of purely visual depths and heights orchestrated by actual depths and heights of paint, embedded figures and raised backgrounds, conglomerations of pigment that catch actual light and cast actual shadows, thus bringing the activity of the medium into the illusion it is to carry at the visual skin in which the painter's art has cast its own spell of light and dark. The activity of the translation is now itself a text to be translated, the terms of the magic translated into the surface of the spell it casts.

*

The play with the terms of the painting extends throughout his concept as he works; he means to release in full the elements of his world into potential meanings. "Figures" are not only elementary terms of the visual gestalt, where the eye reads potentialities of figure and ground in order to apprehend the plastic intent of the artist, but "figures" are also numbers, and where there are numbers given, we might be aware that color and area have in turn their own numbers in sequences, in proportions and ratios, in which there arise rhyme and reason, melody and harmony, disjunction and possibilities of discord, in the composition of the canvas. The play of number is the secret of the music of painting as well as of poetry and the organizations of music proper.

In *The Nonsense School*, figures of the painting are doing their figures: the figure 8 (the number which also appears on the back of the player, the Son of Art, whom we see facing the Lords of Xibalba in *Montana Xibalba*) appears on its side in the figure beyond figuring—the formula for the square root of minus infinity written on the blackboard. Is this nonsense proposition of some time/space, the proposition of the time/space of the world of the painting, the entirely *created* time and space of the merely seen? In *Ex. 6—No-Traveller's Borne,* Jess refers to a "scientific" plate, which, illustrating no known earth in no known space, and, further, no possible earth in no possible space, is a found nonsense object, supposedly showing actual cosmos but actually showing the cosmos of the space and time we know only in the terms of its being painted, having the reality of the fictional. Where Jess allies himself clearly with the grand masters of phantasmal nonsense that arise in the nineteenth century in the genius of the Romantic Movement—with Edward Lear and Lewis Carroll, as, in his translation of the *Galgenlieder* he allied himself with Christian Morgenstern—the modality of the picture is everywhere problematic. It is essential that the figure is absolutely what it appears: it is pictorial, but it is not only pictorial, it is a happening of the painting, but it is also an element in the mode of the picture as rebus. It belongs to a playful nonsense, but this play, like the play in *Alice in Wonderland,* has everywhere a momentous, hallucinatory aura. Its playground the artist reminds us is the playing field of Xibalba. It is in this dimension, in the modality in which art and death confront each other, that the ultimate instrumentality of art is revealed to be a trick or joke, but this is a trick or a joke that is essential to the nature of man's life. The pun—the lowest form of humor—the oracular double-speak in spelling and grammar, the way of telling the truth in what seems to be all an illusion or lie, this is the secret of man's game with the demonic powers. "Remember too," Jess adds, "I configure-eight." The set of Translations and their Imagist Texts as they are presented in this show in this complex game of associations, in which the paintings are cards, the arcana of an individual Tarot, a game of initiations, of evocations, speculations, exorcisms, may be related to the field of dream and magic in art which we inherit in the tradition of the Surrealists. A play at once sinister and rightful, like Lewis Carroll's play with words, but here, a play with the properties of paints and picturing.

*

The "Ex" series are translated from engravings found in scientific
sources, a textbook of 1869 and issues of *Scientific American* of 1887, in
which the illustrations of apparatus and phenomena of the scientific
world operate as pictorial puns to illustrate propositions of the artist's
world, emblems belonging to a second series relating to a process in
vision.
1. "Apparatus for Standardizing Sensitive Plates"
2. "Thermoscopic Balance"
3. "Randall's Lathe Center Grinding Machine"
4. "Laboratory Tromp"[1]
5. "Convex Mirror"
6. "The Earth in Space"
7. "Zodiacal Light"
The painter does not make up the pun, but it comes to him, as
images appear in dreams to haunt the mind with reminders of latent
meanings, where he recognizes in the picture of scientific apparatus the
apparition of his own inner instrumentality as, hidden in the develop-
ment of his work in painting, there is a growing urgency at work in the
art itself to see into itself. We may take the series then as metaphorical,
presenting stations of a passion in painting. The titles and the surround-
ing texts do not explicate but are complicit in the conspiracy whose secret
workings the painter, as agent of an intention of the imagination, obeys.
And where we respond—where our sense of color is aroused to follow
the color, or of forms to carry their imprint, or we are drawn to read and
to wonder—we too become conspirators, linked by a shifting series of
scenes to changes in spirit. Sensitive plates are calibrated for astronomi-
cal observation—so we learn as we follow the legend of *Laying a Stan-
dard;* but in the painting our eyes, if they are to come to see what is
happening there, have their own field of conversions. What in a world of
paintings as objects of value we read as style, in the world of Jess's art
appears no longer as value but as event.

*

His play of properties of vision and of pigment and ways of painting,
his play of visual space and pictorial light and of actual contours and

---

[1] Just as the painter translates into his painting accidents of the original, here he
copies the word *tromp* (*trompe*) as it appears in the *Scientific American* text.

reflecting and shadowing ridges, thicknesses and thinnesses in the work, arises in the process of creating a world—a body or earth, *ge*—that like our earth is not given as a model but is a living form, i.e. a form in process, and has its geology. Areas are geographical, and the realm of meanings we read as we read the boundaries and configurations, the images of the picture dimension, is analogous to the realm of nations, cities, and landscapes which man creates as he sees *his* world. But the evolution of the painting, the geological imagination of the earth, is ever present in Jess's total presentation. Not only depth created in the plasticities of the language of color and mass, but depth of actual pigment, and, further, in that depth, where we see layers of color, we are aware of the depth in the time of painting as a dimension of the visual field.

In the play of time as a dimension of what we see, the series numbers of the Translations are chronological and the progression in time is also a progression in painting. "I am learning how to paint," Jess says of the work, and it is important to realize that in the total project there are to follow this first series a large canvas, *Narcissus,* in homage to Moreau, and then a series of paintings from alchemical plates, and finally, a painting from Dürer's *Melancolia I.* It is a history in which mind and matter come into being in co-operation. Concept and recognition of what is happening, working *with* what happens and projection of happenings. "I am learning to see what is happening in painting," Jess might have said.

*

In the fulcrum of the "Ex" series, Translation 5, *Ex. 4* (where in the numerological play, the sum of five and four is nine) *Trinity's Trine* can be seen in the light of the painter's own personal history as part of his design. For the originals which were "found" as they were recognized to belong to the work of art were also recognized as belonging to the work of his own life—life and art, as one, being the field of a revelation. The work of art here is a primary apparition of what life is about. That is why dream and art seem so close, where we recognize in what we see the creative imagination in its creation of its own world and, at the same time, the dream mechanism in its projection of the life of the artist's soul, where what we see comes to inform what we are.

In *Trinity's Trine* where the painting takes over the picture of a classical experiment[2] to establish, as water, air, fire, and earth are primary

---

[2] *"Trompe.* An apparatus for producing a blast, in which water falling in a pipe carries air into a receiver, where it is compressed, and thence let to the blast-pipe; a

elements of our sensual apprehension of the real, primary elements of its own color universe, we may recall too that the scene from the world of the physics and chemistry laboratory stands at a crucial point in Jess's life, when, as a scientist, he recognized his vocation was to be in art. In his former life, the painter Jess was chemist ("Ex-" chemist, then), drafted in 1943 out of Cal Tech to serve his Babylonian Captivity in the Chemical Warfare Division of the U.S. Army and in the Engineers Corps at Oak Ridge, working in plutonium production, returning after the war to graduate from Cal Tech in chemistry with honor, and serving again in the Plutonic legions of the G.E. atomic energy project at Hanford, Washington. The nightmare gravity that colors Jess's canvases and unites his vision with that of the early Chirico and Max Ernst's hallucinatory collages and paintings has not only its roots in the nightmare gravity that we all know in our childhood vision of the world but also it has its bitter root in the actuality of the grown-up nightmare which the workers in chemistry and physics have brooded in our time. Xibalba, the land of violent death, whose Lords cause bleeding in the road, vomiting of blood, running of pus from open sores, the terrors of revolution and of war, has been known by the artist not only in dreams but in actuality.

Reflecting again upon the artist's titles and texts, we find that these present not only a progress of the artist's vision in painting but also a story of ideas of what vision is as a development of states of Mind in human history. Back of it all, there is the child mind working his serious play and creation of world and self in the concerns of the man in a series of pictures, at once illustrating and story-telling as he goes along, as he did in his own age, where his paints and crayons spread before him a new ground of colors, lines, and areas, of his filling in and his leaving blank, that proved to be, even as he worked there, a ground in which pictures and stories came to him. Close to dream, there is this knowing the meaning of what we see, a message both that we draw from things, giving them identity, and that comes to us from things, giving us identity. The world is a field creative of texts as we see it. Poetry and painting are one in the child's discovery of art, making up the meaning of what he sees in a world he envisions as he creates it. We do not see it yet, but he sees it in the first brush stroke. Jess in his art remains faithful to this first revelation of art, the promise of a world in its fullness to emerge. He populates the area and history of the canvas with events until a context in which they come true appears.

---

water blowing-engine." We are to see all the terms of this definition as carrying a message, ominously informing the painter's own activity in his art. What we see happening in one realm of being is likewise happening in every realm.

Following *Ex.1—Laying a Standard,* in which we see the stage of scientific observation, where the rationalizing eye sets up its ratios in its sight of the light of the stars to establish the world-view we call Science, the painter illustrates a story of Mind in evolution from the vision of the world created by the rule of sensible perception in the empirical mode through a series of conversions in the terms of vision toward the field of the visionary and creative Imagination, where, again, as in the beginning intent, creation and revelation are at one with the eye. First, there is the abstracting and conceptualizing mind, typified by Plato, for whom what we sensibly see but seems, and the truth is found in a metaphysical archetype or idea, whereof what we see is but a copy, and works of art (even as Jess's paintings in this series in which he incorporates ways of seeing so deliberately are) are but copies of copies. In this proposition of the higher rationalism of Greek civilization, true imagination is Reason, as contrasted with a false imagination, which is Poetry or Making-up-what-you-see. In truth, the painter is but an artisan and his work is properly representational—good, insofar as he faithfully copies the archetype as model or paradigm, but evil, insofar as he departs from the original and creates a new vision, insofar, then, as he transforms reality. Second, there follows, in *Ex. 3—Fionn's Finnegas,* the picture of the artisan's lathe grinding machine to illustrate the stage of the phantasmal or faerie world of images, the work of the imagination to trick or amaze the mind, that the tradition of magic and romance as powers of the artist in the Celtic civilization, typified by the bardic poet Finnegas, proposes. Just as the Platonic doctrine of the artist as copyist is playfully incorporated in Jess's painstaking forgery from the photograph or drawing as a model, and the scientific doctrine of empirical observation is incorporated in his close study and translation of elements in the photograph or drawing as a control, so in the sensual lure and keying of colors that is the threshold of his translation of the image, Jess recapitulates the stage of magical art with its spellbinding and its casting of illusions and chimeras in a mirage of images. He works to bring his own fascination with color forward into the activity of the final canvas, to keep this acknowledgment of the working of a wonder alive in the completed realization of what is involved in seeing.

Third, there is the image as symbol in *Ex. 4—Trinity's Trine,* in which the symbolic number plays between the trinitarian configuration of the divine identity which fascinated the Hellenistic mind, typified by Plotinus, and the quaternity of elements in matter in Hellenistic physics. In the Imagist Texts which accompany this icon Jess seems to have found voices speaking of the inner secrets of his art, as in the trinity *I. Atum speaks, II. Plotinus listens, III. Langland's Samaritan describes the Holy Trinity* (as given in Jess's table of contents prepared for my use here). Atum may be the very atomic matter or the world of subatomic particles which in the chemist's knowledge underlies the reality of the pigments and ground in which the artist works, for the god says: "but in the end I will destroy everything that I have created, / the earth will become again part of the Primeval Ocean, / like the Abyss of waters in their original state." In the physical drama of his way of painting, Jess has laid down skin upon skin of paint that in time beyond our experience of time will break, revealing underpainting, widening the life of colors that in our life time we see as an all but invisible excitement at the boundaries of established areas. Behind the meaning of translation the artist senses in the very transformation of world into art the specter of an ultimate return of created things into their original state. If Atum is the person of the matter in art, Plotinus listening to his speech is the person of the artist. In the mystery of his texts Jess here indicates that "If there is to be perception of what is thus present, we must turn the perceptive faculty inward and hold it to attention there. Hoping to hear a desired voice . . ."—the painter's seeing is a kind of hearing beyond sense. "We must let the hearings of sense go by, save for sheer necessity," he quotes from Plotinus. The eye then listens in color for the voice of a long desired color. So, in the ritual of his art—in his mixing of each color toward subtler and subtler advents of color, but also in his actual participation in mixing in each color from the beginning, working in every hour of sunlight through the day, and, in periods of sun, working every day without days off, slowly building up surfaces, layers of work, layers of involvement—Jess works to prolong his life time in the life of the painting, deepening and extending in time his participation in the creation of the painting, for the acts of painting are themselves, in themselves, acts of a personal mystery, for which the words of Plotinus in the Imagist Texts may again speak: "every being of the order of soul is in continuous activity as long as life holds, continuously executing to itself its characteristic act: knowledge of the act depends upon transmission and perception."

In the proposition of the third person of the Trinity which we read in the speech of the Samaritan from Langland's *Vision of Piers Ploughman,* there is the suggestion that the vision of the painter is ultimately poetic, presenting a visible poem, even as the poetry of Langland presents a vision. And in the passage quoted from Langland we find that in the orders of the poetic the Trinity appears as "to a torche or a tapur / . . . likned / As wex and a weke / Were twyned togideres, / And thanne a fir flawmynge / Forth out of bothe," returning our minds to the world of physics and chemistry in their laboratory, where, for the rational mind, the art of vision is one of likening between the world of the senses and the sensible figures of the metaphysical reality.

What brings Examples 1 thru 4 together in one group is the governing rule throughout of the kind of mind in which truth once apprehended becomes dogmatic to exclude as false any further information of the imagination. The Celtic proposition of the imagination as casting an illusion or deceit upon the senses and amazing the mind is but a continuation of Plato's argument against the lies of Poetry. The poets recreate or falsify the myths, is his accusation, in translating them in their works. It is a creativity that threatens the very authority of the state in Plato's *Republic*. So too, the Christian or the Neoplatonic doctrines of the Trinity lead toward a dogmatic reality which must exclude from itself as heresy a world of fantasy and creative imagination. In the extremes of the Hellenistic agony between the absolute and the created, the gnostic cults viewed all Creation as evil in the very fact of creativity.

This group exemplifying an authoritative and collective reality is followed by a second phase in Examples 5, 6, and 7, in which the individual imagination takes over from the collective reality as the principle of truth in vision—from the collective consciousness or social conscience of reality built up in the realm of empirical and logical sciences, accountable to what Freud calls the Reality Principle, the world of actual events, and from the collective "unconscious" stored in the realms of traditional wisdom-cults and revealed religions, the dogmas of the world of communal dream-identities, from the truth of species and tribes, into the truth now of individual revelation.

The transition into the mode of the individualization of Vision and of the Creative Will may be contained in the title of *Example 5—Mind's I,* in which we read that Mind finds its "I" in its invention of seeing. The painting presents the picture of an experiment in presentational immediacy, the projection of an image which has only visual reality by means of a reflection in a convex mirror. The "I" which the painter knows in the individualization of his art, his eye for the realm of his painting, is no longer the substantial "I" of his own body nor of his autobiography. Nor is it the given "I" of an *a priori* being or seeing in their existenz. It is not the "I" of a metaphysical reality, above and behind the reality of the scene. In the work of art, the Mind's "I" is a fictional identity that belongs to the making or fiction of the work itself. It is the identity of a Creator that exists only in His Creation. The truth of the individualizing Vision cannot be verified by facts of the given physical world nor by paradigms existing in eternal verity but only by the works of the individual creative volition in the creation of an individual reality. Once we enter upon the adventure of the individual imagination as a center of creation, all the facts of the collective reality must come to be verified in the light of a personal vision. The "persons" of God in the Christian doctrine of the Trinity may be factors from the mode of the collective that in their personality already lead into the mode of the individual reality. Jess's painting shows the event of the "I" as the magic lantern projection of an image—it is the principle of the Renaissance invention of Athanasius Kircher.

The reference in *No-Traveller's Borne* leads us on further into the falsity of illusion, but in the genius of the Renaissance, the mind turns to find a truth of its own operations and nature in this very world of theatrical illusions—not now the theater of the collective unconscious the theater of the god Dionysus and his dramatists Aeschylus, Sophocles, and Euripides—but the theater of the individual imagination, Prospero's island and the Coast of Bohemia, the world that in Shakespeare's teaching is in truth a stage. In grand canvases and masques, in works of the imagination the gods had returned—creatures now of Mind—and what had been seen as mere illusion, beyond which the true concerns of the visionary lay, is seen now as a play within a play, a locus of the will to see.

In the title *No-Traveller's Borne* we see that the painter would, indeed, have us think here of Shakespeare's "undiscover'd Countrey, from whose Borne / No Traveller returns," the country of an emerging reality that "Puzels the will," where Mind in its own recreation turns from archetypal and empirical models to explore the New World of its own fantasies, raising private and individual—what the Greeks called *idiotic*—realities. This world and this space which serve, in the context of a science textbook, idiotically to illustrate the physics of world and space in three dimensions, in the context of their actual two dimensional page—the third dimension being a projection of the imagination—have the intensified imprint of their belonging to the Irreal of a purely pictorial Space, the spectral imprint upon the Mind of figures that rise from the Mind's own creation, beyond Sense returning to the senses. Enamored, the senses return to the Mind's world in the painting, drawn by the autistic lure of the Mind's vision presented to the sensory threshold, but drawn, also, by the lure in which the senses co-operate in the conception of the painting, by the field of color activities immediate to the eye. But it is the Eye in which we find Mind in Jess's work. The co-ordinating computations of the brain are an extension of the will which is in seeing itself. In *Zodiacal Light,* I would read this development as the original that the painter translates now being informed by "Light," at once phantasmal and nonsensical, beyond the light of the Mind—the suggestions of light that rise from the painted surfaces of the dense matter of pigments he works in and the creations of light that rise in the field of color relationships. For the painter who was once a student of sciences the medium of his art is also a chemical theater—the laboratory of a chemistry and physics now grown phantasmal in the triumph of art. In the allegory raised by the sequence of titles, the eye prepared for astronomical observation, becoming through art converted to—or revealed truly to be— Mind's "I," now sees (as men see figures in the constellations of the Zodiac and are moved to see auras at the horizons of the visible world) the center of Mind is there, where, reaching out from the brain, the brainstalk flowers at the skin where it meets the World in a concert of vibrations and excitements. The Brain but attends and studies. It is in the Eye, in the threshold of color, that the creation and teaching that we know as Mind has its center.

Blake speaks in the tradition of poetry's mysteries of a four-fold vision in reading; and we may likewise speak of a four-fold "reading" of the visual world. The experience of "meaning" is the experience of interrelationships. The "language" of painting in which we read the meaning of the process of art itself, analogous to the meaning of the oral/aural processes of literary poetry, presents itself in the way of painting, and it is important in Jess's work that this "way" is itself a goal of the artist. The "language" of picture arises, as if there were a tongue in the mouth of what we see, and

> *plot or myth, its feel*
> *of what   belongs to it . . .*

There is in Art a primary redemption of the World—but this is only to say that there is a recreation of the World, a play ground, or the creation of a New World in the world, in which the individual human spirit comes to life in its own creation. Here, in the Art of Jess's world, in the autonomy and co-operative identity recognized in each particle, in the love and celebration of the network of the whole, in the freedom of

the creating Mind in its natural pluralities, and in the multiphasic unity—
the confidence of the informing spirit in every event of his work—he
presents a revelation of freedom and individuality as principles of the
social totality, and, underlying all, a Tao of Western Painting replacing
the dialectical frenzy of action and reaction competing in history.

Statement on Jacobus for Borregaard's Museum

Harry Jacobus is a painter in a mixed light; as too, these panels are in mixed media—crayon, pastel, gouache, ink. And color is massed with an activity that comes from undertones and overtones. The light is the sheen of a butterfly wing or it is the diffuse light in a room of late afternoon, sunset or twilight; the light once sought out by luminists in Western landscapes. He sees apparitions of things.

But these are *interiors*, and the concept has a mixed meaning: at once the painter's sensitive, nervous pleasure in ravishing nuances and arrangements as they are revealed in household daily occurrences, splendors of actual things seen in the dying down of the light; and at the same time these interiors are phases of the painter's own inner being and light that finds its affinities or recognitions in what he realizes as he works in color and line in reference to the world about him. These are not abstractions but reciprocities.

In our period that has given rise to career painting and to commodity painting, to the spectacular museum piece, to an art criticism that is all concerned with values and style, with reportage for the marketplace—few painters survive to reveal to us what is moving and eternal, as Harry Jacobus does here. This work is a spiritual meaning; it is poetry; it is an intimation of the beauty around us as it is within us; and the working of the medium tells us that only where the psyche is kept so vulnerable, sensitive, alive to the invasion of things, only in this disturbing area where things mix eternally, can we come upon this beauty.

He relates to other earlier painters who were intimates of the poetic—to the luminists, to the *Nabis* Bonnard and Vuillard, to certain early works of Matisse (*The Blue Window* or the *Flowers and Ceramic Plate* of 1911; the *Poissons Rouges* of 1915; the *Moroccans* or the *Piano Lesson* of 1916), to the *Nocturnes* of Whistler. And there is an important relation too to the San Francisco school of nonobjective painting of the late 1940s

Written in 1961 for an exhibition of Harry Jacobus's paintings at Borregaard's Museum in San Francisco, and reprinted in *Lyn Brockway, Harry Jacobus, and Jess: The Romantic Paintings,* ed. Christopher Wagstaff (Palo Alto, CA: Palo Alto Cultural Center and Wiegand Gallery, 1990).

and early 1950s, where Jacobus was a student—to the early work of Hassel Smith, Bischoff, Still, and Edward Corbett. He has his closest contemporary in the painting of Jess. But I see both Jess and Harry Jacobus in their work as relating in turn to my own development as a poet—for they have brought the imagination into painting again, as I have worked to bring the imagination into poetry. They work with a consciousness of metaphor and symbol, of color and form as terms of a magic.

What is new, what comes as an instruction to us, a suggestion of what his genius strives to get across, is this vision in which inner being and the world about the artist answer each other, correspond or work together in the ground of the painting to reveal a troubled harmony. To reveal, further, that what troubles the psyche is not to be cured but kept, for it is the area too where the beautiful is contagious. The *interior,* Harry Jacobus makes us see, is beautiful where it is moving; is, just so, a matter of radiance and of a delicate edge; is a mixed matter that is a medium for haunting shadows. And we see that the rooms we live in are haunted by our living; that we live in ashes of lavender, in blue lights, in burning orange or luminous gold of ourselves.

Of George Herms, His Hermes, and His Hermetic Art

He is one of that little company of Artists of the Reassembly closest to my heart in my own work. Out of the discarded and unrecognized, he has brought up into the light of the Imagination, at once playfully and devoutly—and out of the Love of the Beautiful, wrought for the Friends of the Earth—a likeness of Earth's humble mysteries. The residues of humanity haunt him. He works with materials fallen away from their original uses, worn until their old useful bodies have fallen away and an other patina alone remains. Or, at times, his angel will lift immediate some element from the context of this world, out of a mere costliness of appearance, the Truth of what we overlooked we now see, into the Romance of Old Survivals. This Renaissance or Recycling of Riches thrives upon the threadbare and remnant. And with all of the fallen world this Angel holds conversation; his Treasury, the dreams and colors the soul knows with; his Kingdom—for here at last each individual man may in his person be his own kingly anarchist Osiris—founded upon Poverty and Childhood. What had been Osiris then is Christ again. What Providence George Herms's transvaluation of Improvidence brings to awaken a new sight and heart in our living in this world informed by the Spirit throughout.

First published in *George Herms: Selected Works 1960–1973* (Davis, CA: University of California, 1973).

Wallace Berman: The Fashioning Spirit

It was in 1954 that Wallace and Shirley Berman first came to call on Jess and me at our Baker Street apartment. Kenneth Anger, who was in the course of realizing his *Inauguration of the Pleasure Dome* in Los Angeles, had talked there about meeting us in San Francisco and visiting the rundown apartment transformed into another world with its suite of rooms painted by Jess, its assemblage of associations, its beginnings of a life exploration of the Romantic spirit—for us, a wisdom of old folk magics, of wonder tales and mysteries, and a keeping open the inspiration of Nature, of cosmos, and of fantasy worlds in the work of art. Through someone in the cast of Anger's film, the Bermans had taken the lead to seek us out. It may have been Cameron, who appears in Kenneth Anger's film as the Whore of Babylon, a creature of old Crowley cult continuities, for it is Cameron whose portrait appears on the cover of the first *Semina*. And it would be a drawing by Cameron, in that issue, that would fatefully lead to the closing down of Berman's Ferus Gallery show when it was included in 1957. The emergence of a new art and a new poetry arising from new life ways in those years was to be written in police attacks and court proceedings against sexual images and the rites of personal mystery cults as "pornography"—the trial of Ginsberg's *Howl*, or in later years, of McClure's *The Beard*. Back of these prosecutions was the war of established religious groups against heretical minorities.

There was only the one visit in 1954, but there was in the course of the afternoon an unfolding recognition that we were possibly fellows in our feeling of what art was. Later that year, "W.B." would send us *Semina No. 1*. In 1955, Jess and I were in Mallorca, returning to San Francisco in the fall of 1956. In December of 1957, Wallace Berman sent *Semina Two* with the appended typed notice pasted on the back cover:

> During the second week of a scheduled month exhibit of my paintings and sculpture, members of the vice squad entered the Ferus art gallery and

First published in *Wallace Berman: Retrospective* (Los Angeles: Fellows of Contemporary Art, 1978).

confiscated a copy of *Semina 1* which was exhibited as an important part of a work entitled *Temple*. Brought before the righteous judge, Kenneth Holliday, who, taking the allegorical drawing in question out of context, declared me guilty of displaying lewd and pornographic matter.

I will continue to print *Semina* from locations other than this city of degenerate angels.

The question of "context" in the affair goes beyond the usual matter of context in such trials, for Berman's very art is the art of context. From the first, the intent of *Semina* was not a choice of poems and art works to exercise the editor's discrimination and aesthetic judgment, but the fashioning of a context. The collage itself, which had been seen by Dadaists and by Surrealists as a mode of attack upon the real or upon established relations, breaking into and deranging sacrosanct images, just as the dream was seen as a betrayal of the nature of conscious life, had, after all, projected in the attack the context of what we recognize as Dada and the Surreal. Now, in our conscious alliance with the critical breakthru of Dada and Surrealism as in our alliance with the Romantic Movement at large, we began to see ourselves as fashioning unnamed contexts, contexts of a new life way in the making, a secret mission.

*

I wanted to turn to electricity. I needed
a catalyst to turn to pure fire,

so Michael McClure begins a poem in that second issue of *Semina* in 1957. Facing his poem is reproduced a drawing from Cocteau's *Opium* series. A new generation was exploring the power of drugs to open up psychic depths and heights, and the lore of drugs in religious ecstasies and in visionary flights of Romantic poets was the lore of the time. "In a twilight spiral," Zack Walsh's poem in the same issue ends: "slowly / roll un-buttoned eyes / beyond our reach, / beyond our arms, / beyond our waving madly hearts." Pantale Xantos (Wallace Berman) announces: "a face hisses rules to cathedrals and prepares the narco myth," and the opposite page presents photos of an addict shooting up—beyond his naked shoulder we see Berman's painting with Hebrew letters. "To prove again fast formulae / for ringing God to make one day," a poem by J. B. May reads. And from a page from *Cain's Book* by Alexander

Trocchi: "It was born of a respect for the whole chemistry of alienation."

Over the years between 1957 and 1964, David Meltzer and e.i. alexander (who were both in *Semina No. 1* in 1954), and John Wieners, Michael McClure, Judson Crews, as well as the originating Pantale Xantos, were frequent contributors. It is a *Season in Hell* period, I think, led on by the specter of the *poete maudit*. Baudelaire, Verlaine, and Rimbaud are there then, and Cocteau; but it is the Artaud who, in breaking with Marxist and Freudian rationalizations of Breton's official Surrealism took his sickness itself to be the new revolution, was the culture hero of this descent. Artaud's *To Have Done with the Judgment of God* (1947) by the early 1950s in a translation by Guy Wernham and preached by Philip Lamantia had become an underground text for us in San Francisco, and, earlier, in 1948, *transition* 48 issued from Paris in English, had presented Artaud's *Journey to the Land of the Tarahumaras*, opening the prospect of a Nature revealed anew by Kabbalah and by the drug peyote. Its opening sentence might describe the works of Berman as they disclose his world: "The land of the Tarahumaras is full of signs, figures and natural imagery, which do not seem to be the work of mere chance; as if the gods, whose presence here is everywhere felt, had wanted to make their powers known through these strange signatures in which the likeness of man is hunted-out from every side."

In late 1955, Allen Ginsberg with the opening lines of "Howl":

I saw the best minds of my generation destroyed by madness, starving
    hysterical naked,
dragging themselves through the negro streets at dawn looking for an
    angry fix,
angelheaded hipsters burning for the ancient heavenly connection to the
    starry dynamo in the machinery of night,

claims his continuity from the *Jubilate Agno* of Christopher Smart, from Blake and Whitman, but we would see also that he follows in the wake of Artaud.

"Morphine mother / Heroin mother / Yage mother / Benzedrine mother," Pantale Xantos chants in *Semina 4:* "Peyote mother / Marijuana mother / Cocaine mother / Hashish mother / Mushroom mother / Opium mother / Mescaline mother . . ."

CHILDREN OF A TIME OF DARKNESS FELT

The art of this generation, of the young men coming into awareness in the postwar period when it was clear that the war had not decreased but increased the feeling of threat thru out the civilization of the West, is distinguished from that of my own generation whose work had taken root before the war by the descent into the underground of the city and by the programmatic use of forbidden drugs. It was not simply a counterculture. Marxist ideas of social alienation may be applicable to the course of an Alexander Trocchi or a John Wieners in their "abuse" of self through drugs, but the positive social values emerging from the art of Wallace Berman must be explained by another course.

I would see the descent as a dramatization of the Jungian concepts of psychic evolution as an alchemical process in which the *nigredo* or *melanosis*, "the horrible darknesses of our mind," is the initial stage of a promised individuation. Significantly, in relation to the self-conscious elements of our period, Jung's *Psychology and Alchemy* was published in the Bollingen series in 1953. But the first drafts of these alchemical essays had appeared in 1935-36 in the *Eranos-Jahrbuch* and in 1939 had appeared in Jung's *The Integration of the Personality* published in the United States. Whatever my quarrels with Jung, quarreling itself is a thorough enough involvement; to know anything about the content at all was generative of new ideas of psychic possibilities in the arts. If there were no archetypes of the unconscious, once they came into the discourse through Jung's inventive doctrines, both the collective unconscious and the archetypes were recreated in the conscious fashionings of the artist. So too in psychoanalysis a conscious pursuit of an idea began. In his work with the French psychoanalyst Allendy, Artaud had gone into psycho-alchemical practices and dramatizations, leading to his actual search for peyote in the land of the Tarahumaras in northern Mexico. What he was seeking was to undo the French concept of *esprit* as Mind—the gains of the Age of Enlightenment—with the other sense of *esprit* as Spirit, but Spirit now darkened by a spiritualism in which spirits antagonistic to the body of Western civilization invaded. It is in the light of or in the darkness of this rising persuasion that we must see the adventure of the new work (where here I mean to suggest the alchemical Work). Jung had seen extreme disintegration as the condition or ground for the psyche-work of a radical reintegration of all elements, a conjunction of opposites.

Semina is to be seen, I propose, and the later work of Berman as themselves "seminal," as the seeding of "that black, magically fecund earth," as Jung describes the alchemical antimony. The milieu Wallace Berman arises as a new world, the world of an invisible "Mother," fashioned within the body of the present world which is experienced as the Terrible Mother. "The artists of the survival," I called us in a poem dedicated to Wallace and Shirley Berman. The world environment—the material world of man's creation evident in the photographic and daily news record was the *nigredo*. If it might have seemed a question of Western civilization, Asia and Africa now emerge in the same state. Each daily issue was filled with "degenerate angels" and the police of that state; each issue of *Semina* projected the suffering of that state as the ground of its spirit-to-survive. "I believe that everything and above all the essential was always in the open and surface," Artaud wrote in 1947 to Breton against the idea of the esoteric and occult: "and that this has sunk vertically and to the bottom because men did not know and did not want to maintain it." The threat we read does not read from some conspiracy behind the scenes, from some content of the unconscious, the hidden, but is seen, where even as we see it we dare not see it, in the public camera eye. So, in the dark intimations of Berman's Verifax series in whose handheld "radio" or "TV," picture after picture of a Revelation is shown, we see the pictures our daily news has openly flooded us with in its trashing of the world-mind.

This time of darkness is also the Flood, especially from the Kabbalistic lore Berman suggests, and his venture can be seen as Noah's. Leaving Larkspur (his Bay Area center) to return to Los Angeles in 1961, he writes in a poem in *Semina:*

> Spurred by what reason
> Do I leave this ark
> For the 'city of degenerate
> Angels' 500 miles south   other than to die.

THE MISSION

"Wherever the seeds of light, the magnificent, falls / Comes change," reads a poem by Hesse ("To a Toccata by Bach") included in the first *Semina* (seed) packet . . . "things are fashioned." This fashioning of things was to be Berman's life mission, and it was our, Jess's and my, sense of his spiritual intent that, for all of our avoidance of the drug culture scene so that we did not cultivate his Larkspur house, made for our lasting alliance. In the fashioning of things, of true goods, our two life ways were united in a deeper way. "The great creative urge," the Hesse poem, outstanding in the initial promise of his journal, tells us: "surges through the inner being of every creature / Toward the Paternal Spirit. / It becomes desire and need, speech, picture, song—"

> It heaps world on world to form a triumphal arch
> Of the vault of Heaven!
> It is drive, it is spirit, it is struggle and joy.
> It is love.

"ART IS LOVE IS GOD" W.B. would print as his motto in *Semina Two* in 1957, following the fall of his *Temple*, his arrest and trial for displaying lewd and pornographic matter among its sacra. He was to become the artist of the outcast.

In the Larkspur refuge or ark, he and George Herms fashioned things of the spirit from outcast objects and "trash" pictures, combing over the city dumps, "working in the dumps," even as Jess combed "as-is" tables of the Salvation Army depots to fashion his household votive objects. Early Bruce Conner assemblages show the same spirit. The word "junk" that in the 1950s would have meant the trashing of the drug heroin, in the 1960s came to mean the redemption of trash in the recognition of devotional objects, emblems and signs rescued from the bottom in the art of a new context. So too, as George Herms writes in his note for the 1977 Berman exhibition at the Stewart Gallery in Los Angeles: "as a photographer he captured the passing parade of angels in human disguise." Wherever he saw the spark, and he had a keen eye for the life-seed needed for the work, he sought to bring it into the assemblage. "As the grain of fire lies concealed in the *hyle* (the city dump, or mire, the trash)," Jung continues:

> so the King's Son lies in the dark depths of the sea as though dead, but yet lives and calls from the deep . . . the darkness and depths of the sea symbolize the unconscious state of an invisible projected content. Insofar as such a content belongs to the total personality and is only apparently severed from its context by projection, there is always an attraction between conscious mind and projected content. Generally, it takes the form of a fascination.

The fascination of these Verifax series of magic "TV" lantern shows, these treasure boxes of stones, of these votive offerings, signals, inscriptions, is that, lastingly, I mean to suggest, of just such an invisible projective content, a seeding then, most invisible in its being so present in the fashioning out of the matter of what is so much seen.

Afterword: Beverly Dahlen's *The Egyptian Poems*

Let the reader go first directly to the text of these "Egyptian" poems to read aloud and find the cadences, seek the potential music in the phrasings, listening to hear the tone leading of vowels, the place of syllables in their word sequences, the inner harmonics, the echoes, the stops—the changing patterns and the centers will emerge. The riming is there but it is slight—nothing must detract from the evocations, the tellings, the keeping of the presence of the gods. In the first poem, "The Opening of the Mouth," the vowel of "coax" will echo the vowel in the word "opening"; the vowels of "dead," "children," and "them" rime; as do the vowels of "we" and "eat": but in the third line "the food," "the bull's leg," "the heart" must stand each as independent as the characters within a hieroglyph. Beverly Dahlen writes in a deep and unfailing sense of the art that she has studied in the cadenced verse that Eliot and Pound, but especially William Carlos Williams and H.D. developed in their late works. Williams in "Asphodel, That Greeny Flower" and H.D. in *Helen in Egypt*—each preparing for death, addressing the core of their feeling—write in essential voice: *from the heart,* as our common speech calls it; but the ancient Egyptians too spoke of Thoth's demand that the witnessing soul speak with his heart in his mouth, or with his tongue rooted in the heart. "Take into the darkness of your mouth / this eye," the first poem in the sequence says. What do you see?

These are poems evoking, and in return belonging to, a mystery. The dead and the gods addresst in this mystery may once have been powers of a religious cult, but they are now eternal persons of a poetry—a poetry drawing upon myth and history—upon what the poet has read—in part, but more importantly, upon dream. "Three gods appear before me. / I have seen their face in dreams," she tells us in "The Gates."

*

First published in Beverly Dahlen, *The Egyptian Poems* (Berkeley: Hipparchia Press, 1983).

In my mind—and I speak here of the realm of thought that involves the deep systems of the body "lost in thought," that stirs at the pulse of nerve energies, that so courses in the blood in its circulations to underlie the courses of words in their circulations—over months of returning to Beverly Dahlen's poetry, what I have to say here slowly has come into place.

Waking this morning in the dark before dawn the blood was rehearsing a kind of speech that came up or came forward as speech does in her speech in these poems that compels us as life compels—fearfully, I realized. I was coming up from the dark myself to come forward into what would be my day haunted by these poems I had asked to be allowed to "introduce," even as, hearing them read sometime in December 1977, I asked the poet to send me a copy of her manuscript. And it has been in light of this set of Egyptian poems, the more strikingly unique that they draw as from a deep well upon the springs of Egyptian theurgy back of her reading of H.D.'s own theurgy. A theurgy? A calling up of divine powers to work in one's life. Needs imagination, needs art, needs prayer.

Back of these Egyptian poems—they are a set, conceived as a set (and in the dream orders from the word *set* the name *Set*, the unnamed, comes forward to take his place with the named: Osiris, Thoth, Shu)— there are two earlier publications: *Out of the Third* (1974), a book of origins in "the memory of my grandmothers," and *A Letter at Easter: To George Stanley*. The three stand as one, even as the oracular saying of Maria Prophetissa which Beverly Dahlen quotes from Jung's *Psychology and Alchemy* informs the reading of *Out of the Third:* One becomes two, two/becomes three & out/of the third comes/the one as the/fourth.

Nothing is incidental in this poetry; everything counts. The poem itself like the body of Osiris must be assembled from each of its parts entire: it is the terms of poetry like a depth analysis reading in psychology.

Go back to search the other two of these three in search of this third. The powers of the Finnish grandmother, of the language Finn rumored to be "a language/that has no root," the powers known by ancestors of Nebraska, of Wyoming, of Michigan, of Montana, of the Great Divide, assemble in Portland, in Vancouver, as they assemble in San Francisco; but it is here in the work that they ultimately stand in the magic with the Other World powers, as with the powers of her fellowship as a poet (writing to and hearing from George Stanley in the Easter Letter), once the work of the three is done.

*

From the two preceding books I would quote passages from two
poems in the context of this book.

From the poem "Black Train," *Out of the Third:*

> My backbone is a black train.
> I start on the grass. It moans for me.
> It will lay down and burn for me.
> You will see its smoke for years and years.

and from the close of "Black Train":

> I will make a voice. It will be alone.
> You will hear it all night long falling away
> towards the west. It will carry you.

from *A Letter at Easter:*

> and then you go away
> And this
> speaks, listening
> in this place, apart
> in the real, immortal world
> finished
> never done

*

What is the nature of this voice in poetry? It is compelling. It comes
from "below"—a speech below speech; it comes from behind speech. Not
from an unconscious below and behind consciousness, for this is a con-
sciousness below and behind consciousness: that is its force. The "I" itself
has undergone a change from the personal "I." Where "I" is an other, as
Rimbaud saw. The psychic life she draws in writing may be drawn from
her own psychic life, but here its body is the text and it speaks to the
psyche of the reader as reader. For the reader too, "I" is an other, as he
or she takes identity in the text.

*

In the Summer Issue 1980 of *Feminist Studies* selections from *"A Reading*—an interminable work begun in June 1978" appear. The very choice of the epithet "interminable" has for me the daring and recognition of what is involved in an open form that only the serious artist (willing to follow the series through to its consequences in full recognition of its perils as well as its lures) will take as the initial proposition.

*

"We cannot refuse it," she writes in the last passage of that selection from *A Reading:* "Freud's prayer to Eros. There is nothing in the unconscious that corresponds to *no."* But isn't it just within the structures of consciousness itself that this idea has arisen? In the field of possible "yeses" and "noes," "no noes" is in order. Even as the idea of an Unconscious is one of the higher elements in the structure of Consciousness generative as it is of fictions that can work fictions.

*

The creative field addressed, worked, and kept at work in *Out of the Third, A Letter at Easter,* and the present set of Egyptian poems sets into motion resonant elements in my own poetic consciousness so that I hear new harmonics. She has deepend my apprehension of the oracular voice in Poetry, and my reading now becomes so confounded with her writing that at the close of these poems with "The Gates," even as I found myself so possessed this morning by reading

> That their eyes look back at me in the instant
> I pronounce these words,
> that I thus draw them out of the darkness
> and enter into their company.

The Delirium of Meaning: Edmond Jabès

1.   In the dedication (which appears in the beginning but is, one knows, so often the after before-thought of a book) of *The Book of Questions,* we read the invocation of powers and spirits to attend the act of writing: "to the high sources of Life and Death revealed"—but just here, the sources seek to reveal themselves in the text we are about to write, and to read. That avowal kept, at once a belonging-to and a keeping-at-heart and in-mind, is an ancient allegiance of Poetry, even as it is an ancient devotional hermeneutics. Each world in Creation seeks to tell us of other worlds or is itself a field of signs of other worlds; and only as we read do we live. Biologically, we read the world in order to survive at all: read dark from light, read weather and soil, and in turn leave traces of ourselves. I read Jabès as if the signs and tracks of my "own" world were drawing me on all the time in just this text. The Book is a Mystery we follow, lured by the ever-present promise of disclosure, drawn into a mesh in which we become such readers in search for meaning. *The Book of Questions,* whatever it means in its transformations of resonances in the commune of French conscience, whatever it means in its recalling the question of the Jewish race in the Diaspora, reaches still to resonances both of French language and of Jewish soul in my own imagination of my deep self—who am neither French nor Jewish. The question of language and of race becomes deeper as it speaks to touch upon something more real in the writer/reader who belongs to the People of the Book. Is the "foreignness" of a language or the "exclusiveness" of a race of the very nature of the frontier of our common humanity?

2.   *The Book of Questions* is meant to arouse, beyond the boundaries of apparent meaning, suspicions and rumors of meaning within meaning, words within words. Jabès writes in order to read, or reading is the order

First published in *The Sin of the Book: Edmond Jabès,* ed. Eric Gould (Lincoln: University of Nebraska Press, 1985).

of his writing, and he brings us back again and again to this boundary of the presence of its being written in the presence of its being read—to the letter the eye sees even as the hand writes the word, to the rhyme or homophone the ear hears even as it attends the message of the voice in the book.

3.   *"A la poussière du puits,"* the second verse reads, and I would recall here Thomas Mann's *Tales of Jacob,* where the appearance of this Well, thematic in the world sage of the Fathers, became for this reader the Well-Sign of an identity of Man deeper than race in our common soul history. In 1934, just as Hitler had launched his program in full to draw the German people into the alienation of a national demon and then into the dementia of a racial identity, Mann had begun in *Joseph and His Brothers* to draw his German-reading followers into the depths of a world soul through an identification with Jewish Old Testament "forefathers," taking Jewish experience and roots to belong to the origins of our humanity. The Well is deep, I remember the book began, or did Mann say "fathomless"?

Returning phrase by phrase, I am returning to Jabès's book always as to a well, and I would read that well and the well in the Dedication to be the very well of Thomas Mann's reflections or of *The Zohar*'s lore. To draw even from the dust (for the oracle has declared, "Regard the dust of the Well") what the Well and the Dust have to tell us. *The Book of Questions,* Jabès writes on the back cover of the book, is *"le livre de la memoire."* In another part of our tradition, out of Hesiod, memory is the mother or matrix of poetries. Is the dust the memorial of the water and of our thirst that was first for milk, water of the mother? Is thirst itself an ever-presence of "question"? Do we thirst in order to come deeper and deeper into thirst? Thirsting for who we are?

4.   Is it a superstition of the poet-reader, excited by Jabès's own declaration *"aux rabbins-poètes"* and the voices of these imaginary "authors in eternity" as Blake called them ("the authors are in Eternity") that I find myself following the rhyme, the foreshadowing and recall, between *la vie* and *puits,* the lovely rhythm reassured as *qui* falls in the sequence of the verse *"Aux rabbins-poètes à qui j'ai prêté mes paroles . . ."* The ear delights in the syncopation in the line, the counterpoint between the significant vowel and the phrase in which it appears. To this ear listening for this tone-leading of vowels, *révélées* is heard again, accented (accidented) anew *j'ai prêté mes paroles et* and then, at each *les, et, les, les, les, et,* I hear

echoes of the key tone lingering even as other tonal keys appear. The text at each level is written in echoes and keys. But the appearance of echoes and keys is the preliminary of a polyphonic reading in which chords emerge, *vie, puits, qui,* for the chord of a message within the message that we hold then in reading memory.

5.   In this close listening to a voice, I hear in reading the mystery of an incarnation or transubstantiation—the responses *"des Rabbins imaginaires dont la voix est la mienne,"* Jabès's says. Throughout, there is at work this presence of a voice of the writing itself and of voices within voice in the writing, so that the narrator, the imaginary rabbis, and Yukel and Sarah, become persons of the voice. This voice of the writing itself is the threshold of a presence/absence in which the creation of person and narrative, melodic unfolding and sounding of chords, can take place. Who is the *je* of *la mienne?* I begin to wonder as I read again. In a book of desert, oasis, sea, and wind, we may be reminded that where paronomasia begins, there may be mirage. This voice and these voices where there are only printed words on the page as I read must be of such a nature, the more so because it is only in the most tenuous reaches of desire, wish, imagination, risk, that I trust I hear, for French is not native to me, it is my "foreign" language, "foreign" to me and then haunting, charged with the over-thereness my native language had only before I could understand and then speak. Oh yes, I can read; the words on the page and their phonetic transcriptions, and the theories of voice, I can read. But this voice and these voices I must hear in an infatuation. This is the language of the "Other," whose ultimate lure is the lure of an other "me." Close then to the very voice or mode of Poetry, for I know in the courses of my work the voice is in one sense more me than I am, in another sense is an "I" beyond me.

   It is, after all, in French, in the oracular voice of Rimbaud, that this *"Je suis un autre"* so strikingly came into our European World Mind, though Baudelaire had noticed that an author is aware that his "I" is an other. In Jabès's dedication isn't this otherness, now between the I and the Thou, between the writer and the reading, in the last verse fused impossibly in the We?

   Et this last verse begins. This last echo of the word *révélées* is not only initial here, announcing its verse; it also stands out in the sequence of beginnings of the verses. *Aux sources, à la poussière, aux rabbins-poètes, à Sarah et à Yukel, à ceux*—all prepositions so that the conjunction appearing in sequence stands out, setting this verse apart, *plus près,* nearer, indeed immediate, to the transport of writing itself—"à toi, à nous, à toi."

"*Tu es celui qui écrit et qui est écrit*" comes the oracular line on the following page, at once the reply (what is an answer? a response? is a presiding question of this book of questions) to the invocation of the dedication and a foreshadowing announcement of the book itself.

6.   Jabès has an affinity with the creative spirit of surrealism, in which the Spirit of Romance of the troubadours was revived, the errant poet following "*chemins d'encre et de sang*," wandering, seeking, questioning— as in the Quest of the Grail—a lost question, or a question not asked and hence fateful, all belonging to the Way or Plot of the Book. The imaginary, the marvelous, the ensorceled, are all evoked by the author—it may be then the Book of the Questionable, in which this Jewish world becomes so fused (*à toi, à nous, à toi*) in the magic of reading with being "ours." To marvel is to bring into question beyond answer; to enchant is to bring into answer without question. Or in the absence of question or answer.

7.   I read here at the level that cannot be translated but can only be related in telling what goes on in the reading, the sounding in which correspondences arise. At this level, where the letters spell and the phones resound, word means to bond to word in inner chords. Is it the wonder-working with numbers and letters of the Book of Splendor that leads into the world of Jabès's "*écrit, récit;*" is my mind reading haunted by Ferdinand de Saussure's anagrams and by his idea of a written language, world in itself, evoking sound as it evokes image, beyond resemblances; or is it—does it go back—the infant mind itself, spelling, misspelling, lettering, finding and losing words and things? How many faces can you find in the tree? "*Je voulais dire que, dans le livre, les choses—les êtres aussi forcément evoluent dans universe de vocable: leur univers,*" Jabès's comments in the interview with Marcel Cohen, *Du Désert au livre*. Even as this writing reading-writing is deeply involved in the Tradition—the *rabbins-poètes* discourse here as they discourse in the counsels of *The Zohar*, and the discourse leads on to oracular evocations of the Universe as a Book to be read—I would recall that God in that telling plays with the letters: a preliterate Baby playing with his alphabet blocks, where each letter is a being, so that He speaks to B and B speaks to him about this matter of the B in the word "Beginning."

8. "But what is it that leads to reading? The text, the word in the text, the text in the word, that is to say all the words in the word and, through these, the interminable cortège of doubts, audacities, questionings, affirmations that the writer assumes because they are from the beginning his?" (*Du Désert au livre*).

9. The white paper upon which the written word appears—in a key scene in the course of Jabès's work, the wall upon which the graffito "Jews go home," illuminated by the swerving headlight of an automobile in passing, written in white chalk upon the darker ground, strikes us: the dark itself as ground may be this white upon which words appear. In English, we alone of European peoples separate all words, word from word, in speech, even as words appear in writing, so that we take for granted the intervention of the ground in the print as a "letter," just as we do not "hear" the juncture or boundary upon silence that punctuates the microlevels of our speech. In typewriting, as distinguished from writing and most printing, there is a space or location in which each letter has its own time, sounded or mute. And the cooperation of these isolations of letter from letter, word from word, accent localites in the life flow of the text as a voice. The white of the page or, in English, the silence between, is not only ground but enters as a part to the essential pattern we read.

    We may miss in Jabès's reiterated *"le mot est lié au mot, jamais aux choses"* the reflection that in speech in France, word is indeed linked to word in the continuous flow of a phrase. So that the eye reading sees breakings through of the page between words, in-ventions of the white, that are not present as a silence in speech but only behind speech. We sound in English an event (the isolate word in itself) that is conceptual only for the reading eye in French.

10. Saussure, Moses of León, whatever be the redirection of each in linguistics or in the creative reading of the Torah—I return to them as if their professions were but screens that allowed a deep reworking in Poetics. Language, for Saussure, is not a means but a realm, a Treasury, in which all words have their account, from which and to which "meanings" come and go. In the Kabbalistic reading there is no "world" that is not such a language or Book—but now a language of letters and compositions of words in transpositions of the alphabet and essential numbers. A third revelation for me is in Freud as he in his initial creative phase sees that the dream-work is such a language—hieroglyphic and yet presenting letters and phones—a rebus that he thinks to be identical with the

poem-work; and his exposition of the polysemous transformations of language into language involved I found before I found Moses of León or Saussure.

11.   In *Du Désert au livre* Jabès recalls the infant's beginning the language-work, word-work (to enter language we rehearse the Treasury): "The child makes up words. As to those which he has stolen from the adults and which have become familiar [I would note here, as one becomes a writer, the writing becomes one's familiar] to him, he tends, once he knows the alphabet—to write them as he hears them. The words make him take consciousness/conscience of his universe."

The universe appears to him only as *his* universe is at work. In this undertaking of consciousness in *The Book of Questions,* to the question *"Quelle est l'histoire de ce livre,"* the response comes: *"La prise de conscience d'un cri."* The poet-reader begins to see that the eventfulness of writing here is not the eventfulness of a personal wit (Jabès's own wit is attentive and graceful throughout) or of a learning in language (again, evident in the pleasure of the text), but the eventfulness of an undertaking of an evolution of consciousness in which to read is to be involved not gradually but immediately. *"Il suffit d'une minute pour prendre conscience d'un siécle,"* Reb Kelab, one of the imaginary informants of the Book, says. It takes but the reading of the vocable to seize upon and be, in that, seized by the consciousness/conscience coming to be manifest in the Book.

12.   The Book's proposition that It has to do with those for whom the roads/ways of ink and of blood *"passent par les vocables et par les hommes"* initiates for the serious reader the mode of the voice—the speaking to us, in us, from us, of What Is—that we in seeking to speak or voice answer, and in ways of ink (drawing, writing) and of blood (ancestral-indwelling and bodily in-dwelling, coming from the pulse and breath) follow. What we take to be race seems at first this "blood," but deeper than race our species, and deeper than species the life-blood. Deepest we know in our present science is the DNA, working signature of life itself. The apprehension of these coexistent realms present in the way of the blood is one not of supercession but of an advancing complexity of presence. *"Il suffit d'un nom"* to paraphrase "it needs only a minute to grasp what a century is"—*"il suffit d'une race pour prendre conscience d'une espèce."*

13.   But these ways of ink and of blood tell ultimately of Life/Death itself. *The Book of Questions* is the book of a Mystery we follow with the

fascination for the detective novel, which we rightly call a mystery, for it is the book of a death or deaths we are to find out. Every phrase, page, chapter will present its clues then. In *"Écrit/Récit,"* Jabès tells us the sole obsession of the writer is the *"parole du livre"*—*"vièrge de toute parole"*—a speech as only the book speaks to us (yes, I understand what it says, I learn from it, but more important, it speaks to me. No, not a matter of my hearing the voice. I can hear it. But, back of the voice, as that tree speaks to me, as that face in the crowd speaks to me, as the voice I heard speaks to me, the book also. It is the resonance, the chord resonant with something I too am, the pure metaphor music in its harmonics knows), virgin in this, immediate. The word itself becomes the act traced or tracked (the ink on the page remaining in the absence of the word) between *"la memoire"* and *"l'oubli." "Et ton salut?"* ("and your salvation?") the question comes, and *"L'oubli de mes paroles"* in thee is the response.

Forgetting one's *own* speech in the Book's speaking: this passing away of one's own *into* the properties of the Book, at once an extinction and a vivification. "Can I enter in here?" the reader asks in this passage: "It so darkens everything—it already is so dark," and the response comes: There is a wick—a wick burns in each word. *"Une mech brule dans chaque mot."* It is in its burning up, its extinction, that the wick bears the light we read by.

14.   In the Tradition the Voice comes out of a "Fire." The writer in his devotion becomes *warm* and then *heated,* as he arranges and rearranges the letters, for he comes nearer and nearer, if he but attend to what is happening, to the First the letters (not only of Hebrew, Abulafia believed, but of languages as such after Babel, Hebrew among them: Jabès's permutations of French then draw near the flame) are articulations of. In childhood's game of this Hide-and-Seek, or Finding, "you're getting hotter, you're burning up, you're on fire," the children would lead us on. In the Story, in the dark before Creation, the points of the letters appear as scintillations, points of fire (as the souls of men, in Gnostic gospel, are sparks of being, immersed in matter). But here, I would see the Matter of the Story as the Mother or Ground in which sparks come into being.

15.   At the "threshold" of the book, Jabès writes, inscribed from Reb Alce in that choral company of imaginary rabbi-poets (*lecteurs privilégiés*): "Mark with a signet of red the first page of the book, for the wound is invisible at its beginning." The spark of red (fire) or drop of red

(blood/ink) finally appears as the opening title of Book VII, as a red dot on the spine, standing alone, and on the cover a subtitle in black: *El, ou le dernier livre,* followed by the title dot in red.

In the accident between languages after Babel, the *blessure* from French appears as a *faux ami* familiar to unwary English readers who read "blessing"; even as between the two religions, Jewish and Christian, this spark (of life, of intelligence, of spirit, of fire) that is a drop of blood, for Jabès, from the circumcision wounding, to me seemed a drop from the crucifixion wound. In both the *blessure* is a "blessing."

16.   In the vocation of Poetry, some poetry yet to be calls us, "wounds" invisibly, or appoints us, and the "I" passes beyond this "we" (in which the intent to write becomes lost in the conflagration of readings) into a void of person where it is the absence of the Book that needs not the writer but the writing in order to present itself. This theme of a void that calls for filling, an absence that calls for presence, a nothing that calls for All, appears in the ground of letters and sounds before the word, as it appears in the love of Yukel and Sarah, as it appears in the narrator's confrontation with narration, and back of narration a Silence that would disclose itself.

17.   Before the writing of the numbers, the *Sefer Yetsira* tells us, before the Creation which the letters of the alphabet attend, there was a "decade out of nothing" (as the Rosicrucian translation by Isidor Kalisch, which my parents followed in their Christian Hermetic studies, translates)—in the analog of the physical body "the ten fingers . . . five parallel to five, and in the center of which is the covenant with the only One" as the hand grasping, the fingers taking hold, is present in the evolution of the mind's grasping, taking hold, in which both Mind and World emerge as if from a point. The hand attending the writing of the book, the account or re-counting of which is memory.

18.   The ordinal numbers (*"Marque . . . la première page du livre,"* the command inscribed at the threshold of the book reads). And in the telling (of the beads or of the sections) there is the numbered sequence 1-2-3-4 of the *Seuil.* In which the cardinal number four is noted: four letters appear in French to be *j-u-i-f;* as in English they may appear to be *p-o-e-t.* *"Tu es Juif et tu t'exprimes comme tel."* Then the response: *"Les quatres lettres qui designent mes origines sont tes quatre doigts,"* leading to five: *"Tu disposes du pouce pour m'ecraser."*

19.   Once Jabès has written these lines, they become announcements of the presence of the Tetragrammaton, in *poet* even as in *juif*. In the matter of the calling to undertake the Jewish conscience/consciousness and in the matter of the calling to undertake the Poetic conscience/consciousness—it is the absence of God upon which the Name calls; the absence of what Poetry is that we know in the commanding need for the Poem or the Covenant. Between the French four-letter *juif* and, for me, the English four-letter *poet*, the point of the mere fourness remains, once it is proposed, as a clue or cue, a suspicion we follow as detectives to that lure: the disclosure of the covenant back of this writing, recounting and spelling.

20.   Abulafia, Scholem tells us in his *Major Trends in Jewish Mysticism*, saw that "every language, not only Hebrew, is transformed into a transcendent medium of the one and only language of God. And as every language issues from a corruption of the aboriginal language—the first Hebrew—they all remain related to it.

"In all his books Abulafia likes to play on Latin, Greek, or Italian words. . . . For, in the last resort, every spoken word consists of sacred letters." So, after Babel, if I read that mystery aright, what we know as Hebrew belongs also, one among all the languages of Man, to the Diaspora of Tongues. There is in the account a language back of tongues, a call-it-Hebrew before the Hebrew, even as before the French which Jabès takes to be sacred, French being native—in each "word": a sign, a name, a signature, and a designation.

21.   At the inscription of the following chapter, *"Et tu seras dans le livre,"* the ordinal is reiterated: "Child, since I wrote, for the first time, my name, I had the consciousness/conscience of beginning a book." And there are seven numbered sections, 1-2-3-4-5-6-7.

"Mon livre a sept jours et sept nuits," a certain Reb Aloum says in the litany of responses in part 3 of the *"Au Seuil"* chapter, *"multipliés par autant d'années qu'il a fallu à l'univers pour s'en délier."* In the *blessure/* blessing of my uncertainty, my stranger-reading out of French, in no way a native, is it: multiplied by as many years as it needs, as the universe needs to free itself in them or through them or from them? Once the reading has so wandered, the "correct" translation remains haunted by the multiplication of meanings only misreading frees in us, who do not misread or mistake carelessly.

Le Retour au livre (volume III) is, Jabès announced when it was published, the last panel or leaf—*volet*—of a triptych or screen. Yet this earlier announcement holds: for the work was to have seven volumes.

22.   Not being French, so that what infancy do I know surrounded by these words and voices, having only the most unschooled romance with the language, and then, having no permission, no initiation—the mystery but increases everywhere, everywhere the dread in reading: to but begin to know the telling echoes and yet having no native permission there, where one does not know the reaches of those correspondences. Slowly, slowly, read over and over again, not all of Baudelaire yet, only the opening twenty or thirty poems. I know so little of the parvis, so little of the Temple. Yet Homer, whom we poets take to be the father of Greek poetry, says "WE who hear only rumor and know nothing."

And here, in Jabès, I take this French to be my "Hebrew," as my *temenos* and dwelling in language.

Yet what in sixty-three years do I know of the parvis and temple of English, who was born into that language? I do not speak of the lore (translation is the mode of learning). I speak of the transport and of the conversation between worlds that we know in how our physical body tells us always of the psyche-world and of the spirit-world (for those of us who are called upon to "be" poets—as one would say "Be a Man!"—how every event of the body predicts, invents, comments upon, relates events in the Poetry in which we have our "Diaspora") and how in turn the poem as a world is so conversant with the actual, the psyche-drama, the spiritual transmutation. Daily events we barely notice present essential configurations—hieroglyph or rebus—of the text we must write.

23.   So that they are like five fingers of a hand; or ten fingers of two hands, of one body. The cardinal numbers—how many—are a "world" as such.

"Il y a deux mille ans que je marche" appears in the litany between the reader (who, I read, is, like me, not Jewish) and the writer. *"Tu es Juif and tu t'exprimes comme tel,"* the reader replies: *"Mais j'ai froid. Il fait sombre. Laisse-moi entrer dans la maison."* Do I overread my own pathos in taking this plea to be mine—having permission neither of race nor of religion nor of language to come in to the depths of this reading? *"Une lampe est sur ma table et la maison est dans le livre,"* the poet replies. Again and again in my own work, to me as I write, to my readers then in the reading, this lamp, this table, this house have appeared.

24.   And, indeed, in my own devotions, having no guarantee or warranty of belief—and *imagining* then in the place of this believing/not believing—even there having no warranty or assurance I would take to distinguish the imagined (or as Jungians, after Corbin, make the distinction, the *imaginal*) from the imaginary. Like Jabès, I would confess the imaginary also I hearken to and take as guide and informant. In my own creational world, in which I know not what I make up that does not make up what I am, the lamp, the table, the house, and the book are immediate to, get warm in the nearness to, "God." They are "home." An absence in any possibility of belief or disbelief, a presence ever to imagination, a ground of affection and awe. "JEWS GO HOME," then, calling up as it does, even as it means to wound, the question of "home" and the *"Mort aux Juives,"* recalling "Death," come as meant to inform the author, for "home" and "death" are the themes of the Book.

25.   In the Diaspora the lamp, the table, the house, and the Book become the "Jerusalem" of the Jews who, in exile, come home to the inner keep of *The Zohar,* or mystical Jerusalem. In this transformation the poet Blake will find his Jerusalem to be state of mind and spirit, in the same time that Baal Shem finds his Splendor to be in song and dance and story. In the currents of a Jewish mysticism, in which the spiritual alchemies of absence and exile, the Book and the Shekinah, the hidden Tzaddik and the mute letter, once that masterpiece of Moses of León begins to work its ferment in the world and time of Dante in the Christian world ("We for whom the world is our native land, as the sea for the fish") and Rumi in the Islamic world: then I hear the beginning of a great change, a rumor going abroad, as in *Les Phares* of Baudelaire.

26.   It is embodied in this tissue of a consciousness in writing, in this creational field that is Jabès-Mind, and *here* French (but as our reading here, over here in English we are there—the events of Jabès's writing altering the consciousness of French, alters our own awareness of English), it is in this medium that the romance of Sarah and Yukel is to be told, "in the course of various dialogues and meditations attributed to imaginary rabbis." *"Le récit d'un amour detruit par les hommes et par les mots."*

What Jabès has done once we but begin to entertain the ideas (sightings of signs and soundings) of this texture itself is to impregnate our reading of French with a "Jewishness" that arises from language itself as race, as nation. The poet Charles Olson in his American vision

Maximus cries out in the concluding passages: We need another kind of nation.

"Le mot est lié au mot, jamais à l'homme, et le Juif à son univers juif." But I read in Jabès's theme of absence, as I read in the Kabbalist theme of the withdrawal/exile, a recognition of that emptiness/need which in the eternal presence of the Universe we must bring into existence.

Emptied of the Jewish universe (his exile from "home," the Jewish community of Cairo, in his actual life, presents an immediacy of this void), Jabès lives now in the creation of his Jewish universe in the universe of the French language. This "Jewishness" is the need for a new universal consciousness/conscience.

27.   Whatever this mystery of blood and of ink, of race and *récit*, it has so entered and impregnated the deep texture of our life-language that at the cellular level of what we are it seems essential. Indeed, as we in our biophysics find in the cell itself the essential life-organization exemplified, we read life, as the scholar of the Tradition reads the Torah, in the smallest jot. And so we search for the Universe.

In *Mon Coeur mis a nu,* which I read as a revelation in Baudelaire of the Angel Syphilis, at the heart of the matter, the hatred of women, the hatred of Jews, the hatred of humanity, and the hatred of Self delineate an auto-destruct in European consciousness. Hatred of the French must be added; deep in the love of the French language and poetry, at this core this *other* presence comes into the void—"The French are the people who hate Poetry." A deep hatred of the body in the worship of the body. Is this dynamic of fire in some phase (but that suggests succession; I mean a phase in an alchemical process), in some aspect, hatred that binds us to the restoration of universe?

28.   The Israelite bears the burden of his "image" as the word carries the weight of its letters, the "author" advances in *"et tu seras dans le livre";* but then the text recalls, *"Je suis la parole."* Reb Josué said: "And you pretend (*pretends*), think, to recognize me by my features," indignant that one could so identify a man. In the seventh volume, the ambiguity between *"Je suis"* I am, and *"Je suis,"* I follow, will be activated.

29.   The presence or mystery of Man has only these individual features in which what is given is constantly recreated to be read by personality, by race, by societal disposition, as well as by physical condition, by the pre-

sent state of the soul, as language is read in the present state of the language.

30. *"Rien, apparemment, au seuil de la page ouverte, que cette blessure retrouvée d'une race issue du livre dont l'ordre et le desordre sont chemins de souffrance; rien que cette douleur dont le passe et la continuité se confondent avec ceux de l'écriture."*

> *Comme de longs echos qui de loin se confondent*
> *Dans une tenebreuse et profonde unité*

31. From *The Book of Questions:*

> I let the words take place in my book and I followed them with my finger. They advanced themselves, two by two, and, at times, by five or six. I respected the affective order of their entrance in me; for I knew, now, that I had carried this book for a long time. (*BQ,* 29)

32. "We" in *The Book of Questions* are people of the book. "The book is my universe, my country, my roof, and my enigma. . . . I am of the race of words with which one builds living places." "The book is the work of the book."

"*'Tu,' c'est quelquefois 'Je'*"—"Thou" is sometimes "I"—is a rule, a perspective point upon the horizon line sometimes of the book. In Buber's *I and Thou,* the writing or work is the Thou rightly. Otherwise the writing is a tool or a projection. It is upon a horizon that the lines of the Book *"se confondent,"* as in Baudelaire's *Correspondences* there is a distance in which the unity of a shadow appears. Yet in the white light of the page or the illumination of the Book, there are neither horizons nor frontiers—another fusion.

33. Race, then, difference or boundary, is a sign in the design of the book that the coinherence of signs has to do with language. The scream or cry of Yukel, creature of the book, comes from beyond the horizon of the Book. Doesn't the narrator meet Yukel on the street? Doesn't he come upon the suicide who has leapt from his apartment house? And are the automobile and the searching headlights and the writing on the wall fictions only of the Book? In this passage, the opening words, *"Les phares d'une automobile éclairent la façade d'un immeuble,"* recall Baudelaire's title *Les Phares,* so that the words of hatred read on the wall excite

another reading in the light of Baudelaire's *Les Phares*, in which, indeed, the cry repeated by a thousand sentinels and the call to hunters lost in the great forests, may be such a cry as the cry in Jabès's Book, a reading of the cries of hatred out of *My Heart Stript Bare,* in which the poet enamored of correspondence and fusions, of expansion, found himself delivered over to a fear and hatred of just that shadowy and profound unity of resonance.

Is the Diaspora an aspect of this *"expansion des choses infinies"*? The violent hatred of Jews is not just of a foreign people, but of a fusion, of the unity that humanity proposes. The burning of books, we remember, was part of the German terrorist possession seeking to purify (burn clean) blood, mind, soul. To draw the line and enclose, to escape the "vanishing point," withdraw into frontiers, boundaries, definitions, and ward off the horizon.

34.   Jabès lives in the French language as if it were the Sea. It is this boundless creational field that the first (last) point—the red dot that appears in the title place of the seventh book of the Book; the *El, ou le dernier livre"* (is *El* here the *elle* we hear when we sound the word? for French is the one language in which the echo of God, *El,* is She, *elle,* the Shekinah then) is the subtitle—that the spark, yod before Yod, the vanishing point upon the horizon, appears, and we begin to see that the intention of the boundless is manifest in the agony and restoration of pages or boundaries or walls.

35.   The cry of Yukel does not echo in the confounding orders the book commands except by the lore of the book. Only as the word *cri* is found in words or reiterated. Only in the vocable can the cry enter. There is a Yukel outside of Yukel, a cry that, in being spoken/written of, we are before in another "world." All of us entering our common humanity have cried out, taken breath, and, those of us who are united in the common Life of the DNA code-creatures hear that cry throughout the community of the living. In the sound field the breath not yet a phone is the point of such a cry, that in the sign-field of writing we see as the red point. The point of blood in the egg, in which the pulsation of an individual life begins, separating itself from the collective in order to enter the collective.

36.   This text must be deeply troubling to the question the Jew has at heart: what is the metaphor of race that this separation from humanity

into the fate of a "being chosen" or called and the keeping of that cove-
nant be so necessary a way to recreate the nature of humanity, this
intensification of an abhorrence of the way of all other men, *goyim,* so
that in not cohabiting with the ways of men, the return from the hubris of
a tribal rejection of commonality deepens the meaning of the Grand
Collective? Man Himself, the species, has just so rejected his common-
ality with the living. My generation but begins to see that in taking the
Grand Collective to be Man, we have been enemies of the commonality of
species. Enemies of our own being creatures of a mystery story in Matter.

37.   For *The Book of Questions* is troubling indeed, as the cry of Yukel
and Sarah proves, unless we read it as "ours"—we who are not by name
or by trait of special breed to be read as "Jews," we who cannot answer to
being "chosen." I am speaking now of this utter humanity of Jabès's
consciousness/conscience in process in the Book, of Yukel and Sarah in
their own "Song of Songs," of this universe in us; of the utter humanity
of being Jewish for us who are not Jewish. Why is this Jewishness—that
for many Jews is a racism—somehow, in its covenant, in its dwelling
apart, so the ground essential to the discovery of our own selves in our
apartness? Is it that the Jews have taken the full burden, the extremity, of
an apartness at the root of Life itself? Every individual is, some biologists
have suggested, in this individuality potentially the beginning of an *other*
species.

38.   If, as Abulafia began to see, all languages belong to the nature of *the*
language of the Book of Creation, all correspond. The drama of the Jews
then is "ours," as the undergoing of all peoples is "ours." As in my
conception, the X-chromosome and the Y-chromosome, not "types" but
unique in their dance together, isolates. To come into the "message" of a
life, "I" is separated from the potentialities of the gene pool into vector of
being chosen, by lot, in that mystery of belonging and not belonging. "I"
am not "Thou," yet in being the "Not-Thou" and then in being conscious
at all of World, "I" is "Thou," where the secret of my identity lies.

39.   To what collective does the cry of Yukel and Sarah belong? It must
belong to what they have suffered as Jews—but that must pale when we
realize that the cry comes, as Jabès tells us, *"plus ancien que la graine."* The
Jews who read their race from the Holocaust and not from the Tradition,
and in Palestine build a separate Survival Nation to take its place among
Nations (even as the Germans, but recently having become a nation, in

the Holocaust sought to enforce a racial purity of their own, separated from the human race by a series of unforgivable atrocities), fail to read or avoid reading depths, for they seek to disown the Diaspora, the spreading throughout humanity of a rumor. It was the contamination of this spiritual rumor of all peoples who were, as the Nazis called them, "international" that was the fear, the abhorrence, underlying the nationalist-racist mania.

40.   The *mute* cry of Yukel and Sarah that has come into question in the Book is a cry in Memory, that the Greek theogony tells us is Mother of Poetry. All of Creation, the Book itself, in the individual incarnation of Man, as in the vocable, to manifest this cry. What I would read here is that in the course of writing we are in the course of this cry. Memory being itself, as faith is, our presence in this cry.

41.   Jabès addressing Yukel says, "I have made the ink run in the divined body of each letter that it live and die by its own sap which is yours, Yukel, in the book and in the approaches and dissimulations of the book."

Then: "Those who do not believe in the book, said Reb Gandour, have lost the faith in man and in the realm [kingdom: *royaume*] of men." That we are man and that there is a realm of men is a proposition of the book, where we take *being* in the name a word is, and live then the story the words tell in their coursings we follow. Jews are not, we find in the terms of modern anthropological study, a "race" as such. "Race" then means here the untranslatable, the following through the fate of a style in writing, an indwelling in the microstructures of a language as the very condition of the story, a letting the microstructures tell the story.

42.   The Book we read is Itself here the threshold of "Book" back of and outside the books we write—the vocable in the sounds of our voicing (crying, howling, murmuring, laughing) is addressed to a cry outside our crying that we know only through our "own" cry. We cry in order to make that distance in which a leap is possible, a withdrawal and separation (at once a hostility and a longing) in the cry and a returning of ourselves as the cry into the field of sound we know the universe to be. The Nazis meant to exterminate peoples in their death camps—not only Jews, but Slavs and Gypsies, not only those of the Jewish religion, but Christian Scientists, Jehovah's Witnesses. But in the case of the Jews, since they were the people of a Story, the extermination became a chap-

ter of the Story. And since the Nazis wanted to erase much of the Story of the German spirit, to rewrite and to do away with the evidence, they may have been jealous in their hatred of those who were faithful to the Story. The inexorable will of Jehovah is the faithfulness of the Storyteller who is also Creator of the Story to the Story itself and its people.

43.   *"Y a-t-il, mon frère, vocable plus attentif et plus rêveur, plus misérable et plus solidaire que celui que tu incarnes?"* (p. 37).

II

44.   In the sixth section of *"Et tu seras dans le livre"* the Book dictates (for so I would read the possibility of the italics at this point) designations of the cardinal numbers.

"If your name has only one letter, you are at the threshold of your name." In English my pre-name (pronoun, *prenom*) has only one letter "I." Can the *y* of *il y a* be a threshold of a name of one letter in French? If one change but the letter *i* for *e*, might one find the name *Elya*, whose book is the fifth in the series of *The Book of Questions*? Am I wrong to follow such questionable leads? to borrow trouble in reading? *"Mais qui réponds/à un prénom/emprunte?"* the Book asks in the following chapter. And in the seventh book, subtitled *"El,"* Jabès, on page 85, placing D-I-E-U out above and D-E-U-I-L below, renders the D, I, E, U out both above and below, and we find L remaining (EL), the one letter name at the threshold of God's signature left below.

45.   The counting rime in *"Et tu seras dans le livre"* has the force of a tune, evoking the presence of the Name in every number: two doors, three masts, four horizons, five books, six sages; open your name, carry abroad your name, drown your name, leaf through your name, interpret your name.

"If your name has seven letters, seven branches burns your name," brings us to the Menorah, the seven-branched candelabra of the Temple. With the publication of *Le Retour au livre*, Jabès announced that this third volume was the last part of the work. But the announcement of there being seven volumes pended throughout. In the formula, there were three, before there were seven.

46.   When in chapter seven of *"Et tu seras dans le livre"* the reader marks the passage of *ses grandes heures* to *des heurts, ses douleurs* and hears an

echo of *seize heures,* the reading may go astray. In this domain of corre-
spondences there is no boundary to homophones. This is the trouble of
expanding the reading below the translatable threshold (*"Aytant l'expan-
sion des choses infinies,"* as in Baudelaire's *Correspondences*). Once aroused,
there is to this suspicion of echoes and shadows a powerful sensuality in
reading itself, only by learned restraints kept at bay.

In our native language, we must close off the pursuit of recogni-
tions, or "age" appears in "language," and we must train the ear not to
overhear "bellow" in reading "below" or "nay" in the word "native."

47.   This delirium of finding meanings beyond meaning is initial in *The
Book of Questions*. The work, Jabès observes, is the tributary not of the
writer as such but of the reader. In the very act of writing his "authen-
ticity," the writer, if he reads, faces not what *he* meant or thought to mean
but what the words begin to mean. In this writing from the first, this
overture, we are led to read as a writer reads who searches the writing for
a revelation or prophecy of self that comes into being only through the
word—or so it seemed at first, but we find that this word comes into
existence by number and letter below the lexiconic level.

48.   The *tu* in *"Et tu seras dans livre"* I took first to be addressed to the
reader, but the *je* in *The Book of Questions* begins to be the voice of the
emergent Book itself, the Self the Book at once creates the writer to be,
speaks from and toward. *Tu* then is Jabès, as he writes in the promise that
he will be in the Book. Wherein I would recall Christ's "Tomorrow you
will be with me in Paradise"—for in Christianity the promise of the book
takes over from the book; the fulfillment of the Word is but announced.
In the mode of *The Book of Questions,* the word is tributary to each
present reading. One reads here as one reads in those poetries where
whatever the message, the words tell, and the reader in turn tells the
words, even one by one, tells the letters as one tells the beads of a prayer
string.

> *Le livre*
> *surgit du cri des pétales sacrifies*
> *de l'incendie de la rose prophetiques.*

49.   This play or possibility of an interchange, an exchange (*"Je revendi-
que, en dernier, mon dû"*) in reading that causes trouble (questions) if it be
not more than a display of wit, we label "the lowest form of humor." But
in deep reading the pun is a key or transport. Freud in his exposition of

the "dream-work" in *The Interpretation of Dreams* made his breakthrough because he took the word seriously, to lead to a seriation of meanings. And in *The Psychopathology of Daily Life,* he began to show that errors, lies, accidents, if they be "chance," chance upon hidden destinies or designs at work toward meaning, if we but read into the text letter by letter and overhear sound by sound. In *Jokes and the Unconscious,* his most ridiculed (rejected) work among these three that came in the period of Freud's first inspiration, he pondered the "joke" as such—not only as a "laughing matter," in which we laugh at what is revealed in order to rid ourselves of the content even as we are entertained, but as a cover-text. He questioned our laughing.

50.   In my intent, I reread toward the event when the finding of words in words begins in the text, as if this way or path followed the scent or trail of a prey or prize (*une prise de conscience*) and must retrace reciting what I see that leads toward that place. *"Il a passé sous des feux rouges, des feux verts"*—one has read a *travers des signes*—he has followed, lost, found again, followed streetlamps (*des réverbères*). As I follow the words, I hear reverberations and in the evening light read *rêve.* This section *"Le Livre de l'absent"* may be addressed to the absence of the reader in his reading. I lose myself in reading.

In this mode of absence, things of Jabès's own past (absent) life appear: the water mills of Africa a buffalo makes turn, who comes forward from the absent to remind him of how the beast gives drink to man who humiliates her. The tenacity of the mute beast becomes the tenacity in service of the race.

Index

[Note: Space limitations have made it necessary to offer an index of "selected names."]